G4/13

D0053889

09   10   ILLO
 l   l   l

5/03

WRITE
Where You
LIVE

SUCCESSFUL FREELANCING *at* HOME

Without Driving Yourself and Your Family Crazy

ELAINE FANTLE SHIMBERG

WRITER'S DIGEST BOOKS
CINCINNATI, OHIO
www.writersdigest.com

Dedicated to Faith,
hope and clarity

ᘒᘏᗒᘉᕀ

Excerpt from *Six Degrees of Separation* by John Guare, copyright © 1990 by John Guare, is reprinted by permission of Vintage Books, a division of Random House, Inc.

Excerpt from Welcome and Introduction speech by Herbert Benson, M.D. at "Spirituality and Healing in Medicine" seminar, Boston, MA, 1997, is reprinted by permission of the author.

Comments by Erma Bombeck from Elaine Fantle Shimberg's *How to Be a Successful Housewife/Writer* (Writer's Digest Books, Cincinnati, OH, 1979) are reprinted by permission of The Aaron M. Priest Literary Agency, Inc. on behalf of Erma Bombeck.

Excerpt from *100 Ways to Motivate Yourself*, by Steve Chandler, copyright © 1996, Career Press, 3 Tice Rd., P.O. Box 687, Franklin Lakes, NJ 07417, 1-800-CAREER-1, is reprinted by permission of the publisher.

Other fine Writer's Digest Books are available from your local bookstore or direct from the publisher.

Visit our Web site at www.writersdigest.com for information on more resources for writers.

To receive a free biweekly E-mail newsletter delivering tips and updates about writing and about Writer's Digest products, send an E-mail with "Subscribe Newsletter" in the body of the message to newsletter-request@writersdigest.com, or register directly at our Web site at www.writersdigest.com.

03 02 01 00 99   5 4 3 2 1

Library of Congress Cataloging-in-Publication Data

Shimberg, Elaine Fantle.
    Write where you live / by Elaine Fantle Shimberg.
        p.   cm.
    Includes index and biographical references.
    ISBN 0-89879-872-8 (alk. paper)
    1. Authorship—Vocational guidance. 2. Home-based businesses.
    I. Title.
PN153.S55   1999
808'.02'023—dc21   98-54787
                                                                          CIP

Edited by David Borcherding
Production edited by Pat Beusterien
Production coordinated by Kristen Heller
Cover illustration by Tom Post

ACKNOWLEDGMENTS

I thank, as always, my husband, Hinks, and our five children, Kasey, Scott, Betsy, Andy and Michael, who cooperated so I could write at home for so many years and who provided so many subjects for me to write about. Thanks also to all the professional writers who took time from their own work to share a few thoughts so that I could include them in *this* work. Special thanks go to the many at-home writers who have corresponded with me over the years, especially to tenacious Nancy Pistorius. I appreciate all the prompt and courteous help given to me from the staffs at the Tampa/Hillsborough County Library and the Scarborough Public Library in Maine. Thanks to Faith Hamlin, as always, for keeping me busy and laughing. I am especially indebted to the trio Bill Brohaugh, Jack Heffron and David Borcherding, all of Writer's Digest Books, for giving me the privilege of writing another book for them about one of my favorite subjects.

ABOUT THE AUTHOR

Elaine Fantle Shimberg is the author of seventeen books on health care and family issues, including *Blending Families*; *Living With Tourette Syndrome*; *Depression: What Families Should Know*; *Strokes: What Families Should Know*; and *How To Get Out of the Hospital Alive*. She is past president of the Florida Chapter of the American Medical Writers Association and is a member of the American Society of Journalists and Authors. The mother of five adult children, she splits her time between Scarborough, Maine, and Tampa, Florida.

TABLE OF CONTENTS

Introduction 1

SECTION ONE

Writing Issues.. 3

ONE   **Do You Have the "Right Stuff"**

To Write at Home? 4
• Figure out why you want to write • Know your goals • Analyze your motivation • Be realistic • Create your personal motivational mission statement • Understand the importance of self-discipline • Value your time • Channel your energies • Learn the importance of patience and persistence • This is a test; it is only a test

TWO   **Weighing the Pros and Cons of**

Writing at Home 14
• The positive aspects of writing at home • Weigh the savings in transportation and clothing costs • Consider the flexibility • When you're a caregiver too • Is working evenings and weekends a plus? • Can you control your work hours? • Mine the wealth of ideas • The negative aspects of writing at home • Discipline is needed • Fighting loneliness • How to separate work and home • Respect as a "real writer"

THREE   **Making Family Part of the Writing Team**...................... 29
• Anticipate changes in your family dynamics • Communicate your intentions • Protect your time and use it wisely • Get family involved • Beware of saboteurs

FOUR   **Handling Interruptions**.................................... 38
• Telephone distractions • Say no • Look in the mirror • Schedule breaks • The Hansel and Gretel gimmick • Start something • Skeletonizing

FIVE   **Doing Household Chores and**

Other Have-To's 45
• Do what has to be done • The clutter question • Timesaving devices • Ask for help • Aim for the bull's eye • Change with the times • Inner clock • Two-box approach • Housework • Four dozen super cleaning tips

SIX   **Taking the Leap** 71
           • Visualize yourself as a writer • Remove barriers • Make changes • Focus

SECTION TWO
Technology and Business Issues 77

SEVEN   **Finding a Room of One's Own** 78
           • Claim your space • What to look for • Be creative • Don't overlook
           the little rooms • Protect your turf • Settling in

EIGHT   **Equipping Your Office** 87
           • Furniture • Where to find it • Importance of a chair • Lighting
           • Computer vs. typewriter • Other plug-ins • Extras • Supplies • Storing
           the "little stuff" • Reference books • Keep track of pencils and pennies
           • Business hours

NINE   **Laying the Groundwork** 105
           • Know your markets • Market guides • Read the darn things • Narrow
           focus • Check the competition • Outlines • Wide-open spaces • Titles
           • The query

TEN   **Researching** 115
           • Why do it • How to begin • Talk about it • The library • Networking
           • The Internet • Government agencies • Keep track of sources
           • Reminders

ELEVEN   **Interviewing** 126
           • Why interview • Who to interview and how to find them • Research
           your subject • Different types of interviews • Where to conduct the
           interview • Plan specific questions • How to look professional • To
           tape or not to tape • Written notes • Listen • Don't talk about yourself
           • "Say good night, Gracie"

TWELVE   **Showtime! Time to Write** 144
           • The query • The lead • Confetti your work • Leave something behind
           • Begin in the middle • Read aloud • Rewrite • Rejection

THIRTEEN   **Making It Your Business to Be Businesslike** 152
           • Management and labor • Practice punctuality and peak performance
           • Follow a routine • Be flexible • Build in breaks • Establish a quitting
           time • Handling mail • Money in, money out • Watch your pennies
           • Cushion your deadlines

FOURTEEN **Making It Pay** 163
• Time is money • Costing out a project • Multiple sales • Use your
expertise • Speak up • Publicize • Expand your talents • Photography
• Desktop publishing • Diversification • Advertising • Annual reports
• Brochures • Collaborations • Columns • Corporate histories
• Ghostwriting • Greeting cards • Manuals • Newsletters • Press
releases • Speeches • Subsidy press • Self-publishing

SECTION THREE

Emotional Issues 182

FIFTEEN **Staying in Touch With Friends** 183
• Organize your break time • Meet with the upbeat • Organizations
• Writers clubs • On-line

SIXTEEN **Believing in Yourself** 188
• Positive thinking • Visualization • Confidence • Role models
• Handling rejections

SEVENTEEN **Preparing Your Mind and Body** 196
• Control stress • Relaxation techniques • Relaxation response
• Progressive relaxation • Yoga • Massage • T'ai Chi • Daydreaming
• Aromatherapy • Nature • Exercise • Self-talk • Eating properly

EIGHTEEN **Doing Good Through Volunteerism** 205
• Why volunteer • Protect your time • Know when to say yes • Include
volunteer writing samples in your portfolio • Put something back

NINETEEN **Following the Leaders** 209
• Bette Greene • Erma Bombeck • Wendy Wasserstein • Sue Grafton
• Teresa Bloomingdale • Mark Fuerst • Dodi Schultz • Patricia O'Brien
• Judy Blume • Lisa Iannucci • Susan J. Gordon • Christine Adamec
• Sandy Frye • Cady Bissell Ferguson • David Schaefer • Jeff Berner
• Shirley Linde

TWENTY **The Beginning (Not the End)** 225
• Write now • You're not alone • The secret to becoming a published
writer • Praise and garlands at your feet • Why write? • Define yourself
• Writing gives pleasure

Suggested Reading 230

Index 231

INTRODUCTION

Almost twenty years ago, my first book was published. It was called *How to Be a Successful Housewife/Writer: Bylines and Babies Do Mix*. The publisher was the same as for this book, Writer's Digest Books.

A lot has happened since that first book came out. Back then, a "web" was something a spider left and a "hard drive" referred to any trip of more than two hours with all the kids in the car. My five kids have grown into adults, and two of them have children of their own. The dogs and cats that napped on top of my manuscripts have gone to dog and cat heaven. My IBM Selectric, carbon paper and yellow second sheets have given way to a laptop computer and 3.5-inch disks, and I've written and had published sixteen more books.

When the last child went off to college, we sold the house and moved into a two-bedroom condo. And, although I do have a room in my husband's office building where I store the bulk of my personal research library and do some writing, I still write at home. The second bedroom has become my office/guest room/grandchild's nursery/massage room. That's a lot of slashes, but the arrangement works.

One thing that hasn't changed over the past twenty years though is the need for discipline, persistence and motivation. These qualities are always necessary when you're writing, but especially when you write at home. This book will tell you why and how to master them.

Since the publication of *Housewife/Writer*, I've received and am still receiving letters and calls from men and women who want to know how to begin to write at home. Many have offered to take me to lunch in return for my telling them "all I know." Since I'd weigh twice as much as I already do (something else that has changed over twenty years) if I accepted all those invitations (not to mention having no time to write), I'm offering this book, *Write Where You Live*, instead.

Think of this book as our having a friendly conversation over lunch or a cup of hot tea. Relax, get comfortable and start reading.

I'll "talk" you through what you need to know in order to write at home.

It's just like taking a hike through the woods: It may seem scary at first, but when you put yourself in the hands of an experienced guide, you can relax and become more aware of your surroundings, learn what you need to know for survival and, most importantly, have fun.

Writing Issues

CHAPTER 1

Do You Have the "Right Stuff" to Write at Home?

Talent isn't enough. You need motivation—and persistence too. . . .
— Leon Uris

M otivation! Confidence! Persistence! That's what you need to become a successful writer at home. If that's what you want, why not get started today?

WHY DO YOU WANT TO WRITE?

It's probably a safe bet that you're interested in doing some writing or you wouldn't have picked up this book. Unless, of course, you just liked the cover or needed a book in this specific color to fill a spot in your home library. But have you ever thought about *why* you want to write? It's really an important question for you to address because unless you know why you want to write, you won't be able to plan your motivation for doing so. And if you can't sustain your motivation, it's doubtful you'll succeed as a writer.

People have a variety of reasons for wanting to become writers. Some want to write for the money that they fantasize making or just because they think they could produce a lot better material than some of the "stuff" they read. Others want the fame and the opportunity to appear on television talk shows. Still others want to write because they have a message they need to share or just because they feel they must.

There's really no right or wrong answer. Just your answer. But it's important to know why you want to write in order to stay motivated to do so. Like any traveler to a foreign country, you'll be better prepared if you've given some thought to your trip and know how and why you're going there. You also need to consider language differences, how much time you can spend on the journey and how you're gong to get there, in order to know what to pack.

MOTIVATION IS YOUR DRIVING FORCE

Your motivation is the fuel that can propel you into your future as a writer. But just as some cars run on gasoline and others on diesel fuel or electricity, your motivation for writing my differ from that of other writers. Read their biographies and study their motivations. You'll find a wide variety of influences. Some wrote simply because they needed or wanted the money; others, to carry them out of their unsatisfying existences. Some writers admit that their driving force was their desire to prove to their fathers, mothers or spouses that they *could* become published writers. For still others, writing was their only form of self-expression.

Writers have often attempted to crystallize just why they wrote. Author John Cheever said, "The need to write comes from the need to make sense of one's life and discover one's usefulness." Carson McCullers explained her need for writing as, "I live with the people I create and it has always made my essential loneliness less keen."

Anne Morrow Lindbergh wrote, "I must write it all out, at any cost. Writing is thinking. It is more than living, for it is being conscious of living."

Elie Wiesel said, "[T]he act of writing is for me often nothing more than the secret or conscious desire to carve words on a tombstone: to the memory of a town forever vanished, to the memory of a childhood in exile, to the memory of all those I loved and who, before I could tell them I loved them, went away."

And Tennessee Williams once said, "When I stop [working] the rest of the day is posthumous. I'm only really alive when I'm writing."

As for me, I write "because I find humor in the absurdities of daily life. Sometimes I feel sadness too, and I find I can write my tears away. I write when I'm angry and feel I must right a wrong. I write when I'm touched and want others to see beauty and gentleness. I write, as so many others do, because I must." I wrote those words twenty years ago for my first book, *How to be a Successful*

Housewife/Writer. As I reread them today, I realize that my motivation for writing has not changed.

Be Realistic

Be honest with yourself as you try to determine you motivation. Be realistic as well. If you're driven by the thought of the big bucks you've read that some authors make, remember that many writers struggle for years before they finally make a sale and it's usually not for those big bucks. The majority of writers who sell their work on a somewhat frequent basis still often realize so little profit that they must teach or get other jobs to support themselves and their families.

If your main motivation for writing is your burning desire to appear on some of the major talk shows, you should know that many successful and prolific writers whose names you know have yet to get a booking on *Oprah* or the *Today* show. On the other hand, that doesn't necessarily mean that you won't be widely successful with your first book and that it won't immediately be optioned by Robert Redford or Barbra Streisand. You might be that lucky. Just don't count on it.

Write Your Motivational Mission Statement

Successful companies, both large and small, and most nonprofit organizations, all spend a great deal of time and effort creating and perfecting their mission statements, their purposes for being and how they intend to achieve their goals. A mission statement helps everyone to stay on task and remain focused. It also helps in making decisions that will insure that mission. When you begin to write at home, you also need a framework to plot your direction and help yourself stay motivated.

Create your own motivational mission statement by putting your strategy in writing. Make it concise and to the point. It could be as brief as, "In order to realize my desire to become a published novelist, I will write two hours three times a week in order to complete my novel." Note that this statement doesn't say," I'll try to write two hours three times a week if I can." It offers no wiggle room; it declares, "I *will*. . . ." It also reaffirms the goal, that is, to become a published novelist.

Your motivational mission statement does more than just keep you on track. It helps remind you why you are spending those long hours staring at the computer screen while the rest of your family is downstairs eating popcorn, laughing and watching *Seinfeld* reruns. It serves as a motivational mentor to help push you out of your warm cozy bed at 5 A.M. so you can write for two hours before everyone else wakes up. It is the traffic cop blowing the whistle and telling you that you've dawdled over your coffee and the newspaper long enough and that it's time to get back to the typewriter or computer. Your motivational mission statement helps to keep you writing.

To illustrate how long I've been writing, my original motivational mission statement (we called it a long-term goal back then) was "to get into the card catalog." You may remember the card catalog as those wonderful little wooden boxes on stands that held thousands of cards with authors' names and the book titles printed on them. When I got the call from editor Carol Cartaino telling me that Writer's Digest Books wanted to buy my first book, the only person who was at home with me at the time was my seven-year-old son. I turned to him and proudly announced, "Mommy's going to be in the card catalog." He just looked at me and said solemnly, "I don't think you'll fit." It's hard to be a hero at home.

DISCIPLINE KEEPS YOU GOING

Discipline. For most of us, the word itself conjures up negative connotations, primarily that of punishment. But for those of us who want to write at home, self-discipline can mark the difference between becoming a published writer or remaining a wanna-be writer. When you write at home, there is no boss telling you to sit down and get back to work. You have no copy chief reminding you of deadlines. You have no peers to bounce ideas off or to tell you how to spell a word that you can't find in the dictionary because you can't spell it.

When people discover I'm a writer, the two most common comments are, "Oh, I've always wanted to be a writer, but I never found the time," and, "I started to write a book once, but I never got around to finishing it." Both of these remarks reflect why the individual has never been successful as a writer: a lack of self-discipline. The sad truth is that regardless of how supportive your family and friends are in regard to your writing, no one really cares whether you write or not. Actually, if you *don't* write you'll probably have more time to help with household chores, take your kids to the movies, exercise, play golf, learn bridge or mah-jongg, wash the car, put all those photographs into albums, call your mother and thousands of other items on your "to do" list.

When you think about it, there are probably more reasons you shouldn't try to write at home than there are to do so. But—and it's a most important "but"—there's one great reason why you *should* write at home: If what you really want and need to do is to become a published writer, there's no reason you can't do it. Just be certain you have both the motivation and the self-discipline to *make* (not "have") the time and to stave off procrastination. If you're not really sure just yet, don't quit your day job to become a freelance writer.

Writing at home is more difficult than writing in a business office because of all the temptations around you. There's no clear division between your private life and your work time. What's more, family and friends often don't think you're really working and feel more inclined to interrupt you because you're at home. Chapter two goes into more detail about the pros and cons of writing at home, but the most important asset to develop is self-discipline. Fortunately, you are in control of your destiny. You can learn to become more self-disciplined if that is your desire.

Value Your Time

Time is a limited resource. Each of us has only twenty-four hours each day, and there are numerous demands for every hour, with obligations chipping away at our time rock until often there's not even a pebble left for ourselves. But successful writers have learned to value their time and to preserve blocks of it for themselves and their craft. If you don't value your time, no one will.

Obviously, your present responsibilities dictate how much time you can carve out and preserve for your writing, but it's often a matter of *when* that time will be, not *if* you'll have the time. If you're a full-time homemaker with small children running around, you may find it difficult to write a novel during the daytime. But you can work on the chapter outline and editing during the day, reserving time in the evening or during the early morning to actually do more of the creative effort. You can also hire a high school student to come in for two hours in the afternoon to watch the kids so you can go into another room and write.

If you're a businessman or woman, you may want to use the early morning hours to write before the rest of the family gets up. Many individuals who do this swear it gets them charged up and ready to face whatever crises exist in their offices. Those who commute by train or bus find that the travel time allows them a specific designated period for writing. (Warning: Do not attempt this when driving your car.)

I know a television executive who used to spend every Saturday working on his detective novels, which he sold on a frequent basis. Retirees often schedule specific periods in which to write, finding that when they don't adhere to their agendas, the days tend to slip away from them.

If you are caring for a chronically ill loved one, you may find it difficult to preplan stretches of time in which to write because medical problems tend to pop up when you least expect them. But there are bound to be periods of inactivity from time to time when you can sit down and do some writing. If you have your work within reach, you can map out the beginnings of an article, write a query, outline a chapter for your book, write a few verses for greeting cards or begin to edit what you've already written. It may take you longer to complete a piece if writing in bits and snatches like that, but you'll be writing. And the more you write, the sooner you'll have something to send in to be published.

Don't be disheartened by the fact that it's taking you a long time to complete your article or book. Focus on the goal of finishing it. According to B. Eugene Griessman, author of *Time Tactics of Very Successful People*, "One of the biggest time-wasters is quitting too soon. Too often people do 90 percent of the work, but fail to do the final 10 percent that would take them to success." Go for the finish. You'll be glad you did.

Channel Your Energies

Don't waste your precious time and energies trying the shotgun approach to writing. I did this in the beginning, trying to write articles for almost every magazine that was on the newsstand. It was frustration and unrewarding. "I'm a generalist," I explained to my writer friend Linda Albert, author of the *Coping With Kids* series.

A teacher first and writer only later in her career, Linda gave me the best advice I've ever received on writing: "Write about what you're interested in and about what you know best. I write about kids and education. That's what excites me. What excites you?"

I considered her words for a long time and came to the conclusion that I really wasn't that fascinated writing about camping outdoors, sports, science fiction, mysteries, automobiles or gardening. A light turned on. Maybe that was why I had never sold any articles dealing with those subjects. On the other hand, I was really excited about medical issues, relationships, parenting, writing, travel and self-improvement. It was not surprising for me to then realize that the articles I had been able to sell all dealt with themes about which I felt passionate.

Your time for writing is precious and, like most precious things, is available in a limited amount. Don't waste your efforts trying to be all things to all people. It's expensive not only in the monetary outlay for postage, paper and toner for your printer, but also in the unwise expenditure of your most valuable commodity: time.

Think about the type of fiction and nonfiction you enjoy reading. If you don't like to read it, don't try to write it. That would have been good advice for me to take early in my career when I tried to write a science fiction short story, quitting only when I realized that even if I had been successful in writing it, I wouldn't have enjoyed reading the darn thing.

List some of the issues you are or have been dealing with in your life. Because of your experience, you may have a great deal to write about on a particular subject. Many of the topics I selected for books and magazine articles, including carpal tunnel syndrome, periodontal surgery, Tourette Syndrome, strokes, sending kids to camp, accidentally poisoning your child and stepparenting, were drawn from my own personal experience. So is the topic for this book.

Develop a Thick Skin

If you want to be a writer, you need to develop thick skin to protect you. Against what? Against the teasing by others who are jealous that you are even attempting to write. Against the lonliness that comes when friends drop you because "you're always writing" and never free to shop, play golf or whatever. Against the doubts that plague you when a character doesn't come to life or a final paragraph lacks zing. You need to be resilient when your manuscript comes back, rejected once again, and you wonder if anyone even bothered to read it. You need a shield of steel when your work's rejected by editors and you feel it was the best writing you've ever done or when a book comes out on the same subject as yours the day you mail your manuscript to that publisher.

"Tell them it's not easy being a writer," a number of authors urged me. They weren't being discouraging, just realistic. They know just how badly it hurts to have your work rejected. It's a part of you, like your kids, and no matter how impersonal you try to keep things, the rejection still hurts. Will you sob into your pillow and quit, or sniffle and continue?

Don't think the picture changes once your writing is published. Friends and family members may think your book or article is lousy and feel duty bound to tell you. Others may think your characters were based on them and get their feelings hurt. Some folks may bore you with how they would have written it better . . . if only they had the time.

Criticism hurts most of us, even if we don't think much of the critic's ability. One author, who received wide acclaim for her latest book, told me she was upset by her only bad review. "I know it's the only lousy one out of all the good ones," she confided. "But I keep thinking about it and it hurts. I wonder why he didn't like it."

That's why you've got to be thick-skinned when you're a writer, and most of us aren't. We're sensitive, emotional, creative beings who love to be loved, and we're grieved, shocked and surprised when we're not.

Learn Patience and Persistence

Remember the nursery tale about the tortoise and the hare? Well, the little known aspect of that story is that the tortoise moved slowly because he was carefully editing the final draft of his book as he crawled along. But as you know, the tortoise made it to the finish line first and had his manuscript published while the hare was still hopping around chasing his tale [*sic*]. The moral? If you're going to stick your neck out and be a writer, you have to have patience and persistence.

Persistence also helps you overcome any physical limitations you may have. It allows you to create new ways to interview or handle research if you have hearing difficulties or visual deficits. If you have arthritis in your hands and fingers, persistence lets you master the complexities of a computer that may require a lighter touch to type on than a typewriter. Where there's a will, there's a way to write.

THIS IS A TEST; IT IS ONLY A TEST

How can you know if you have the "right stuff" to write at home until you give it a try? You really can't. But by answering the following questions, you might get a feeling for whether or not you have a good chance of success. Be forewarned, however, that a high score doesn't assure you that you'll be published the first time out. Neither should you let a low score alter your course if you really feel motivated to write at home. Instead, use the test to help you determine your personal strengths or weaknesses so you know where you need improvement.

	Yes	No
1. Can I discipline myself to stick to a writing schedule?	☐	☐

	Yes	No
2. Am I assertive with those who want to infringe on my writing time?	☐	☐
3. Am I really motivated to write?	☐	☐
4. Can I organize my time?	☐	☐
5. Am I able to enlist my family's cooperation?	☐	☐
6. Am I willing to take risks?	☐	☐
7. Do I really believe I can become a writer?	☐	☐
8. Am I in good health?	☐	☐
9. Can I avoid procrastination?	☐	☐
10. Am I persistent?	☐	☐
11. Do I have a sense of humor?	☐	☐

The more yes answers you have, the more likely you'll be able to successfully write at home. While you probably don't really need a sense of humor, I think it helps to reduce the stress in this writing business. (Oh yes, we'll talk about stress in a later chapter.) It helps to be able to laugh to reduce tension when problems arise. When I sent the proposal, for my first book to Writer's Digest Books, I was very nervous every time the phone rang. I got home one afternoon and one of my kids said offhandedly, "Oh, by the way, the digest called."

I also had a proposal out to *Reader's Digest* at the time. "Which digest?" I asked. "*Reader's, Writer's* or *Science?*"

My kid shrugged his shoulders. "I don't remember. Does it matter?"

It mattered enough to me that I could have exploded. Instead, I thought it was funny, which it was, and I knew that whichever digest it was would call back, which it did. But a sense of humor prevented my doing physical and emotional harm to my son, and the story has brought laughter whenever I retell it. Keep laughter in your life. It eases every load.

CHAPTER 2

Weighing the Pros and Cons of Writing at Home

If one advances confidently in the direction of his dreams, and endeavors to live the life which he has imagined, he will meet with a success unexpected in common hours.

— Henry David Thoreau

enry David Thoreau, of course, had it fairly easy writing at home. Walden Pond, where he spent two years, was a quiet place, and although he did have visitors there, he lived alone in his one-room cabin. What Thoreau emphasized, which is applicable to those of us who want to write at home, is that we must simplify our lives in order to preserve the time and energy we need for writing.

This isn't a suggestion that you should pack a knapsack, grab the raisin and nut mix and head for isolated ponds in New England—although I'm quite partial to that area. And you don't need to strip your home of all your photographs, candy dishes and the china pig collection. Forget about becoming a recluse. You should, however, consider some personal decisions that are bound to affect your ability to write at home.

Begin by weighing the pros and cons of writing at home. Obviously, I have a strong bias for becoming a home-based writer as I have been one for more than thirty years. But I think it's only fair to let you know some of the negatives as well. As you read the list, consider your personal situation to determine how you will be affected.

THE POSITIVE ASPECTS OF WRITING AT HOME

Many of these pros are more definite for those who write at home full time than for the weekend writers who, like the weekend athletes, give their all over the weekend and wonder why there's a sense of total exhaustion on Monday. As with the athletes, it's often better to spread out the activity and make time midweek as well.

Offers Savings in Transportation and Clothing Costs

It's fairly obvious that you won't have any transportation expenses if you work out of your home, unless, of course, you have a toll booth between one room and another. But you may not have thought about the wear and tear you'll spare your car, as well as the time you'll save by not having to leave home to get to your office. You also won't have to worry about parking fees.

When you work at home, you don't have to worry about what to wear, although most home-based writers stress the importance of showering, shaving or putting on makeup, and getting dressed rather than lounging around in your pj's and bathrobe all day. I think you tend to consider yourself more professional when you're dressed, even if you're just in blue jeans and a T-shirt and are barefoot, which has always been one of my favorite writing outfits. While you'll need a "big person" outfit for interviews and TV appearances, you certainly can dress down and be more casual when you write at home.

Allows Flexibility

There's little doubt that writing at home gives you a great deal of flexibility: You can move around and take your "office" with you as needed. Although we live in Florida, my husband and I spend the better part of four months in Maine every summer. For the last eleven years I've taken my laptop computer with me and finished whatever book I was working on as I listened to the harsh cries of seagulls and the moan of the fog horn and watched the surf roll in, caressing the sand on our beach. Editors don't need to know or care where I am, only that my work is in on time, which it always has been.

Provides Ease of Caregiving

Despite what you may think, I believe it is far easier to care for small or sick children (or elderly parents) when you write at home. If you worked out of an office, you would still have to be home or find alternate child care when the kids were sick, but you'd have none or few of your essential papers with you so you would be unable to do much work. The same is true if you are caregiver to an elderly parent or other relative.

When I first began writing at home, I had only a newborn to look after. It was fairly easy to find writing time then as she did little but sleep and eat. By the time she was fifteen months old, there was yet another newborn to look after. Two additional babies came in rapid succession, and after a four-year hiatus, one more.

The type of writing I did in those early years varied somewhat. For the most part, what I wrote required a short attention span, such as 500-word newspaper and magazine articles, fillers and greeting card verses. These were projects I could quickly put down when things got too quiet and I guessed the kids were pulling toilet paper off the roll and stuffing it into the toilet or smearing baby lotion on the bedroom wall. (Usually my intuition was right.)

I did much of my concentration-intense work during the kids' nap times. How I hated to see their morning naps end. When they stopped taking afternoon naps as well, I still required them to have some quiet time in their rooms, for their benefit as well as my own.

Writing at home was the best of both worlds for me. It allowed me to become a productive writer and, at the same time, gave me the opportunity to be available when the kids got home from school. I was there to console when one was cut from an athletic team and to wipe away tears when another didn't make the cheerleading squad. I was there to congratulate when some won school elections and to praise when a difficult term paper was rewarded with an A. Because I was my own boss, I also could take off work early when one of my kids had a sporting event or was in a school play.

But the important message here is that although I was home with my kids, I also was writing. My mother once asked why I didn't wait to "become a writer" until the kids were older. I replied, "What would I write about?" Because in those early days, while I was learning and perfecting my craft, I also was writing about what I was living. I wrote about my concerns over child rearing, about children's health care issues and about selecting the right play school, school or camp for each kid's specific needs. I wrote about my need for some time alone and with my husband. I wrote about my family relationships. Our family became (and often still is) a well into which I frequently dipped for ideas.

Learning to write continually and effectively with little ones racing around my feet was a great training program by total immersion. It taught me to focus on my work and to ignore all background noises other than the sound of dripping blood. Writing in the trenches gave me the confidence to write and the experience to improve my writing skills. Looking back, I'm glad I didn't take my mother's advice on that issue. (There were other times I also didn't and should have, but that's another story.)

Writing at home also gave me the flexibility in later years to help care for my parents as they grew older and often needed rides to medical appointments and other assistance. Because I had no time clock to punch, I was able to sit with them in waiting rooms, sometimes editing manuscripts and sometimes just sitting and talking with them.

Enables Evening and Weekend Work

When you write at home, you're never far from your office. You can wander in after dinner to rewrite a paragraph that didn't really work for you or add a thought on a Sunday morning that popped into your head while you slept the night before. You can spend a rainy Saturday afternoon purging your files and cleaning off your desk—which for me is often merely a matter of condensing stacks in order to see more desktop space. I must have been absent the day they talked about paperless offices. When you write at home, the entire house can be yours. I recently had an extra modem jack installed near the breakfast table so I can sit in the family room and watch/hear television while I roam the Internet or rework a chapter.

Makes It Convenient to Be There for Repair People When Appliances Die

My grown children often complain that they have to take time off from work when they need something repaired in their homes. "They say they'll come in the morning and they don't show up until four in the afternoon. I've wasted an entire day," is a familiar refrain. In my case, I haven't wasted the day. I've been home working.

I have learned, however, to try to schedule more than one repair person on the same day, as usually we do have more than one item in our home that is dysfunctional. (Fortunately, it isn't either of us.) If you double-book repairs, only one morning or afternoon is shot. That way I can patiently explain to one person that the dishwasher motor usually sounds as though it is chewing up the dishes and I can't imagine why it isn't doing it now, while demonstrating to the other that I always thought window shades should be able to be opened and closed and mine can't.

If you don't schedule repairs around times when you are least likely to be doing productive writing, you may find that you're more likely to figure your day's been ruined anyway and take off and go fishing or clean out a closet. Don't let household repairs take top priority over your most creative time.

Allows Control Over Your Work Hours

Writing at home is ideal for people who march to a different drummer and prefer to work "odd" hours. While others may be toiling a 9–5 day, you can work 5 A.M. to 1 P.M. and go skiing or sunbathing in the afternoon. Or, you can sleep till noon and work into the evening hours. Whatever schedule you prefer, it's your body rhythms that dictate your hours, not those arbitrarily assigned by someone else.

For years I have been at my desk at 8:30 A.M. or 9 A.M. and write until about 2 P.M. or 3 P.M. Any later than that and my mind gets fuzzy. I can file papers, type letters, pay bills or tear out magazine articles to be saved, but that's about all the creativity I can muster after 3 P.M. The few times I've tried to work in the evening, I've either messed up something on the computer by calling up some obscure code with the three fingers I use for typing or I've written something that looks like it was originally written in French and was translated poorly.

It may take a while for you to figure out your prime time. It differs for all of us. It's the time when you most feel like completing projects, such as repairing the fence, painting a room, cooking up a storm or repotting all your plants. If you don't think you ever feel a spurt of energy like that, try scheduling your writing time during different parts of the day. Stay with each time period for a week or two. Record how you felt when you began working (excited, motivated, nervous, tired, etc.), how long you felt you were able to concentrate and what work you actually accomplished.

Study your time sheet. Are there any periods where your productivity seemed higher than others? Did the writing seem to come easier during these periods? What time of day held the fewest distractions for you? Rank these different parts of the day from one to ten, with ten being the peak of production for you and one being a time when you are really dragging.

You should quickly see one section of the day with higher numbers than the others. This is most likely the best time for you to be writing. Try to schedule your other activities and responsibilities for the remainder of the day. Note: If the entire day seems to be about a three or four for you, perhaps you should consult your doctor. You may have a case of the ho-hums.

Offers a Wealth of Ideas for Articles and Books

Your home is a treasure trove for ideas for books and articles. Why? Because home is where you live, love, eat and play. And so do millions of other people. The issues that confront you each day within the walls of your home are similar to those most of us are tackling. We can identify with them. And when you write a piece that speaks to the "you factor," editors and readers respond favorably.

Ideas, like dust mites, are always around you. You just have to be susceptible to know they're there. Once you begin to look for them and make note of them, you'll find that rather than having nothing to write about, you have more far more ideas than you can ever possibly use.

- **Listen for ideas**

If you have kids, you've struck it rich because you'll never lack ideas. Children give you aggravations, headaches and heartaches as well as great joy, comfort, new perspectives and good old-fashioned belly laughs. All this is grist for your writing mill. With kids around, you have a continuous natural flow of good in-house ideas if you stay tuned in to them. What are your kids talking about? Dating? Drugs? Smoking? Movies? Teenage pregnancy? Sports? School? What are their biggest gripes? Teachers? The drinking age? Teenage curfews? Dress codes? Lack of "wheels"? What are their fears? Low SAT scores? Not being "normal"? Not being accepted by their peers? What questions do they ask or not ask? What makes them laugh? What makes you laugh about them?

My adult children have always known that there was a good chance they'd read about themselves (disguised, of course) in the newspaper, a magazine article or a book. I figured that was only fair since they talked about me and their father (undisguised) to their friends. My kids' concerns about giving a speech in class led me to write an article on how to do that for *Seventeen*. One child's interest in learning to play chess turned into an article for *Jack and Jill*. When one of my toddlers climbed up on a chair and got into the baby aspirin, I turned that experience into both a newspaper article and one for *Essence* magazine, as well as a women's magazine in England.

When you use your children's lives as springboards for articles, don't abuse the relationship. Laugh with them but never at them. When you have multiple children, as I do, it's better for all concerned to refer to them as "one of my sons" and not single anyone out by name.

If you don't have kids of your own, get to know the kids down the street or in your apartment building. Kids have a special way of looking at life that we adults seem to have lost. They're honest, direct, funny and often very touching.

As you sit around your dining table, tune in to conversations by other members of your family too. What concerns your parents? Aging issues? Poor health? Money matters? Loneliness? My ideas for two of my books, *Strokes: What Families Should Know* and *Depression: What Families Should Know*, came directly from my parents' worries and experiences.

Once you develop the habit of listening to others, you'll begin to eavesdrop on other conversations as well. Many of the originations for magazine articles were triggered by something I overheard from the next table at a restaurant or while standing in the checkout line of a grocery.

• **Keep a journal**

Although many writers recommend keeping a journal to record thoughts, ideas and character sketches, I suggest using one strictly to record one-liners that you find memorable. Kids especially have an uninhibited and wonderful way of expressing themselves that you may be able to work into an article one day, and if you don't write it down, you'll forget it.

On Mother's Day, my kids offered to bring me breakfast in bed. "Just point us to the kitchen," one laughed.

I did just that, but I also captured the remark in my journal and sold it to Hallmark Cards as a greeting card verse. They've reprinted it many times, not only as the original Mother's Day card but also as a mother's birthday card.

At the dinner table one night, my kids were talking about their report cards. "I'm getting straight As," one bragged. "I'm getting straight As too," another added. My then five-year-old was bursting to be part of this "adult" conversation. "I'm getting curvy As," he piped up. We all laughed, and I added his comment to an article I was doing for a parenting magazine.

• **Tune in to yourself**

Don't neglect to get ideas from the person you know best: yourself. You may not think you've done anything special that anyone else would want to read about. But you have. We all have. While each person is unique, we still have much in common with our neighbor. It's our humanness.

That's why Betty Rollin's book about her breast cancer, *First, You Cry*, became a bible for so many women who had learned that they too had breast cancer. It's why Stephen R. Covey's book *The 7 Habits of Highly Effective Families* has touched so many people. It also explains the success of William J. Doherty's *The Intentional Family*. These books reach out to us. Because they are based on the personal experiences of the writers, we feel as though they are speaking directly to us. And in so many ways, they are.

Think about what you have done this past week. Did you visit a loved one in the nursing home? Scream at your teenager? Put your beloved family pet to sleep? Learn to use the computer? Lose two pounds? Continue your exercise regime? All of these experiences are familiar ones to thousands of other people, all possible readers for your article.

A few years ago, Sheldon Blau, a physician, got in touch with me through my agent to ask if I'd write a book about his difficulties while he was in the hospital. A series of mishaps had almost cost him his life. The more we talked, however, the more I began to feel that the real story was not just his unfortunate experience but how others who were not doctors could prevent accidents and mistakes from happening to them while they were hospitalized. Dr. Blau's story became the opening anecdote for our book, *How to Get Out of the Hospital Alive*.

- **Reminisce**

While your kids and spouse may tune out when you start reminiscing about what happened to you way back when, your readers may find it new and interesting. Spend time thinking about yesteryear. Keep a notepad handy, or "doodle" on your computer as you tune in to your subconscious. What was special or memorable? What made it so?

Reminiscence is particularly effective when you're writing about holidays and for scenes in a book or article. You also can use it to trigger ideas for a humorous or inspirational article. Best of all, you don't have to research your memories, go on-line for them or leave home.

When my kids were little, one of them complained when I forgot to give him his allowance. That triggered the memory of my childhood when I had the same complaint. When my mother forgot to hand out the allowances, my father said (as he did many times), "When I was a boy, my mother lined us up every Sunday afternoon by her desk and handed out the allowances." By the time I was through reminiscing, I had almost completed a humorous yet nostalgic article called "Sometimes You Have to Make Allowances," which sold immediately.

- **Confess**

I confess. They're two little words that boost TV ratings and sell tabloids, magazines and books. Everyone loves a good confession, especially when it's someone else's. It's not only good for the soul, but it's good for the pocketbook.

You don't have to leave home to find a confession to write about. My article "Will You Poison Your Child? I Did" was my personal confession of how my toddler got into the baby aspirin. I used statistics from the National Safety Council and interviews with pediatricians and poison control centers to gain the expertise I needed for the story.

Sometimes, however, you're the only expert that's needed. My qualifications as mother and driver gave credibility to my humorous article "Carpools Drive Me Crazy." A series of inexpensive costume parties my husband and I had given gave me all the authority I needed to sell an article, "I Was a Party Smarty," to *Woman's Day*. My attempts to get my home office organized led to an article, "How to Avoid Mess Stress," which was published in a military magazine.

Look around your home for additional ideas. On days when you confess that you can't think of a thing to write about, your confession may be the answer.

THE NEGATIVE ASPECTS OF WRITING AT HOME

Now that you've caught on to the fact that I'm enthusiastic about writing at home, I'll share some of the negative aspects about it to keep things somewhat balanced. Oddly, many of the same issues that are positives about writing at home can also become negative.

Discipline Is Needed

It's that *D* word again. If you don't have the discipline to keep working without someone else cracking the whip, you're going to have problems writing. There are so many temptations at home. You can procrastinate for hours and it doesn't seem like it because you are doing necessary things like putting clothes in the dryer, changing a burned-out lightbulb in the hall, pulling weeds, walking the dog or eating. You also can spend a great deal of time just chatting on the phone or watching TV. Before you know it, the day is over and you haven't written a word.

You need to be disciplined when your neighbor comes to the door, fishing rod in hand and confides, "Fish are biting. How about it?" And you have to stand firm when your mother calls to chat or your best friend arrives with a just-out-of-the-oven coffee cake and some great gossip.

If you have a retired spouse or small children at home it's difficult to shut them out and focus on writing. But it can be done. In *A Memoir of Jane Austen*, her nephew James Edward Austen wrote, "She had no separate study to repair to, and most of the work must have been done in the general sitting room, subject to all kinds of casual interruptions."

Although I prefer to work in total silence and isolation, I have learned to turn inward, concentrating on what I am writing. I've succeeded to the point that often I drive my family wild. They may be talking to me and I don't hear them. I've "gone into my head," as they call it. That technique served me well to block out shrill voices and barking dogs when the children were little, and it helped them to grow into independent youngsters who didn't need to be watched or played with every minute of their waking day.

While you don't want to drop out and become a hermit, you do need to protect your time because no one else will. Author Marjorie Holmes knew of the frustration of interruptions when she wrote, "I learned not to fret and fume and scream that 'Life won't let me write.' Simply to realize that life didn't care whether or not I wrote— but *I* cared, and somehow, some way I would do it. This steely 'just try and stop me' attitude is very important. It develops the patience a writer must have for the long, long haul. . . . And just as important—perhaps even more so—it establishes the writing *habit*."

"The writing habit." That's the essence of what you need to create when you write at home. Although throughout this book I will share with you what worked for me, you need to discover what works best for you. Don't get discouraged. It takes time to develop any type of habit, regardless if it's an exercise program, new dietary guidelines or even hanging up your clothes rather than tossing them in a pile on a chair. It takes time, patience and discipline to write at home.

It Can Be Lonely

Although I love the cloistered feeling when I'm writing—I adored studying in the library stacks in college—I'll admit to sometimes feeling a need for human contact. Writing at home can be lonely, even if you have kids around. It would be nice at times to have someone occasionally ask, "How's it going?" and then disappear. Perhaps I'll create a series of audiotapes for lonely writers that would say, "Hey, that looks great," and, "Can't wait to read it."

Some people find the isolation of working at home more than they can handle. That's when it becomes tempting to invite a neighbor over for coffee and conversation or to pick up the phone to call a friend. Some people begin nibbling constantly or drinking excessively. Others become depressed. Some give up writing at home or just plain give up writing.

But you can prevent these negative reactions by being aware of the problem and heading it off before you get cabin fever and it interferes with your writing. Use some of these suggestions:

1. If you have little ones at home and yearn for the sound of an adult voice, take the kids to a park or playground for a few hours. You can soak up atmosphere, talk to other parents and enjoy watching your kids at play in the fresh air.

2. Schedule a lunch date with a fun friend (one who is upbeat) once a week, but have a definite "got to go" time.

3. Try to relax and enjoy the weekend (or if you write then, a few weekdays). Don't do any errands. Just unwind and refill the creative reservoirs. Sometimes I've come back to a page or two that just didn't work out on Friday and found that it almost wrote itself

on Monday. I've never questioned why that is, other than to attribute it to my strong belief that time off gives your subconscious a chance to work.

4. Accept an occasional speaking date. Avoid scheduling too many or you'll find that you're talking about writing rather than writing. By speaking to groups about writing or a particular topic on which you're working, you'll break the isolation barrier and recharge your enthusiasm. You also may get ideas for new articles from those in your audience, an unexpected but delightful plus.

5. Join a professional organization in your community. Most areas have some type of organizational groups for writers. There are some for beginning writers and others for those who have made a specific number of sales, such as the American Society of Journalists and Authors (ASJA). Some groups, such as the American Medical Writers Association (AMWA), have both state and local chapters as well as the national organization.

6. Attend writers conferences sponsored by your local colleges and universities or the writers organizations in your area. You'll not only build up a support network but may gain valuable tips from the speakers and other attendees.

7. Try to get some physical exercise each day. It doesn't matter if you jog, walk, jump rope, ride your bike or just climb the steps in your home. You'll keep the blood circulating and keep yourself from getting stiff as you work at the computer or typewriter.

8. Run away from home from time to time. Since home is also your office, you need to get away for a change of pace. Visit the aquarium, go shopping or wander around a used book shop. Consider it a reward for good behavior (and writing). Just don't treat yourself too often or you'll never finish a project.

There's No Separation of Work and Home
While the lack of separation of work and home may seem like (and can be) a real benefit, it's also a potential negative for workaholics (like me). It's very tempting to wander into your home office to sharpen a pencil and then turn on the computer to clean up a few paragraphs. Before you know it, you've spent two hours working. Now that isn't too bad if your spouse is snoozing in front of the

television set and your kids are grown and gone. If not, however, becoming addicted to your work means you're taking important time away from your family.

Even if your office is a separate room, which is the ideal, paper tends to insidiously work its way into the rest of your home like a lava flow. Before you know it, everything is buried under a cover of your papers, reference books and multicolored Post-it Tape Flags.

Every week I scan a number of magazines for articles on health care that could be used as future reference and mark the pages to be filed in one of my over two hundred medical-related file folders. Usually I do the brainless work of tearing out the pages during the multiple commercial breaks while we're watching TV at night. But if I don't put them in my guest bedroom/office immediately, the couch and coffee table in the family room quickly disappear under a blanket of my clippings. Occasionally I'll find a reference book misplaced in the bedroom or kitchen where I must have dropped it when the phone rang or I otherwise got distracted. I don't chalk these wandering texts up to advancing age, by the way, but rather one of the many mysteries of life that poses more questions than answers.

Harder to Gain Respect as a "Real" Writer

Over the years, I've come to realize that this negative aspect of writing at home—lack of respect—may be geographically based. My writer friends in New York City don't understand what I'm talking about since most of them—as well as many of their agents— work at home. In New York, Boston and other metropolitan areas, writers are accepted as writers and it really doesn't matter where they plug in their computers. I've found the same to be true in Maine, where writers (and bookstores) seem to be as plentiful as blueberries and mosquitos, and are far more welcomed than the latter.

In communities without a number of writers, however, the individual who writes at home is considered unusual and not really working or, as it's put generously, "just writing as a hobby." Since there is no visible product until a manuscript is published, you appear far different from someone who gives piano lessons, tutors, throws pots or makes wedding cakes at home. It wasn't until my twelfth book was published in 1993 and received a great deal of publicity that local people stopped asking me, "Are you still writing?" and finally accepted that I indeed was a writer and that professional writers *still* write.

Despite the negatives I listed, I still feel that the positive aspects of writing at home outnumber the problems, providing you have the necessary motivation, discipline, confidence and persistence. It always comes back to these, you see, these four horsemen that carry you to success. Helen Adams Keller expressed it well by saying, "We can do anything we want to do if we stick to it long enough."

CHAPTER 3

Making Family Part of the Writing Team

Synergy is not just teamwork or cooperation. Synergy is creative teamwork, creative cooperation. Something new is created that was not there before.
— Stephen R. Covey

The word "synergy" is high-priced terminology for working together. Scientifically, it means a cooperative effort of two or more muscles or organs working together in order to perform specific actions; in lay terms, "two heads are better than one." Its actual definition is "combined action." And this combined cooperative action between you and the rest of your family members is required if you are going to successfully write at home.

ANTICIPATE CHANGES IN YOUR FAMILY DYNAMICS

Most of us find it difficult to handle any type of change. But it's especially troublesome when it has to do with our routines at home. The known is comfortable. It's become a habit or "the way we've always done it." Think about it. Move a chair to a different position in your bedroom and you'll probably find yourself unconsciously tossing your jacket to the spot where the chair used to be. Rearrange your glasses and china in the kitchen cupboard and you'll reach in the wrong spot for weeks. Decide you'll park on the opposite side of the garage and you'll still automatically pull into the former side.

Is it any wonder, then, that your kids may feel uncomfortable or even rebel when their always-available mom suddenly says she is writing and is too busy to carpool or be homeroom mother and bake cookies for thirty? Or when dependable dad announces he'll be writing at night and can't coach the Little League team? The youngsters may act out their disapproval through misbehavior or actually voice their displeasure by asking, "What about us?" (The innuendo, of course, is that you have abandoned all responsibility toward them and will let them starve, wander the streets in unironed clothes and flunk out of school because you won't help with their homework. The intent, of course, is to make you feel guilty. Don't let them succeed.)

Kids aren't the only ones who may feel shortchanged, however. Some spouses also resent the time their mates spend at their keyboards instead of with their husbands or wives. "I could almost understand it if my competition were 'another man,' " one husband complained. "But it's a Smith Corona."

Every marriage is unique and, therefore, so is the response of each mate to the writer spouse and the couple's particular situation. Some spouses gladly serve as proofreaders or editors. Others may decide to make writing a team effort and join in as coauthor, collaborator, photographer or illustrator for the project. While some read everything their spouses write and mumble, "That's nice, dear," others make constructive suggestions that serve to strengthen a manuscript or add to its salability. A few husbands and wives transfer their resentment of their spouses' preoccupation with writing to the work itself and tear it apart verbally or sometimes even physically.

With family cooperation so vital, it's important for you to get family members to buy into the idea that you're going to be writing at home and that you need for them to be supportive. You aren't asking for their permission, just their cooperation.

Don't keep your intentions a secret or expect your family members to read your mind. It's unlikely that any of them are gifted with ESP. Give some thought and consideration to how your family dynamics will change. Because they will. You can't be two places at once and if you are in the den, bedroom or wherever busily writing, you certainly are not going to be as available to the family as you formerly were.

Don't think in absolutes, however. Writing at home doesn't mean that you'll *never* be able to play a game with your kids, read them a bedtime story or attend their sporting events. It certainly doesn't mean that you and your spouse will have to turn down invitations for dinner out, stop taking vacations or give up going to the movies together. It does mean, however, that the rest of the family may have to help pitch in with some of the responsibilities you formerly took care of, such as fixing dinner, washing laundry, shoveling snow, doing yard work, cleaning the pool and so on.

But you know what? It's good for your kids to have a little more responsibility at home. It helps them develop self-confidence and bolsters self-esteem, which is vital for their well-being. It makes youngsters feel needed and an important part of this organization we call family. By observing one or both of their parents writing at home, your youngsters will see by your example the importance of writing skills, careful research, motivation and self-discipline. What you do will have far more effect on them than what you say.

Communicate Your Intentions

Effective communication is the power that makes families run smoothly. It clarifies values and expectations so that all members know what is required of them. But effective communication requires more than just telling people something. It also requires your inviting feedback to determine whether or not your message has been received the way you intended it to be. Remember the children's game of telephone in which a phrase is whispered from one person to another around a circle? The last person who repeats the message aloud often recites something quite garbled from what was originally said.

Most people think of good communication as using words. But it also involves good listening skills, not only of what is being said but also of what is being expressed in body language or nonverbal language. Over 50 percent of our communicating is nonverbal, such as sighing, frowning, crossing our arms across our chests, maintaining or avoiding direct eye contact, or fiddling with rings or objects on a desk.

Think about the nonverbal clues your family members give to each other, when someone is speaking. Do the members of your family really listen to each other or are they preoccupied thinking of a snappy comeback or what they want to say next? Do they interrupt? Do they give verbal cues, such as "Oh, I see," and, "All right"?

You need to set aside time to talk to your family about your desire to begin to write at home. The best time to discuss these changes that will take place in your family is at a family meeting. If you haven't held this type of meeting before now, it's a good time to begin doing so. The rules for a family meeting are fairly simple. Everyone has an equal opportunity to give an opinion, no one will be criticized for doing so and each family member must be treated with respect.

Hold your family meeting at a time that is convenient to everyone. Plan an agenda that includes ample time for you to discuss why you want to write at home, when you plan to do so, where you will work and what the rules will be about interrupting you. Obviously, fire and injuries involving bleeding should be high on your list, but you may have to contend with a lot of "what if's" at your first meeting: "What if Johnny takes my truck and won't let me play?" "What if I need to ask you something?" "What if I'm hungry?" Think about your policy ahead of time and expect the kids (and, possibly, your spouse) to test you in the beginning.

Listen to your family's concerns about what this new activity means to them and try to reassure them. Make compromises if you need to in the beginning to help everyone reach a comfort zone. You might begin your writing-at-home career with a shorter time span at first, such as an hour, to get your family used to your being near but not available. Then you can expand your writing time to two hours, then four or even more.

Don't be surprised if the other family members begin to request regular family conferences to discuss additional issues that arise. We started this type of family get-together when the kids were young, to review allowances and budgets, household chores, family vacations and rules. As they grew older, our meetings were filled with dating issues, rules on car use and bigger allowances. Now that all the kids are adults, we still get together for Sunday dinner to catch up on what everyone is doing and enjoy general conversation. It's kept our family close for many years. I highly recommend adopting this tradition, even if your children are grown with their own children. It's never too late.

There's little doubt that improved communication skills are the key to getting cooperation from your family. They can't respect your writing time if you haven't communicated to them what it means to you and how important it is. At future family meetings, you can talk about other issues, such as respecting each other's space and property. You may be thinking about a hands-off policy for your work supplies so that your scissors, paper clips, dictionary and favorite red pen don't disappear from your desk. Your kids may interpret what you're saying more personally, about respecting a sibling who's on the telephone, knocking before entering a room or asking for permission to borrow a favorite audiotape or CD. This, in turn, could open the door to further discussions about relationships and traditions within a family. This is just one way in which your need for time and space in which to write can have a positive rippling effect on your family. Just the act of seeing you motivated and working to meet a deadline could encourage your youngsters to plan their own time more efficiently when faced with homework assignments. It also gives them permission to reach out and ask for help from other family members when it's needed. *Help* It's one of the good four-letter words.

Protect Your Time and Use It Wisely

All right. You've taken your case to the family and they've agreed to cooperate by leaving you alone so you can write. Be sure that you live up to your end of the bargain too. It's so easy to hide behind that closed door and sharpen pencils, string paper clips together, read a magazine or gobble up a Snickers bar.

Once, when my kids were little, I was attempting to finish the final chapter on a manuscript at the same time the kids were on a school holiday. They kept running back and forth through the house, standing outside my study door arguing and playing air force in the hallway with my door being the supply depot.

I tried to stay focused, but my concentration was shattered with bombs bursting outside my door. Finally I gathered the troops together. "This book is very important to me," I said, "and my editor is waiting to get it. I really would appreciate your help in being quiet so I can finish this chapter."

They accepted the challenge and for two days tiptoed back and forth whenever they even came close to my door. They spoke in whispers. At the end of the second day, one son asked how the chapter was coming.

I had the decency to blush. "I . . . ah, I didn't work on the chapter actually. I was making notes for my column."

"Mother," he interrupted in youthful exasperation. "You were supposed to be working on that chapter."

I felt properly chastised and went back to work on the chapter immediately and finished it the next day. I could tell that the kids were disappointed with me. They had taken my work seriously, but I hadn't.

Don't let your family down. When they cooperate to give you the time and space you need for writing, make good use of it.

You're not altogether "safe" just because your kids are grown either. If they have been used to your baby-sitting, waiting for repair people at their homes or going over to feed the cats while they're away, they may not understand your suddenly setting limitations on the use of your time. If you have been at your adult children's beck and call, there may be some resentment for a while when you say no to them. But just as you need to discipline young children, you need to let the grown ones know that you have the right to protect your own time.

Having said this, I confess that I often drop what I'm doing or take my laptop with me to help my kids when they're in a pinch. My schedule is more flexible than most of theirs, and as my writing now is primarily full-length books, it's fairly easy to stick notes for a chapter in a briefcase and become mobile. When the chore is baby-sitting until the regular nanny comes, I'm suddenly thrust back in time, trying to write with a little one at my knees. The difference is that I'm now a grandmother, and I find that I often put my papers back in the briefcase and gather my grandchild up for a cuddle, a kiss and some story time. I may be a disciplined writer, but I'm also human.

Get the Family Involved

Some writers disagree with my belief in getting their families involved in the writers' work. But I think sharing what is important to you helps to cement any relationship. I like to know about my husband's work. If I know the obstacles he runs into on a daily basis, I can be more interested and sympathetic and, occasionally, may offer a suggestion that he, being too close to the subject, may not have thought of.

My husband has always been extremely supportive of my work. At times, he has mentioned the names of various people I might interview for a particular article or book. Often he has suggested ideas for books. Last summer, when I was in Maine publicizing my book *How to Get Out of the Hospital Alive*, he drove me to various interviews and waited patiently until they were over to drive me home. Although he's not a writer, he often offers a layperson's insights that help me focus a book to better serve my intended reader.

I also enjoy hearing about my children's work and what it involves. Their experiences are so varied. Their professions include a development officer at a major university, a home builder, an elementary school teacher, a computer specialist and a restaurateur. Even though I don't understand much of what the computer kid tells me, I still like to hear about it.

My kids also feel a part of my work. Just yesterday, one of my daughters drove me to a speaking engagement almost two hours away. It gave us a good opportunity to catch up on each other's lives. It helped me to be relaxed by the time we reached our destination. But it also gave her a glimpse of her mom in the role of a public speaker, something she had never observed before. I enjoyed having her there, and she admitted that it gave her a chance to view me in a totally different way. She had known me as a writer from the time she was a little girl, but she had never witnessed sixty people listening intently to what her mom had to say. It was a growth experience for us both.

As I've mentioned, my kids saw me working as a writer as soon as they were old enough to peer through the bars of their cribs. For the most part, we coexisted peacefully. I wrote and they played happily nearby. But they seemed to sense my tension as deadlines approached. Skirmishes broke out, with fits and accusations flying. After quickly discovering that yelling only added to the noise level, I learned to be creative in those situations.

When they were little, I'd put each in a different room and tell them to draw pictures and tape them on their doors. The judging came after I finished my work. Guess what? Everyone got blue ribbons.

As they outgrew the picture contests, I tried reason. I reminded them that Daddy had his work, they had school as their work and I had my work. I was glad that mine could be done at home so I could be around if they needed me, but they had to help me. I compared my deadline to their homework assignments or team competitions, anything that helped them relate to my situation. I appealed to their sense of honor, responsibility, decency and, as a last resort, guilt. I also was not above using bribery.

I still remember trying to complete an article on speculation for *Essence*. I was typing (it was before computers) my final draft, and my typing was, and still is, painfully slow as I only use three fingers. The kids were arguing outside the door to my study. Suddenly, the door flew open and one of the "defenders of truth and justice" came in to lodge a complaint against the other siblings who seemed to represent evil and destruction.

"Play a quiet game," I said with sudden inspiration. "If I don't hear any noise, I'll treat everyone to ice cream."

There was an immediate peace treaty. I finished typing the manuscript without any more interruption and mailed it. We all got ice-cream cones. The kids considered that article "theirs," and when it sold, they couldn't wait to see "their" article in print. And no, I never felt one bit guilty for using bribery (or eating the ice cream). Any port in a storm.

The point of all this reminiscing is more than just sharing fond memories of my kids when they were little. It's to illustrate that your family members can be brought into your working life so that they feel as though they too play a part in your success. It makes them more cooperative in taking on more responsibility and more supportive of you and your need for quiet time. It also helps to break up the loneliness of writing when you know you have your own personal cheering section.

Beware of Saboteurs

Be aware of subtle messages—verbal or nonverbal—that may suggest that your family may not be so delighted with your decision to write at home. While they may tell you how pleased they are and wish you great success, their actions may say otherwise.

A wife complains to friends supposedly in jest that she has to tiptoe around the house on the weekends because her husband is writing. "He might as well be out of town. I never see him," she adds. A husband feels neglected even though he tells people he's proud of hs wife's published work. But when complimented on his loss of weight, he may jab, "It's not from dieting. My wife's just too busy playing writer to cook for me anymore." These comments are spoken in the voice of anger and resentment.

Watch too for put-downs, such as, "He's got a new hobby. Writing. Certainly cheaper than golf." Or, "She says she's home writing all day, but I think she's napping or watching TV." These and similar comments can be very destructive, not only to a relationship but also to your writing.

Don't ignore statements like this or try to laugh them off. Be assertive and tell your spouse (or kids) the message you are receiving and how the comment makes you feel. You may be told that you've misunderstood or that you're too sensitive. More likely, however, your loved one may not have even realized that he was so resentful. Spend some time talking about these feelings and discuss how you both can compromise so your family doesn't feel abandoned while, at the same time, you can begin to accomplish your goals.

Your family can scuttle your writing plans if they have a mind to and if you stand passively by. It's worth taking some time to clear the minefield before you start moving forward.

CHAPTER 4

Handling Interruptions

Nothing interferes with my concentration. You could put on an orgy in my office and I wouldn't look up. Well, maybe once.

— Isaac Asimov

Unfortunately, most of us would and do look up more than once and it doesn't take an orgy in our office to distract us. When my children were little, too much quiet distracted me because I sensed (correctly) that they were into some mischief. Sounds of the dryer also caught my attention when I knew I hadn't been the one to start it. (I was correct again. The kids were making scrambled eggs in the dryer to surprise me. They succeeded.)

DISCONNECT FROM TELEPHONE DISTRACTIONS

Even with an answering machine to catch my calls, the sound of the telephone ringing still distracts me. I worry that one of my kids needs me. (They're all grown, but I *am* a mother. I worry.) When my parents were still alive, I worried that one of them was ill and needed help. I used to fret that the caller might be an editor calling to say she wanted to buy my latest proposal. Even now that I have an agent who has to answer *her* phone, I worry that if I don't answer mine, she may be calling to say that Sir Anthony Hopkins wants to buy the rights to my latest work, but he has to know my answer immediately. (Just to be safe, I've told her the answer is always yes.)

There are three ways you can minimize telephone distractions. The first is to have an emergency code for those calls you want to take—from your kids, spouse, parents, agent and so on. The easiest code is to have them call, let the phone ring twice, hang up and then call back. It means you have to listen and count the rings, but otherwise, it does work.

You can get a second line that can be used only for "have to talk to you now" calls. It's more expensive, but when the red phone rings, you listen.

The third way to minimize telephone distractions is to get a caller ID device. In some areas, you can get it through your telephone system. Otherwise, you can get the box at stores such as Radio Shack, Office Depot or Staples for about twenty dollars and up. While you'll still hear the phone ring, all you have to do is to glance at the caller's number to decide whether or not you want to pick up the phone. It does interrupt but in a less obtrusive manner.

It's hard to believe how much time you can waste chatting on the phone unless you actually document it for a couple of days. Try it. Talking to a friend rehashing a movie or football game: thirty minutes; thanking someone for a gift or dinner: fifteen minutes; talking to your mother: twenty minutes. See how fast it builds up? Scary, isn't it? You can easily spend two, three or even more hours on the phone each day. That's enough time to make real headway on an article or book chapter. People have written complete novels with no more daily allowance of writing time.

How can you use the telephone more efficiently? Here are a few suggestions:

- Schedule your calls in one block at a specific time each day.
- Use a timer so the minutes don't slip away.
- Learn to say good-bye first and hang up.
- Eliminate calls whenever possible by writing thank-you notes, memos or E-mail messages.
- Confirm details on future dates with friends so you don't need to make additional calls to confirm.

LEARN TO SAY "NO"

My science-oriented friends tell me that Newton's third law of motion says, in effect, that for every action there is an equal but opposite reaction. That's pretty much what you can expect when you announce to the world that you're finally going to take your writing seriously and that you need some time and space, thank you. As you begin to withdraw a little from the world around you in order to have some solitude for writing, you'll suddenly find yourself in greater demand than ever before.

You'll be overwhelmed with offers to play golf or tennis or to go sailing with your buddies. Friends want you to go shopping with them and may feel cross and a little resentful when you turn them down. Grown children, who haven't called you between Thanksgiving and Valentine's Day, suddenly begin checking in on a day-by-day basis. Organizations, who once counted on you and your writing talents, may be confused when you turn down requests to write skits, the newsletter and publicity releases because you need to stay focused on your writing. And the strange thing is, the more you say no, the more they all want you, grabbing at your time allotment as though it were a big bowl of popcorn.

But you have to keep saying no, if you want to make the time for your own writing. It's difficult. How can you escape without hurting some feelings or feeling as though you are letting others down? The answer is, you can't. The trick, as magician David Copperfield must have said, is in making sure you *do* escape.

That's not to say that you should tear up your address book and never see friends. They're an important part of your life, so much so that an entire later chapter is devoted to ways you can stay in touch with friends and still have time to write. But you need to control the interruptions so they don't interfere with your work.

If you find that you're always available to your friends and you secretly feel they're taking advantage at times, ask yourself to seriously consider whether or not *you're* the one using your friends to keep from writing. Possibly you are because deep down you're afraid that you might not be a good writer. But if you don't give yourself the proper time to try, you'll never find out, will you? Don't be afraid of failure. As Henry Ford once said, "One who fears failure limits his activities. Failure is only the opportunity to more intelligently begin again." Author Ilka Chase echoed those thoughts by saying, "The only people who never fail are those who never try."

LOOK IN THE MIRROR

Usually, our biggest distractor can be detected by looking in the mirror. It's us. We take one phone call and decide to call everyone else we haven't heard from in weeks. Someone sticks his head in to ask a question and we figure, "Oh, well, as long as I'm interrupted, I'll go get a bite to eat." Or we stop to watch one favorite television show and lose two hours watching the junk that follows.

We have to take ourselves in hand (isn't that a great image?) and give ourselves a good talking to, remind ourselves to focus on the task at hand. I have a sign above my desk that I cribbed from one of the earliest and best time management books, Alan Lakein's *How to Get Control of Your Time and Your Life*. The sign reads, "What is the best use of my time?" When I glance at that, it's as though my better self is standing over me shaking her head. It does keep me on task.

My biggest distraction is the mail. As soon as it comes, I want to stop and go through it, even if I'm writing and the thoughts are flowing well. Usually, there's nothing more than magazines, which I then stop to thumb through, or bills, which I immediately put in a file to pay later. If the Pulitzer prize committee has sent a letter to tell me I've won, it got lost in the mail, so there's really no reason to stop to look for it. I've had to discipline (that word again) myself to ignore the sound of the mail truck and wait until I'm ready for a break.

SCHEDULE BREAKS

This is the part you were waiting for: break time. That's right. The discipline for writing at home isn't just for keeping your nose to the grindstone. It's also about knowing when to come up for air. Sometimes giving yourself a little distance from a project gives your subconscious an opportunity to wrestle with the tough parts. Many times I've gone to bed frustrated about a lead that doesn't seem to click, only to wake up and find the elves have left a tight little bundle of perfect words on the tip of my tongue or fingertips. The same wonderful magic has worked when I've left the computer for the kitchen, and as I sautéed the chicken breasts in wine and garlic, the answers that had eluded me in the study seemed to flow up with the steam. Why? I have no idea, other than to say I think it's because I rested one area of my brain by scheduling a break so then another area kicks in with the solutions.

The trick, of course, is to schedule these breaks judiciously. If you take more breaks than work time, you'll be relaxed but probably not a published writer.

PRETEND YOU ARE HANSEL AND GRETEL

Remember that frighteningly grim Grimm fairy tale about the two little kids lost in the woods who find the witch's house in the middle of the forest? She wants to eat them while they want to eat her house. It's one of the early dietary tales, like "It's a dog-eat-dog world." Anyway, the siblings leave cookie crumbs as they walk along in the woods so they can find their way home.

That's what you need to do when you're interrupted. But rather than leaving cookie crumbs, which will just make you thirsty so you need to get another drink of water, which interrupts you all the more, leave cues to remind you where you were so you can quickly get back to work. Put a light pencil mark or a Post-it flag to mark the line of the reference book you were reading, or write a few words to help you recapture a thought you were developing before you were interrupted. When I have to interrupt my writing to start dinner, I often leave myself a memo. It lists two or three things I want to do first thing in the morning, such as add two ideas to a chapter, get information I want for an upcoming chapter or ask my agent a question. By leaving these starting-gate messages, I'm ready to go first thing in the morning, rather than wasting time trying to remember where I was.

When I was little, I had a book mark that read, "Here I fell asleep." I always liked the idea of marking my ending point. Now that I'm grown, I prefer the marker that says, "Here I begin again."

START SOMETHING

Procrastination is the ultimate interruption because it keeps you from even beginning. When you're writing at home, it's easy to find reasons to procrastinate. There are so many things that you "have to do" before you sit down to write. You have to do the dishes, read the paper, toss another load of clothes in the wash, oil the screen door, pay some bills or water the plants. You see how busy you can be? And it's just the beginning. The list of possible chores is endless.

Most people procrastinate because they're afraid to begin. After all, if you don't begin, you can't fail. You can still say you're a writer because you haven't set anything down on paper to prove yourself a liar. But then you'll never know, will you? What's more, you'll never write anything if you don't get started.

You may feel overwhelmed because you don't really know where to begin. You stare at the blank computer screen and eventually decide to play solitaire or one of the other computer games instead. Or you roll a clean sheet of typing paper into your typewriter and then wad it up in frustration because there are no words magically appearing on it.

Think small. What may be making you procrastinate is the size of the job ahead. Cut it down to size. Make confetti of it. Write a sentence. Any sentence. It doesn't have to have any significance. Most of my original first sentences or even first paragraphs don't. But at least you'll have broken the ice. You'll have something written on the page. Keep writing until you have a paragraph. Then begin again with a new sentence, and before you know it, you'll have a second paragraph and then a third. Don't try to make your writing perfect. It doesn't have to be, and unless you're a most unusual writer, it probably won't be. That's why we all have to rewrite, even though our work still seldom reaches that lofty perch we call perfection. But you will have made a start.

On more than one occasion, I had to reorganize and rewrite one or more chapters for books I had sold to publishers. The first time it happened, I spent two days worrying about it. I found myself incapable of beginning the rather tedious job. I transferred all the names and addresses from one address book to a new one, put plant food on my dead cactus, rearranged old copies of *Reader's Digest* into chronological order and washed out all the mugs holding my pencils and pens.

As my deadline approached, I knew I had to take action. I outlined the chapter, writing the main idea of each section on a slip of paper. Then I spread all these scraps on the floor and moved them around like chessmen until they (at last) followed in a natural order.

A sneeze or a strong wind would have set me back days. Then, taking each piece of paper in its turn, I wrote a paragraph or two, explaining the idea.

Before I knew it, I had outsmarted myself. By making confetti out of chaos, I had been able to work on the chapter, piece by piece, rather than by trying to tackle the whole chore at once. I was able to stop procrastinating because I was faced with only a series of small and nonthreatening writing tasks. So often we procrastinate because we have so much to do we don't know where to begin. So we don't.

SKELETONIZE, EVEN THOUGH IT'S NOT HALLOWEEN

I still use the piecemeal method of writing, only now I use Post-it Notes because they stick to my desktop and don't slide around as the strips of paper and index cards did. It's a generic form of outlining that I call skeletonizing. It involves the bare bones of an article or book. It's no different if you're talking about a house, human being or book. You have to first form the skeleton before you know the shape of what you're creating. While you might not want to connect the kneecap to the chin or stick a front door on the second story, you have the freedom to rearrange the bones of your article or chapter until you think the skeleton can stand on its own. Then you begin to flesh it out.

Skeletonizing works for me because it's user-friendly. I think we all get a little uptight when we think about outlining before writing something. It takes us back to our elementary school days when we learned to create a formal outline with roman numerals, indented *A*s and *B*s and so on.

Use whatever works for you to get you rolling, to put something down on that bit of blankness in front of you, even if it's no more than "The quick brown fox jumped over the lazy dog." It's not too original, but it's a sentence and that's a start. Put your goal in writing and paste it on your computer monitor or over your typewriter so it's the first thing you see when you sit down to write.

In 1508, Erasmus, a Dutch scholar said, "The desire to write grows with writing." Remember that books are written by chapters, chapters by pages, and pages one by one. It all begins with that first word and sentence. So writers, start your writing.

CHAPTER 5

Doing Household Chores and Other "Have-To's"

Work expands so as to fill the time available for its completion.

— Cyril Northcote Parkinson, Parkinson's Law

It might surprise you to know that writing at home is probably most difficult for those of you who are retired or who have no children. You may think it should be easier because you have nobody to interrupt you. The day looms large with no blips on the horizon. But it is just this lack of structure that makes scheduling time to write like trying to throw your arms around an elusive fluffy cloud before it drifts away. Because you feel as though you can catch the proper amount of time whenever you want it, you don't harness a specific amount, and before you know it, it all floats away from you and the day is over.

But those with kids around can also find themselves being carried off course by the demands of their youngsters and The House. While the appetites of both are seemingly insatiable, The House, regardless of its size, tends to scream for more attention, like a spoiled child. No matter how often you do household chores, there always seems to be more to do. Dust settles back on the furniture almost before you can put the rags away, and the just-empty laundry bin fills up as quickly as the bill box. Family members who easily exist on a two-week vacation with nothing more than a pair of jeans, two T-shirts and a bathing suit seem to feel that at home a shirt's dirty after an hour's wear and a towel used to dry a just-washed body needs to immediately be thrown into the hamper.

If you wait until The House is immaculate and consider yourself a contender for the Perfect Home and Hearth Award, you probably will never get around to writing. If, however, you can put household chores in their proper place—something that must be done eventually—you can make and stick to a writing schedule that works for you. Do what needs to be done as it needs to be done, then do it as efficiently and effectively as it needs to be done and nothing more. I call it planned procrastination so it sounds official. And it works.

DETERMINE WHAT *HAS* TO BE DONE

The main criterion for chores in and around the house is, Does anybody notice? If nobody notices that you spent the better part of a day repainting the mailbox, it probably didn't really need it. The same goes for rearranging your bookshelves so everything's alphabetical by author. Perhaps the kitchen floor doesn't really need to be scrubbed as often as you think it does. In her book *How to Be a Mother—and a Person, Too*, Shirley L. Radl wrote, "If my feet stick to the kitchen floor, I mop it." I've taken her philosophy to heart.

On the other hand, you or someone else needs to take the garbage out on a daily basis, provide something to eat and do the laundry when everyone's run out of something to wear. Note I didn't mention making beds; just close the bedroom doors.

Call a family meeting and enlist everyone's help in drawing up a list of necessary chores. Then see if they fall into any type of logical order. For example, the day the bed sheets are changed is probably a good day to wash them. Dry cleaning can be dropped off on the way to someone's work, school or exercise class. Grocery shopping can be done in the evening or midweek, rather than on Friday when the supermarkets are jammed. Fill the larder whenever it's convenient for you or there's nothing left to eat but peanut butter and pretzels.

Forget Granny's rigid routine of Monday we wash, Tuesday we iron and so on. Times have changed and you need to schedule chores to suit you and the rest of the family. What's more, there are many chores you really don't have to do. If you immediately take clothes out of the dryer, for example, you can smooth many of them out so you don't have to iron them. You can soak pans in dishwasher detergent rather than scrubbing them. Friends don't inspect your home with white gloves, and if they do, perhaps you should take a good look at your choice of friends. For the most part, if your home is reasonably neat and you're content and able to write, your pals will be far more impressed with the smile on your face than the shine on your floor. Remember that people aren't supposed to eat off your floor. That's why we have plates.

ANSWER THE CLUTTER QUESTION

I prefer the term "clutter question" rather than "simplify." The reason is personal bias. I really don't like the word simplify because too many people translate it to mean radically paring down one's environment to the barest of essentials. The followers of the recent simplify fetish strip their bookcases of books and knickknacks, their kitchen cupboards down to one bowl and one knife and their closets to two shirts, one pair of jeans and two pairs of shoes. Their dwellings may be easy to care for and the dwellers can pack up and move anywhere within hours, but their homes resemble museums without warmth and the personal touches that make a house a home.

As you may surmise, I tend to go for the comfortably controlled cluttered look. And to be totally up front with you, I do have a collection of more than two hundred glass, ceramic, wood and metal hippos. Nevertheless, you should do as I say, not as I do. It's easy to keep clutter from gaining the upper hand.

Begin by taking photographs of each room. What our eyes get used to, the camera reveals most vividly. It shows the pile of unread magazines teetering perilously on the kitchen counter, along with two tennis balls, a pencil with broken lead and pictures of a friend's grandchildren that you really didn't want to keep but felt guilty throwing out. It exposes the mess on your bedroom dresser that includes unpaid bills, a tube of ointment for some forgotten itch and a brochure for a theater event long since over.

Check the photograph for too many objets d'art (and photographs) sitting around and accumulating dust. If you have collections of little things (other than kids), consider putting some away and rotating them. Unless indoor gardening is your thing, toss the violets that have given up the ghost and deserve a proper burial.

Do the same with the straggly plant of unknown origin. Although I still nurse my late mother's Christmas cactus and am amazed when it rewards me once annually with a magnificent array of colored blooms, the bulk of my plants are silk or plastic. I have even given up on trying to landscape the outside balconies of my high-rise home and have put fake trees and bushes there. I have a simple philosophy about pets, plants, piles and hodgepodge: If you have to dust, water, polish or feed it, you don't need it. Notable exceptions, of course, are your spouse and kids, if any.

If you have children, help them to control their clutter too, but make it easy for them to do so. Give them containers for their possessions. Buy colored baskets, buckets and plastic washtubs for toys, blocks and books. Lower the closet rods in the closets so the kids can hang up their clothes. Put a plastic washtub on the closet floor for dirty laundry.

Use plastic boxes for your own shirts, shoes and out-of-season items to keep them dust-free but in plain sight so you don't buy duplicates. That advice earlier might have prevented my now owning three pairs of black midheels.

Clear your kitchen countertops, which seem to attract clutter like a magnet. If they're anything like mine, they are usually topped with old newspaper clippings that I can't remember why I kept, keys to unknown locks, half-empty medicine bottles, cookbooks and a burned-out lightbulb I need to take with me in order to buy a new one in the same shape. Clearing flat space, such as coffee tables, countertops, dressers and desks, makes it easier to clean your home quickly and gives the appearance that things are neater, and for those of us writing at home, illusion is the name of the game.

TAKE ADVANTAGE OF TIMESAVING DEVICES

Use timesaving devices, such as electric brooms, microwaves, pressure cookers and slow cookers, to keep you out of the kitchen and at the keyboard. Take advantage of the precooked entrées you can find in most groceries, or cook in quantity and freeze for other meals. Remember that others in the family—male and female and children of almost all ages—can be "cook for the night."

The U.S. Postal Service feels your panic, and that's one reason it's instituted the "buy postage stamps by mail" system. Pick up a couple of mail-in envelopes the next time you're at the post office, or call and have some sent to you.

Stop running around the house looking for frequently used items. Buy duplicate scissors, for example, and mark them with permanent ink by location so you'll know (and be able to scream) if the kitchen scissors have made their way to the family room or the stapler from your office mysteriously makes its way into one of your kids' rooms.

Post a grocery list on the refrigerator and insist that family members write down what they need. Let all drivers in the family take turns going to the grocery. It's great training for kids and is a simple way to educate them on the cost of things. Grocery shopping becomes such a habit that we tend to always buy the same things and don't even see new products. By sharing the shopping chores, you may discover something yummy you've been missing.

My family calls me the Catalog Queen, although one of my daughters-in-law is threatening to steal my crown. I find it's much more relaxing to shop by catalog than to fight your way through crowds, especially during the December holiday season. You also can find food items, furnishings, stationery and, yes, even silk plants within the pages of the catalogs. Just be sure you keep your order form with the date you ordered the item, the person's name taking the order and the order number in case you need to check on it. I have learned, however, to toss the older catalog when the new one comes in so we're no longer in danger of being crushed by the catalogs.

ASK FOR HELP

I doubt that it's written anywhere that a particular chore can be done by only one person in a family. So why not rotate jobs? Our kids really can do many of the tasks that we as parents take on because it's often easier to do the chores ourselves than to ask for help. But as Eleanor Roosevelt so aptly stated, "When we make it easy for our children, we make it hard for them." We need to teach them responsibility because it is only through taking responsibility that young people can develop a sense of self-esteem and self-accomplishment. So stop feeling guilty about asking your kids for help. It's their home too, and doing chores is just part of family life.

Be careful that you don't assign certain chores by gender. Girls as well as boys can take out the garbage, and all your kids should learn to cook and clean up afterward. When my kids were young, all but one had a culinary specialty. A friend quizzed them.

> "I'm the brownie maker," said our oldest, then thirteen.
>
> "I'm the omelet maker," boasted the oldest boy, then twelve.
>
> "I'm the bread maker," said the youngest daughter, then ten.
>
> "I'm the hot dog maker," said our little guy, just five.
>
> The middle son, then nine, was silent. "What about you?" my friend asked.
>
> He thought for a minute, then smiled. "Me? I'm the troublemaker."

They're all grown now and I'm pleased to say their cuisine has gotten a little more sophisticated. And the middle son? Although he still doesn't like cooking, I'm happy to report he's no longer the troublemaker.

Parcel out age-appropriate chores to the younger kids. If they are eager to help, make it seem like a real treat as you wrinkle your brow thoughtfully and say, "Well, maybe you *are* old enough to run the vacuum and empty the dishwasher." They can help strip their beds when the linens need changing as well. Let teenagers who can drive have the car to help run errands, such as picking up dry cleaning and going to the shoe repair.

Institute a weekly rotating duty roster for the kids' chores. These could include such tasks as table clearing, loading the dishwasher or washing the dishes, sweeping after the meal, taking out the garbage and feeding the family pets. Be wary, however, of a possible devious streak in your children. When mine were little, I had a paper clock with hands pointing to the various jobs. But my older kids moved the hands around to suit themselves, leaving the younger ones in tears and seemingly responsible for the dirty jobs. When I switched to index cards marked with the various chores and alternated them under the children's names, my offspring re-shuffled the cards. It's hard to stay ahead when there's more of them than you.

Snap out of your rut when it comes to household chores divided between you and your spouse. Since we scaled down, moving out of our big house and into smaller quarters, my husband has begun taking the shirts and sheets to the dry cleaner. Grocery shopping is appropriated to whichever of us has the time to do it, although sometimes we go together. We make the bed together and do laundry whenever the hamper is full.

You can also barter or hire extra hands to help you. Cleaning services are available in many areas. During the summer, you can often find teenagers or teachers who are interested in making extra cash helping with housework. Ask around or put an ad in your neighborhood newspaper. Be sure to check references, though, before letting strangers into your home.

The important thing to remember is that household chores need to be relegated to their proper position. While many of them need to be done in order to keep your home running smoothly, they don't have to be done all the time or by you. And they should never consume so much of your time and energy that you have nothing left for writing.

AIM FOR THE BULL'S-EYE

Picture your neighborhood as a dartboard with your home as the bull's-eye. When you have errands to run, try to keep them within the same area as your home. If you have to go out of the target area, visualize another concentric circle and try to incorporate all your business in that section so you don't find yourself running to one end of town for letterhead, another for dry cleaning and still another for the shoe repair shop. Before you go anywhere, remember the telephone yellow page slogan and "Let Your Fingers Do the Walking." Always call first to see if an item's available and, more important, if it can be delivered. Time spent in your car is time away from your writing.

CHANGE WITH THE TIMES

One of the most difficult adjustments for me has been trying to get used to a household with only two people in it. It's not the empty-nest syndrome. I love returning to the way we were in the beginning, just the two of us. It's that I can't remember how to cook for two. I still think in sevens and, of course, am in my glory when we have all the kids and their spouses and the grandkids. Then I have a flock to cook for in quantity once more.

But I've learned that I need to change with the times because it will save me time. For years I kept my biggest mixing bowls and institutional-size pans in the lower cupboards, despite the fact that I had to climb up on a step stool to reach the ones I now use daily for the two of us. Now that I've rearranged my kitchen back to a "tea for two" room, it's far more efficient and effective.

Consider other ways you can control your space. Throw away (or store) things you don't need, use or have an overwhelming attachment for. Ideally, of course, you should toss those items, but since I still have a chipped orange-colored pitcher from my childhood vacation home in Okoboji, Iowa, my old much-loved teddy bear and my high school letter sweater, I'm really in no position to advocate such a radical thought.

Think about how you are living right now. Has anything changed in the last five years? Ten years? What are you still doing that could be altered to better suit today's living style? For example, where are your bed linens? In a linen closet down the hall or in each bedroom where the beds are? How many sets of towels do you have? How many do you really need? Where do you pay bills? Is that where you keep the envelopes and postage stamps? Where is your mending kit? Where do you put the extra buttons that come with so many of today's outfits? What can you do differently that would be more efficient or effective? Don't let old habits steal time that you could be using for writing.

LISTEN TO YOUR INNER CLOCK

Since household chores don't go away, you will have to do your share of them, but you don't have to use your most creative time to do so. Know when your energy level is highest, and spend that time writing, even if it means leaving dirty breakfast dishes soaking in the sink. Don't wash the car during your peak period over the weekend. Use that time for writing. The chores can wait until later in the day when you feel sluggish and need some physical work.

USE THE TWO-BOX APPROACH

The two greatest solutions for handling household chores constitute what I call the two-box approach. The two boxes have worked for me since I first started using them twenty years ago, so I pass their functions along to you.

The Gift Box

I created the gift box idea when my kids were little and I was constantly interrupting my work to run to the store to buy gifts for them to give at birthday parties they had forgotten to tell me about. Rather than running out every time to find a gift, card and appropriate paper (it seems you can't give a boy pink wrapping paper with cute bunnies on it), I began buying an assortment of new and clever items at discount stores, at drugstores and when I was on trips.

I kept a large box filled with gifts for the kids' friends along with little things, such as coloring books and games, plus tape and scissors. I also purchased individual enclosure cards with each child's name printed on them. When there was an occasion for a gift, my child could rummage through the box and "shop" while I was happily writing. It saved time, gas, money and energy.

Today, the kids are on their own when it comes to gift giving, but I still keep a gift box filled with boxes of pretty note paper, fancy pens and other small gifts that can be given when the occasion calls for it and I have no time to shop. It's stored along with wrapping paper, gift cards, scissors, ribbon and tape in the dresser in the spare bedroom. It was too good an idea to grow out of.

The Tidy Box

The tidy box and its companion, the dump-it drawer, are exactly what they sound like: places to hide things. They make tidying up a breeze when company's coming. The tidy box basically is a covered box, basket or trunk kept in the family room or bedroom. It can be slid under the bed or used as a nightstand or end table.

As you walk through a room, you can put magazines, sneakers, catalogs and keys into the box. It removes clutter and gives you and your family a central lost-and-found depository. It also saves you from "Have you seen my . . ." discussions because everyone knows to look in the tidy box. The dump-it drawer operates on exactly the same principle, but it's a drawer, usually found in the kitchen. Try to keep only one dump-it drawer per room. They tend to breed like mice.

You may have spotted the inherent weakness of the tidy box and the dump-it drawer: Eventually both of them are filled to overflowing and you have to empty them. (It's much the same as the laundry hamper, when you think about it.) Usually you dispose of 75 percent and put the rest back in the box or drawer.

WHAT TO DO WHEN YOU HAVE TO CLEAN THE HOUSE

The ideal solution to cleaning the house might be to move out. But until we have disposable houses, you eventually may have to do some household chores. There are many good books available on how to clean your home and what utensils you need. Most of them probably tell you more than you want to know about cleaning and dusting everything but the dog. And they do tell you which to do first, dust or vacuum, but I'm not going to spoil it by telling you.

Instead, I'll share with you my four dozen super cleaning tips for the man or woman who wants to write at home and needs to get those pesky cleaning jobs done as quickly and efficiently as possible. Follow these and you can change from mild-mannered household cleaning person to Superwriter faster than you can find a phone booth. Note: These tips are in no particular order of importance.

1. Have the proper cleaning tools.

While you don't want to invest in every cleaning device you see advertised, it helps to have the right tool for the particular job. Carpenters and handymen (and women) have known that for years, although my mother could fix almost anything with a bobby pin. If you live in a two-story house and can afford to, buy a second vacuum cleaner, do so and you won't have to haul that awkward and heavy thing up and down stairs. I'm not singling out any particular brand. They're all awkward and heavy. I use an electric broom for quick jobs, such as sweeping up the last bits of broken glass, cleaning under the dining room table and picking up sand that comes in with shoes and toys.

2. Be selective about appliances and gadgets.

They're supposed to be timesaving devices, but much of the equipment cluttering our kitchen counters takes longer to use than, and actually duplicates, something we already have. That's why I gave away my electric hot dog cooker and the bread maker. (Our groceries sell wonderful bread.) I relocated our unused pasta maker to our summer home in Maine, and I haven't used it there either. I moved my electric mixer from its perch on my limited counter space in the condo to the bottom shelf of a cupboard in the family room. I only use the big mixer two or three times a year to make meringues so I want to keep it, but it doesn't have to take up counter space the other 362 days of the year. It's far faster to whip out the portable hand mixer for mashed potatoes and cookies. Since we stopped drinking coffee, I put the coffee maker away too and only get it out for company.

Go through your kitchen drawers and throw out or give away extra spoons, spatulas, graters, carrot peelers, peanut butter spreaders and other hand appliances that seem to multiply in the darkness of the drawers.

3. Weed out books.

If you're a book lover as I am (and most writers are), books tend to follow you home from bookstores and used book shops like lost puppies. You become addicted to library book sales. But books require maintenance—storing and dusting—and there is a limit (although I've pushed the envelope) to how many bookshelves you can squeeze into a room.

Weed your bookshelf on a regular basis as you would your garden, removing the "slugs" and the "dead leaves" (books you know you'll never reread). But don't throw them away. Recycle them by giving the books to your library (so somebody else can buy them during the next sale) or donating them to a local hospital, retirement home, youth center, nursing home or nonprofit group's garage sale.

It will make cleaning your bookshelves much easier and even give your room a less cluttered look. Vacuum or blow the dust off those books you're keeping. Keep your books free from moisture, and store them upright so the air can get to them. Do *not* stop to thumb through them or you'll never finish.

4. Reevaluate magazine subscriptions.

Magazines, once let into your home, seem to take on their own lives, breeding and multiplying at an amazing rate and taking up residence on your tabletops, floors, countertops and even in the bathtub. I constantly find myself on the receiving end of magazines I've never heard of and know I never subscribed to. Some I've actually enjoyed and renewed. Others I put in the recycle bin as fast as they arrive.

When you get a renewal bill, check to see if it's actually due. Many magazines begin sending notices months before the actual expiration time. Stop before checking "bill me" and mailing it back in the ever-so-convenient postage paid envelope and determine whether you really want to renew a particular magazine. Does it come weekly and get buried under each new issue without you even glancing at it? Do you enjoy reading it? If you subscribed to it for your kids, do they read it or have they outgrown it? Is it a magazine to which you hope to submit manuscripts?

Make sure every magazine subscription is one you welcome into your home like a favored guest. Otherwise, banish it to "occasional visitor" status by making it a newsstand purchase. (Note: If you want to minimize the number of unwanted catalogs and unsolicited advertising materials that appear on your doorstep like a baby in a basket, write to The Direct Marketing Association, Mail Preference Service, P.O. Box 9008, Farmingdale, NY 11735-9008 and ask that your name and address be deleted from mailing lists.)

5. Minimize your bathroom cleaning time.

My selection for invention of the year is the sponge on a stick that can be used to clean out the bathtub without climbing into it. You also can keep a squeegee inside the shower stall for occupants to use on the glass door after their showers. Keep a toilet brush in every bathroom so you don't have to tote a dripping brush throughout your house. Store extra soap and toilet paper in each bathroom in a basket or on a shelf, not in a hall linen closet where no one can get to it when it's really needed.

6. Bare your floors.

I used to think the ideal would be to have carpeting throughout my house. Just plug in the vacuum and take off with it. Now that I can look back on almost forty years of housekeeping, I realize that carpeting often cost me a lot of time in its upkeep. The kids lost bits of Legos and contact lenses in it, spilled liquids on it and tracked mud through it. The various dogs and cats got sick on it, left fleas in it and tracked mud through it. Unfortunately, wisdom came late. Now I opt for wood floors if possible, as they can be cleaned with a swipe of a damp mop. Vinyl and slate floor coverings also are a breeze to keep up, as long as you change the water frequently in the scrub bucket.

Although I've done away with rugs in my bedroom because of my asthma, we still have them in the family room and living room. While you need a vacuum cleaner for heavy-duty cleaning, I love the electric broom or carpet sweeper for quick pickups. They're both lighter than the vacuum. The electric broom I have in our Maine summer home is battery operated and plugs into an electric base to recharge.

If you're redoing your floors, there are many types of flooring that resemble wood. If you prefer carpeting, select a color and style that will be relatively easy to maintain.

7. Declutter your closets.

Books have been written about cleaning your closets. But if you're trying to make time to write, you don't want to spend too much time in your closet. There are just a few basics to remember. All closets need to be cleaned once in a while, and that's best done by taking everything out of them. In a clothes closet, you also need to wipe off the clothes rod. Sweep or vacuum the floor. Don't bother with shelf paper. If the shelves are nasty, paint them with high-gloss paint so you can just wipe them off.

Finally, only put back those things you really want to keep. It's true that if you haven't worn or used something in a year, you probably never will. When my husband and I shared a small closet, I got into the habit of getting rid of an old outfit whenever I bought a new one. I still try to maintain that practice even though I now have the luxury of my own closet.

Don't be tempted to put the rejects in the basement or attic because you'll just have to go through them again at a later date. Give unwanted clothes and shoes to a charity or recycle them at a secondhand shop. Without all the clutter, you'll be amazed at how much closet space you actually have.

If you have small children or grandchildren who visit, put a lock on one closet so you can store cleaning products there.

8. Dust 'cause you must.

Dust happens. It's almost impossible to keep it out of your home, so you have to dust often unless you plan to write your manuscripts in it. Most people I talked with said they dusted and then vacuumed but there's no federal law either way (yet). To help keep the dust from getting an upper hand, replace the vacuum bag often. Use a silicone-treated dust rag so you aren't just moving the dust around. Rather than using chemical aerosol products, make your own polish from a combination of one tablespoon of white vinegar to a half cup of olive oil. And to make dusting easier and faster, minimize the number of collectibles you have sitting around on coffee tables and dressers. Yes, I know I mentioned the hippos, but no one's perfect, you know.

9. Patrol the nightstand.

On the first of every month, go through the strange-looking items that have found a home on your nightstand. This cuts down clutter and makes it easier to keep your nightstand dust-free, which is important because your pillow and head are nearby. As I write this, my bedside table this morning harbored

- a two-cent postage stamp
- a paper clip
- an unfilled prescription for an ailment I forgot I had
- four books I haven't read since they've been sitting there (two of which I probably will never read)
- a piece of memo paper with some unknown person's phone number on it
- a pair of broken sunglasses

- the instructions to my camera, neither of which I've used recently

10. Raid the refrigerator.

If you think about it, the refrigerator is just one more closet that needs to be cleaned regularly. Unlike the others, this one happens to be cold and doesn't have your shoes inside—hopefully. But if you attack the refrigerator on a monthly basis, you'll be able to get through the task quickly and reasonably effortlessly.

Turn off the refrigerator and take everything out. You're bound to be surprised what crept into the back and hid. Throw away any brown lettuce (it's supposed to be green) and mayonnaise with rust spots on it. Check the salad dressings for end dates. If the eggs are cracked or smell funny, toss them too. If there are moldy spots on the cheese, throw it away. (I know "they" say you can cut the bad spots off and eat the rest, but the only time I like green on my cheese is on Roquefort.)

Wipe the shelves with baking soda and water. Put all the similar type food in one spot so you don't end up buying a third bottle of catsup or mustard. Be sure to empty and rinse the drip pan at the bottom of the refrigerator. While "they" say you should vacuum the vent on the back of the refrigerator, they never suggest how you should pull it out to do so. I read somewhere that you can use a hair dryer to blow out the dust, but I haven't tried that yet.

Don't forget to turn the refrigerator back on when you're finished. If you attack your refrigerator on a monthly basis, it will take less time to win the war.

11. Ban those washday blues.

You can drastically reduce the time you spend on laundry by sending it out. If that fails as an option, however, always pretreat stains before washing and fold clothes smooth as soon as they are dry so you don't have to iron. If you have to iron something, be careful, as electricity and water from the washing machine can be a deadly combination. Better yet, don't have an iron. Then you'll *have* to smooth things out as soon as they finish drying. Without an iron, you'll send some items, such as shirts, to the laundry, but the cost of cleaning the shirts may be less than the value of your time when you could be writing.

Read the printed care labels before you toss a new article of clothing into the washing machine. Don't overload the washer or dryer. When you overload the washer, the clothes don't get totally clean; when you overload the dryer, it increases the drying time and your clothes will have more wrinkles in them.

Use white vinegar or baking soda in your wash instead of bleach and other chemicals. If you prefer using bleach, keep it and other cleaning supplies in a high and preferably locked cupboard if you have small children or visiting grandchildren.

Use cold water to remove blood stains, white vinegar and water for chocolate or coffee stains. Buy one of many good spot removal guidebooks for the laundry room and keep it there for a reference.

12. Love oven cleaning.

Two luxuries I once considered highly overrated were automatic garage door openers and self-cleaning ovens. I take it all back. There is nothing as sweet as pushing a baffling array of buttons and then sitting down to write, knowing that the automatic oven-cleaning elves are fast at work.

If you don't have a self-cleaning oven, you have two choices: Either don't use your oven (which is the choice made by a relative of mine), or put some ammonia in a glass bowl (not a drinking glass) in the closed oven overnight. Be careful not to inhale the fumes. By morning, the baked-on stuff should be loose and you can wipe it off with a damp sponge or rag. I don't like commercial oven cleaners because they make me cough and my eyes water. If you do use them, however, wear gloves and be careful not to inhale the fumes or spill the chemical on your skin.

13. Clean your windows on the world.

You really don't have to clean windows often. Doesn't that make you feel better? On the other hand, if a bird messes them up or you find the world's going dim, it may be the time to do it. Wait for a cloudy day. Otherwise, the sun will streak the windows. Use vertical strokes on one side of the window and horizontal on the other. It helps you to see where the streaks are.

Use a squeegee with vinegar and water or the blue stuff from the grocery. People disagree which is best between drying with a newspaper, paper towels or cloth. I have no opinion and use whichever is handiest. Leave the upstairs outside windows for a professional window cleaner and take thee back to your writing.

14. Ban dirty pans.

Don't waste time scrubbing pans with food stuck or burned on them. Sprinkle some dishwasher detergent in them and add some water. Let them sit in the cold oven overnight. My mother and I used to call this oven surprise, as we often forgot about the pans and were surprised when we opened the door a few days later. But the good news was the pans were easy to rinse without scrubbing.

If the coating on your nonstick pans is coming off, replace your pans. You and your family shouldn't be eating that stuff. If the size of your family has grown or shrunk, invest in some appropriate-size pans.

15. Clean up and down the staircase.

Keep the staircase free from obstruction. Don't let children play on the stairs. They could fall, plus they might leave small toys on a step, which could cause someone else to trip. If the treads are carpeted, be sure the carpet is firmly tacked down.

Clean the staircase with a small whisk broom or a portable hand vacuum. Many of the more recent models work off batteries so you don't have to worry about tripping over the long electrical cords. Never polish wooden steps.

16. Clean garages.

Your garage should be cleaned when there's no room for the car(s) or the kids need money or something to occupy them. Metal shelving can double storage space. Throw away empty or dried-up paint cans. Return disposable bottles to the grocery. (Let offspring do the returning and keep the money.) Take newspapers to the recycling center. Put all repair equipment (hammers, screwdrivers, bicycle pump, etc.) in one spot. Peg-Board is ideal for this.

When everything is out of the garage, sweep the floor with the largest pushbroom you can find. If the floor's really dirty, use the hose. Take items nobody wants, such as old bikes, wagons, tools and sports equipment, to a secondhand store. Don't get talked into a garage sale. They take far more time than the amount of money taken in.

17. Get to the bottom of things, the baseboards.

Although my husband and one son are in the home building industry, I've never really understood why we have to have baseboards. They just sit around collecting dust. And eventually you need to remove that dust. Many vacuum cleaners have special attachments just for baseboards, and the illustrations that come with your vacuum will show you which one that is. You also can use a damp cloth, which keeps the dust from falling on the floor so you have a second chance to catch it there. If you have inside cats and dogs or fluffy carpeting, you may have to dust more often.

18. Unearth the dump-it drawer.

Go through your dump-it drawer monthly and discard as much as possible. Keep unidentified keys for one year. Then if you still don't know what they unlock, toss them. If you discover their identies, mark them with metal tags.

19. Go on a "junk it."

Either read and throw greeting cards away after you get them or put them in a specially marked box for unforgettable cards and put it on a closet shelf. Note: If you keep cards from one kid, though, make sure you've kept some from the others. Kids keep track of things like that.

Tear interesting articles from magazines and throw the remainder of the magazine away. Toss out-of-date catalogs when the new ones come. Recycle newspapers so they don't pile up.

Have specified places for things—a bill drawer for bills, a bulletin board for invitations, a container for pencils and scissors. If you see something that you know belongs in another spot, put it there. Junk breeds.

20. Don't bypass the heart of the house: your kitchen.

The kitchen is the heart of most homes and so the clutter tends to hide out in the kitchen along with the members of the family.

Get a long phone cord for the kitchen phone or use a cordless so you can wander while you're on hold. You can clean out a drawer here, a cupboard there while you're waiting or talking.

Be sure you have things in the proper place for you. Everyone's needs are different. I'm a short southpaw. My kitchen looks backward to many people, but it works for me.

Keep one area for entertainment supplies, such as candles, coasters, cocktail napkins and matches, and another for paper clips, notepads and pencils.

Toss empty vanilla extract bottles and stale dried herbs that have lost their flavor. Clean your pantry using the same techniques you used with your other closets. Be sure you have no cleaning supplies under your sink if you have small children or grandchildren visiting.

21. Never clean draperies.

A drapery expert to whom I shall always be indebted once told me, "Never clean draperies. Just take them down once a year, take them outside, and shake the dust off." You can also vacuum them if you have the proper attachment. Dust rots draperies eventually, but by then you might be ready to get new ones anyway.

On the other hand, if your drapes are really curtains and they're machine washable, go ahead and wash them. But be absolutely sure they're washable, or you may end up with a handful of shrunken, limp curtains.

There are some dry cleaners who specialize in cleaning draperies, but always check their references. I once got back drapes resembling Swiss cheese, and they weren't even dotted Swiss.

22. Use your head with lampshades.

Dust your lampshades with the special vacuum attachment, or use a large pastry brush to get at the dust in the folds. Note: If you use the same brush for pastry, your cookies will taste dusty and your lampshades will be greasy.

Be sure to use the proper watt bulb in each lamp. It's usually marked on the lamp. I once burned a shade by using a 100-watt bulb when its maximum was only 60 watts. Occasionally wipe dust off the lightbulbs, but be sure the bulbs have cooled before you do.

23. Clean the basement.

We definitely don't have basements in Florida because they'd be filled with water, but we do have one in our Maine home. And I've learned that basements quickly become a natural resting spot for many items, including bikes, sleds, empty glass jars, Christmas decorations, dollhouses, old boots and workshops. For many people, the laundry room is in the basement.

But unless your basement is finished (paneled or otherwise made livable), it's probably filled with partially filled paint cans for rooms long since wallpapered, picnic baskets and other part-time paraphernalia. Sweep the floor from time to time, throw away newspapers and other potential combustibles and knock down the cobwebs, but otherwise don't spend a great deal of time cleaning this area unless you're working on an article titled "I Held My Daughter's Wedding in Our Basement."

24. Attack the attic.

As we usually don't have attics in Florida, we can't fill them with junk we probably should have thrown out years ago. To compensate, though, we Floridians tend to rent storage units that serve the same function. Both need to be uncluttered from time to time, rather than cleaned. Use large plastic bags for throwaway things and a box for items you can give away. If you feel the need to clean your attic on a weekly basis, consider seeking therapy.

25. Do more than bake with baking soda.

Baking soda is a safe product that cleans a myriad of things in your home without any chemical smell or side effect. Mixed with vinegar, baking soda can clean your bathroom and kitchen drains. Toss a bit of baking soda on your rug and then vacuum it up to remove built-up dirt. Baking soda is also good for removing odors in your refrigerator, baby's room or bathroom.

You also can bake cakes and cookies with baking soda, but then you'd have less time available for your writing. If you must bake, be sure you're satisfying a sweet tooth and not a sweet way to procrastinate working at your computer.

26. Bag it.

The word is *plastics*, just as Dustin Hoffman was told in the movie *The Graduate*. I use plastic bags to keep my clutter somewhat under control. Index cards? Keep them together in a plastic bag. Rubber bands and paper clips? Ditto. The same for plastic forks and spoons, straws and other seldom-used picnic items. I put silver candy dishes in plastic bags to prevent tarnishing between uses. Many brands of bags come in a variety of sizes so you can fit larger silver items in plastic bags as well. Small self-locking plastic bags

can be used by non-toddler-aged children to contain crayons, miniature cars, toy people and puzzle pieces.

27. Get things off ice.

When you notice little fuzzy things floating in your iced drinks,
it's past time to wash out the ice cube trays. Just empty out the ice
and rinse the trays in warm water. Never put them in the dishwasher
or use hot water; you'll remove the coating on them. But don't
think you can relax if you have an ice maker in your refrigerator.
Ice makers need to be cleaned too. Just dump the ice in the sink,
rinse the container and put it back.

28. Count on cleaning the countertops.

Use a paste of baking soda and water on a paper towel to clean
your kitchen countertops. White vinegar also can be used to remove
spots. *Never mix chlorine bleach with ammonia.* Don't use steel
wool or other similar products to clean your counters because you'll
scratch them. If you wipe your counters with a sponge, clean the
sponge daily in the dishwasher or you'll spread bacteria.

Women should keep their purses off kitchen counters. We often
put our purses on the floors in restaurants and rest rooms. You
don't want to transfer those germs to your kitchen counters. In fact,
try to keep your kitchen countertops free of all the clutter that seems
to naturally accumulate there. You probably won't totally succeed,
but make a stab at it.

29. Clean the microwave in microminutes.

It comes as a shock to many that even if you use your microwave
only for popcorn, it occasionally needs to be wiped out with a damp
rag. Never use chemical cleaners on your microwave. Check the
seal twice a year for radiation leaks with a gadget you can buy at
an electronic store. I borrowed one from a friend and discovered
to my horror that my ten-year-old microwave *was* leaking radiation. Very scary.

30. Sterilize the medicine cabinet.

Well, you don't actually sterilize the medicine cabinet, but it is
one area of your home that you should clear out fairly frequently.
Your good health may depend on it. If there are half-empty bottles
of old prescriptions, dump the remaining contents in the toilet,

wash out the bottles and throw them away. (Next time finish the medicine entirely as the doctor told you.)

Check the labels of all medications (over-the-counter as well as prescription) for expiration dates, and toss those that have expired as they may either lose their potency or, in some cases, may become more potent as the ingredients break down. If it's a medication you need from time to time, such as for asthma or allergies, ask your physician for an updated prescription. Actually, the bathroom really isn't the best place to keep medications because the steam from the tub or shower can dissolve tablets. We keep ours on a shelf in the kitchen.

Throw away last year's cosmetics, dried-up skin cream, worn nail files and rusty razors. Then wipe each shelf with a warm, soapy rag and rinse thoroughly.

31. Choose your shoes.

Most of us have too many shoes that take up room in the closet and get dusty when they aren't worn frequently. Go through yours on a regular basis. Throw away those you don't wear anymore even if they were once loved, and keep the others in good repair. Store polish, rags and buffer in one spot. If you run out of white polish, you can use toothpaste on white patent-leather shoes. I often use black markers in an emergency to cover scuffed spots on my black leather shoes.

32. Talk pillow talk.

Every so often (more often if people snack on the couch or you have inside cats and dogs), toss the throw pillows in the dryer on low heat. It fluffs them up. Some people wash bed pillows and put them in the dryer too. Since mine are feather, I haven't tried that.

33. Talk trash.

One of the easiest ways to look as though you've spent the day cleaning your house is to get rid of all the trash—garbage, boxes, old newspapers and stuff overflowing from your wastepaper baskets.

When it comes to wastepaper baskets, buy big. The dainty ones may be pretty, but they're not functional. Use plastic liners if you prefer. I don't. I think it makes a home look too antiseptic, and it's just as easy to empty all wastebaskets into one big garbage bag at once. It's cheaper too than buying little plastic bags to go into little plastic wastebaskets and then putting the little plastic bags into a larger plastic bag to dump them. Recycle grocery bags whenever possible.

34. Get the lowdown on upholstered furniture.

Take cushions off your couch and chairs once a week and vacuum after picking up the popcorn and stray pieces of change you discover there. If you're buying new furniture, remember that dust shows up more on dark furniture than light.

Clean spots off your upholstered furniture as they occur. Use a clean rag with a mild detergent solution. If there's a tear or a spill beyond your expertise, call in an expert. The service is bound to be cheaper than having to recover your furniture.

35. Never mind singing about rag mops.

If you like string mops (I don't), rinse them in warm water or vinegar after use. Otherwise, you'll just transfer the dirt from one spot to another. I use sponge mops that need to be replaced frequently, but at least they don't leave telltale strings to show where you've been.

36. Toy with the toys.

Your kids' toys can squeeze you out of living space if you don't take charge of things. They also make the house look cluttered because they (1) tend to be big, (2) have many parts and (3) replicate themselves in the dead of night.

Sort the toys on a regular basis, and throw out the ones that are broken or have missing parts. Recycle toys your child has outgrown by giving them to younger offspring, a friend's children or thrift sales. Urge your children to help decide which toys (that are in good shape) they'd like to donate to less fortunate children at holiday time.

If you're like me, you'll also save some favorites and box them up to hand down to your grandchildren. Mine now play with a complete set of Star Wars figures, a GI Joe and Tonka trucks that their parents played with many years ago.

37. Assign the yucky job.

Yucky things need to be cleaned too. Fortunately, one person's yucky job is often another's "I don't mind doing it." But when nobody wants to do it, trade off, barter, hire someone or draw straws. I usually end up doing it myself as quickly as possible. When we had a single-family house, I hated taking the garbage out at night because there often were possums or other things creeping in the night. Now that we live in a high-rise, I just lean out our back door and drop our garbage down the handy garbage chute.

38. Say good-bye to the bag lady (or man).

In my mother's day everyone saved string. Not that you couldn't buy it if you needed it, but if you had string, you saved it. Today, we all save shopping bags—both paper and plastic. And no matter where you store them, they multiply. What's worse, in warm climates cockroaches lay their eggs in the folds of the paper bag bottoms. When you store the bags under the sink, you create a perfect incubator for them. Save a few bags to dump the cat litter in or to hold muddy shoes. Recycle the rest. Use reusable cloth bags whenever possible.

39. Don't be a wall washer.

You can write a lot of words in the time it takes to wash a wall. Do maintenance washing only. Paint what you can with semigloss paint so you can easily wipe off spots that appear out of nowhere.

Vinyl-type wallpaper is good in the kitchen for the same reason. While you can clean some spots from some walls with an art gum eraser or a mixture of baking soda and water, call a wallpaper store first and ask for advice, as different types of wallpapers respond to different cleaning treatments.

People who wash their walls say to wash from the bottom up so dirty water doesn't run down. I just attack spots as they appear and change from 100-watt bulbs to 75-watt so nobody notices. I'd rather repaint than wash walls.

40. Become a clock-watcher.

Set a kitchen timer when you're picking up clutter, cleaning or doing laundry. If you know you have to complete a task in five or ten minutes, you'll do it faster to beat the clock. Otherwise, you'll slow your pace. Follow the movement of the hands on the clock and clean or tidy up moving in a clockwise direction. That way you won't wander around a room, wondering where you left off. It saves time and time saved means more time at the computer.

41. Win the silver.

If you have silver items that you hate to polish and never use, be a winner by giving them to your grown kids, a relative or close friend who would like the items. You'll gain added space and a grateful recipient of the gift. You also can sell your silver, but don't expect to be paid even a fraction of what it's worth.

42. Improve your reception.

If your reception seems fuzzy, dust the television screen with a clean, soft cloth before calling for repair. Do not use window cleaner. Stick all the TV clickers in a basket so they're easy to find.

43. Don't abhor a vacuum.

While nature doesn't think much of vacuums, we need to use one from time to time to pick up dust and dirt in our homes. Experts disagree if you should vacuum before dusting because you stir up dust or dust first so what you drop on the floor can be vacuumed up. I prefer the latter, but I think it's like the argument about which way to hang toilet paper. It really isn't important enough to fight about. Do whichever you prefer. Just be sure to put in a clean vacuum cleaner bag *before* you clean.

44. A penny saved is a penny cluttering up your dresser.

"A penny for your thoughts?" wouldn't buy you even a hint of a thought today. But those pennies do add up, usually on the top of your dresser, in a jar on the floor (collecting dust) or overflowing the ashtray on your desk. The first of every month, take the pennies to your bank and cash them in for "real" money. If your bank won't take them loose, roll them in coin wrappers. Let the kids help if you have kids. Otherwise, roll your own in front of the television set. You'll be surprised how much cash those pennies can turn into.

45. Don't make a mess of things if you smoke.

OK, so I have a bias against smoking. Not only is smoking bad for the smoker, but the secondhand smoke is dangerous to the rest of the family as well. It can foul up your computer too. But smokers also can create a mess for someone (probably you) to clean up. If you haven't turned all those pretty ashtrays into candy dishes and you really need one for smelly cigarette or cigar ashes, toss the dainty ones and get one big ashtray so you don't get ashes all over everything.

46. Don't do spring-cleaning.

If you keep up with household chores, doing a little each week, you won't have to do spring-cleaning. That mania is just a plot to keep you from writing.

47. Quest answers to questions.

You probably have a great many questions about specific cleaning problems. You'll find everything you want to know (and more) in the housecleaning books by Don Aslett, Jeff Campbell and the Clean Team and others listed in the Suggested Reading portion in the back of this book. One caveat, however: Don't get so caught up in cleaning techniques that you overspend the time needed for these chores. The idea is to make your home livable while still giving you time to write. Keep your priorities in order.

48. Destripe the zebra.

A man came home from work and found his wife busy scrubbing their zebra. "I've been working all day, and it's still not all clean and white," she sobbed.

He took her in his arms. "Some things don't have to be," he said gently.

And so they don't. Just get your household chores done as quickly and effectively as you can in the shortest amount of time so you can focus on your career as a writer, not as a housecleaner. From my Suggested Reading list, select those tips that can help you. Leave the "everything must be cleaner-than-clean and white" to the announcers in television's laundry soap commercials, and just settle for the sentiments printed on a plaque in my kitchen: "My House Is Clean Enough to Be Healthy and Dirty Enough to Be Happy." It reflects the state of my home too, and its policy grants me time to get some writing done. And that makes *me* sparkle.

CHAPTER 6

Taking the Leap

As a man thinketh, so is he, and as a man chooseth, so is he.
— The Bible

Becoming a writer is one of those cases where thinking docs make it so. Once you begin to really think of yourself as a writer, you will start making choices that send you along the path of becoming one. So begin right now.

VISUALIZE YOURSELF AS A WRITER

That famous person Anonymous once said, "If you wait for inspiration, you're not a writer, but a waiter." So right this moment, start to visualize yourself as a writer. Close your eyes for a moment and visualize yourself sitting down in front of your typewriter or computer and running your hands over the keyboard, the instrument of your craft. Feel yourself feeding paper into the typewriter or turning on the computer. Sense that burst of excitement as your adrenaline starts flowing. See yourself taking that first step along the well-worn path trod by thousands of writers before you by putting down that first word. Then make it a complete sentence, and from that, a paragraph. Visualize yourself continuing to write until you have completed your article or novel, feeling the momentum, getting caught up in the pace of your project.

What you are doing is exactly what actors, public speakers, top salespeople and athletes do to enhance their performances. They first see themselves performing successfully in their minds, visualizing their actions step-by-step, and then mimic the actions with their bodies. Now this doesn't mean that you can bypass motivation, self-discipline and hours of practice and doing nothing but sitting on your couch visualizing yourself writing the Great American

Novel. But unless you can see yourself positively working step-by-step toward your goal, even if it's only with baby steps, it's unlikely you will ever achieve success in your work.

I feel so strongly about the relationship of visualizing yourself performing in a positive manner to success in your writing that I've included more detail about it in chapters sixteen and seventeen.

REMOVE BARRIERS

Be sure you have cleared the path so you don't trip as you begin your journey into what I think is a fantastic world of writing. Begin by asking yourself some questions and answer them honestly, not just the way you'd like things to be.

1. Do you know why you want to write?

You need to understand your motivation for wanting to write at home if you are to sustain the effort. Don't just think about what your motivation is. Actually write the words so it becomes your personal mission statement. Post this statement over the mirror in your bathroom and over your desk. Say it aloud often so it becomes real to you. Repeat it as you sit down to write each day.

2. Is making time for your writing a definite priority for you?

Everyone has the same amount of time, just 168 hours a week. But if you wait for a definite block of free time to just pop up and say, "Here I am, take advantage of me," you'll never write. You need to put writing high on your list of priorities, knowing that if you do so, it will have to be at the expense of other pastimes, some of which will probably have a more immediate pleasurable response.

When I was completing my first book, we were vacationing at Martha's Vineyard, my first time on that beautiful island. Unfortunately, I didn't get to explore much. While my family was having fun at the beach, I was rearranging chapters. When they went fishing, I was rewriting parts of chapters. When they went sailing, I was proofing chapters. I actually only got to the beach once. Why didn't I play by day and write at night? Because even then I knew how my inner clock functioned. I do my best writing between 9 A.M. and 4 P.M. At night, I'm beat. If I try to write in the evening, I usually make mistakes and get error messages on my computer screen. My priority that summer was to complete my book by dead-line, which I did. I rewarded myself by having time with my family in the evening. And yes, since I'm not a masochist, I really did feel sorry for myself.

While I don't advocate working during vacations, sometimes you have to. For some reason, many of my recent book deadlines have been in August and September when my husband and I summer in Maine and enjoy our children, grandchildren and friends visiting. Fortunately, I can take my laptop computer with me to Maine and finish my work there. It means shipping some files and duplicating some reference books, but it's worth it. Along with scheduling time for my writing, I also make time for walking on the beach, hunting for antiques and, of course, eating lobster. As long as you have your goal in mind, you know where you have to go. You just need to plan how you're going to reach that target.

My goal right now, for example, is to write this book and have it completed before its deadline. My plan is to write at least four pages each day. That's approximately 1,000 words. My contract calls for the book to be about 280, pages which means between 70,000 and 90,000 words. Most days, I do write four pages. Some days I write fewer than that, and often, I write more. And yes, there are days (other than Saturday and Sunday) when I don't write anything. But I know that staying on schedule is an important prior-ity for me. And, as I have my plan written on a large easel right in front of me, I can keep myself on schedule. Each day I record the number of pages I wrote that day, how many I have completed and how many I have yet to go. It keeps me focused on my plan for reaching my goal. Other writers have other tricks to keep them from straying, but this one works for me.

Think of those four pages as the steps you take when you're walking from one place to another. Sometimes you may think you misjudged the distance and aren't sure you can make it without getting exhausted. But when you begin to count your strides, going from one to ten over and over again, you quickly find that you can cover the distance and, possibly, even go a little farther. I began using that little device to motivate myself in my exercise plan and soon discovered that I could easily fool myself into walking three miles, rather than the two I was used to.

3. Have you discussed your desires with your family?

If your family doesn't know about your desire to write at home, they can inadvertently undermine all of your best intentions for self-discipline in your writing. Yet many people feel embarrassed to share their secret with their families and somehow just expect their loved ones to know exactly how they, the writers, feel. Since most of us are not equipped with ESP, that experiment is doomed for failure. The family is confused and the writer-to-be is resentful that the family is sabotaging him.

Share your desire to write with your family, and suggest ways in which the members can be supportive of you in your new venture. Be specific. Don't just say, "I need time to write." Instead, offer some possible action cues by saying, "If you all would do the dinner dishes Monday, Wednesday and Friday nights, I could start writing right after dinner."

4. Is your family supportive of your desire to write at home?

What if you've clued in the family and they still aren't supportive? Unfortunately, that does happen to many beginning writers, many of whom just throw up their hands and sigh, "Well, I guess I just can't do it right now." (It also happens to more experienced, published writers as well.)

Don't allow yourself to be passive. If you have the desire to write, then you certainly have the right to do so. As I stated before, you don't need your family's permission, but you do need their cooperation. Perhaps you weren't clear when you first announced that you wanted to write or you need to say it more assertively. Restate in specific terms what you need from your family members. Is it more help with housework? Refuge from toddlers? A place to work where your papers are safe from prying (and grimy) hands? Quiet time?

If the lack of cooperation is from your spouse who feels left out and somewhat neglected while you are writing, be sure to plan for some together time to compensate for the time you need to be by yourself. Plan to see a movie or to have a quiet dinner together after you have spent many of your evenings and weekends writing. Be sure to thank your spouse for being understanding and for helping you carve out your writing time. We often take our loved ones for granted and forget to say those magic words, "Thank you."

In his book, *Love Is Never Enough*, Aaron T. Beck lists qualities needed for a happy relationship. Among these are the following:

- commitment
- sensitivity
- generosity
- consideration
- loyalty
- responsibility
- trustworthiness

These, along with the ability to laugh together, cooperate, communicate and compromise, are important to develop when you suddenly change your goal and your spouse must get used to sharing you with the typewriter or computer. By working together to strengthen these qualities in your marriage, you'll not only reduce stress and conflict within your family but will also find yourselves becoming closer and more caring for and of each other.

While it's important to put writing time high on your priority list, you need to put your family relationships even higher. While that doesn't mean that you have to be at everyone's beck and call, it does mean taking the time to let those you love know that you do. While it's easy to say, "Of course they know I love them," kids and spouses don't always know. When you're closeted behind a closed door, they may feel ignored and unloved. Tell them often that you love them and that they're important to you. Share what you're working on so they have the opportunity to feel a part of your writing. That way they can take pride in your success and feel an ownership in your writing efforts. "I was quiet for a whole hour until the timer rang so Mommy could write," one of my little ones once told her grandmother proudly.

5. Have you made at least two changes in your lifestyle or living habits in order to carve out a specific time to write?

If you have made at least two changes in your lifestyle, you have probably cleared the way for or made a good beginning in creating a time to write. The time doesn't just appear magically because you want to have it. The changes may be as minor as bringing in dinner one night a week so you don't have to cook and can spend more time writing. It may be as major as changing jobs so you have less daytime pressures and can write in the evenings or hiring someone to sit with your chronically ill parent for a few hours. Whatever these changes, be sure you have selected them in order to give yourself a definite period of time for your writing and that you don't end up with more responsibilities and less time.

6. Are you focused on your goal?

If you are focused on your goal, you will be able to maintain regular writing hours and overcome procrastination. You will feel yourself running with open arms toward your goal, more than ready to put your plan into action.

7. Can you maintain this focus for at least six weeks until writing becomes something of a habit for you?

My habit. That's what your writing time becomes very quickly once you have determined a time for it and are loyal to your schedule. You'll be surprised how quickly it does become a habit. Many experts say you only need to repeat an action for six weeks before you have set a mental pattern for it.

If you stay focused for those six weeks and don't falter, I promise that you'll look forward to your writing time just as a runner craves a workout. Best of all, you don't need special shoes and you won't get sweaty.

Ready? Then on your mark. You're set, so go.

Technology and Business Issues

CHAPTER 7

Finding a Room of One's Own

A woman must have money and a room of her own if she is to write fiction.

— Virginia Woolf

I've always known that anyone—man or woman—needed a room of his or her own in order to write anything, fiction or nonfiction. Almost twenty years ago, I wrote this as my fantasy:

> "Last night I went into my study to work. As always, it was spotless. Leather-bound reference books filled floor-to-ceiling bookcases. Pristine pale yellow wallpaper descended to immaculate off-white wall-to-wall carpeting.
>
> Soothing symphonies filtered in through the well-modulated music system. Ignoring my well-stocked refrigerator, I turned to my secretary, Robert Redford's twin brother, and smiled. He nodded, then lifted the telephone receiver.
>
> "No calls, please. Ms. Shimberg is about to create."

I sighed. Something was tugging at my arm. I opened my eyes.

"Mommy," said a small figure, digging jelly-covered fingers into my stomach. "The dogs messed in the kitchen again."

The strange thing about rereading the above flight of fancy is that it still sounds pretty good to me, although I have yet to acquire that magnificent study with floor-to-ceiling bookshelves or, for that matter, Robert Redford's twin brother.

My office in our condo is in the second of our two bedrooms. My desk shares space with the guest bed (queen size), two campaign dressers, a small writing desk that was my mother's so I can't give it away, a folded massage table, a plastic foot locker filled with toys for my grandkids and a crib for the baby grand-child who doesn't use it that often but it's easier to keep it up than to find a place to store it. There is not a great deal of space for pacing. My reference books nestle cozily alongside those written by Dr. Seuss and the brothers Grimm on bookshelves built in by the former owner.

In our summer home, my "office" is at one end of the kitchen counter, located between the refrigerator and laundry room right next to the garage entrance. It obviously is in the main line of traffic. When we have kids and grandkids in the house, it takes a great deal of concentrating to write. I'll admit, I'm not always successful, especially when the grandchildren are around.

But regardless of where your work space is located, you do have to set up shop somewhere. Nonwriters glamorize the flexibility aspect. "Oh, it must be great to write anywhere," they gush. They visualize you sitting by the sea, clipboard in lap, churning out words as you're caught up with the rhythm of the surf. Or they picture you reclining on your chaise lounge, eating Malomars as you peck out the next scene for your novel. Maybe this works for some, but personally, I don't like Malomars, have no room in my bedroom for a chaise lounge, and the one time I tried to write out-of-doors, I spent most of my time blowing flies off my papers and chasing notes across the lawn.

CLAIMING YOUR SPACE

Note that I didn't say, "Finding a space." Unless you live in a castle, there probably isn't vacant space in your home just waiting to be appropriated. So you have to search and then claim a spot that will work for you.

Where should you put your office? Often the question is not *where* but *how* you can make a place for it. You may have to be a little creative, but it's there, hiding, like the key you dropped in the grass. You may have to move things around a little or even look for it from a different angle, but it's there. You'll find a work space if you really want to.

The best home office or study has the following five common characteristics.

1. Availability

The office space you select has to be one that is available when you are able to make time to write. If it's located in your family room, for example, you won't be able to use it until the kids are in bed and no one is watching television, unless you can develop strong tunnel vision so you're not distracted by the noise and commotion. Most of us who began writing with toddlers and little folks under-foot did develop this type of focus out of necessity. You can too, if you have to. But if you work at another job all day, you may be too tired to wait until ten or eleven to start writing. On the other hand, if you put your office in your bedroom, you'll have to put off your weekend writing until your partner gets up.

2. Accessibility

You won't spend much time in your office if you have to move suitcases or boxes to get to your desk. The dining room, which is always a good starting point for a mini-office, is useful only if you eat most of your meals in the kitchen or have a chest or storage spot nearby where you can easily place your writing materials during dinner.

Having said what I have about accessibility, one of my favorite stories from authors about their writing places was the woman who made herself an office in the attic of their house. When she was working, she pulled up the ladder so the kids couldn't bother her. Her office was accessible to her but not to her children. Unfortunately, I've lost track of her over the years, but I'd love to know if she's still up in space.

3. Comfort

If your office space isn't comfortable, you're going to have difficulty making yourself go there to write. It's important to have a comfortable chair and a desk that is the proper height for you (I'll discuss ergonomics in more detail in chapter eight). If you use a computer, as I urge you to do, your desk should be at least 20 inches deep to hold the monitor. If you use a laptop computer, the desk doesn't need to be that deep. The room or area needs to be well ventilated and have proper nonglaring lighting. Most experts suggest both overhead general lighting and task lighting.

4. An atmosphere conducive to concentration

You need to experience a sense of safety and security in your writing locale. The ambiance of a room can actually play an important part in freeing your creativity. Although I can write, and have written, on airplanes, poolside during my kids' swimming meets, in the family room with five kids under age ten alternately playing and fighting, sitting bedside in hospital rooms, in doctors' waiting rooms and in libraries, my preferred writing site is a cave, that is, a quiet room with no windows and no other people present.

Yet many others would feel claustrophobic in such a room. Some people prefer pleasant views to help them think, while others (including me) find that distracting. Many writers work best with loud music blaring with a strong beat. Still others prefer soft music or no music at all. Think about your own personality. How do you function best? If you've never thought about it, do so now because it can affect your ability to concentrate and maintain your focus.

Also become aware of the noise level in and near your home office. Too many decibels and you may have trouble concentrating. It also can cause noise-induced hearing loss (NIHL), which is suffered by ten million Americans. If your office is next to your neighbor's yard where he constantly uses a lawn mower and grass blower, or there's a barking dog, loud traffic noises or construction sounds, or you're right next to the dishwasher, consider relocating to another part of the house.

5. Storage space for the tools of your trade

Chapter eight is devoted to describing the items you'll need for your office. It's vital to have storage for them wherever you decide to put your office. Storage is available in many different forms, such as baskets, file cabinets, dressers, washtubs and dividers. Create unique solutions. Proper storage not only reduces clutter so you can find things easier, but it also protects your work and your equipment.

Be Creative in Searching for an Office Location

Over the years I've collected a number of wonderful stories describing unique sites writers have used to carve out that special place for them. (I've included many of them in chapter nineteen.) Many locations were created at great expense, such as building a loft in the bedroom (like a tree house) so the writer could climb up and be alone with his muse. Some cost only a few dollars, such as hanging two shower curtains at one end of the bedroom so the curtains could be pulled when the writer was on the job.

One writer I know made herself an actual closet case. She confiscated a long, narrow closet on the second floor of her home that was used to store Christmas tree ornaments, suitcases, leftover wallpaper rolls and outgrown clothing waiting to be grown into by another child. She removed the lower shelves, piled everything into the back of the closet and hung a beaded curtain to divide the storage area from her "office." Then she moved in her typing stand (no, she wasn't computer literate), file cabinet, books and a $19.95 electric fan, and began writing.

Her kids tell callers, "Mom can't talk now. She's in the closet." But my friend doesn't care. She's writing and she's being published.

Check out the forgotten areas of your home too. There usually are many sections in the basement, attic or garage that can be cordoned off and used for an office site. If you set yours up in the basement or garage, however, be sure to use a dehumidifier. Otherwise, your books and papers may get moldy. Dampness also is a no-no for your computer.

Some older houses have ample landings on the second floor or separate outbuildings, such as a toolshed or gazebo. If these can be enclosed to protect them against changing climate conditions and heated and/or air-conditioned, they might work well as offices.

Consider too the little rooms, such as the laundry room, mudroom or walk-in closet. One writer, displaced by a new baby from the second bedroom, said he now works out of the dressing room, which has its own window and a nice view.

If you decide to commandeer part of a room that serves another purpose, put a divider screen around your area or hang curtains on hooks (like the privacy curtains in hospital rooms). Some screen dividers come equipped with slots to hold photographs. You can use them for index cards instead to keep important phone numbers in front of you.

Most writers who use parts of their bedrooms for offices suggest using some type of divider to visually block the sight of the office from the rest of the bedroom. They claim it's hard to sleep or to feel sexy in bed with your work staring you in the face.

A Lap Does Not an Office Make

Laptop computers are great. I use one myself. They give you mobility so you can work as you sit on the couch half watching your favorite TV show. They can be moved to the game table in the family room when you're feeling lonely. But you're just putting off the inevitable. Eventually, even laptop computers need to be set on some solid terrain where they can hook up (literally) with a printer. That means you're going to have to find an office somewhere.

If you've looked all over your home, apartment or condo and can't find an inch of space to call your own, then use the kitchen or dining room table. But make it easy for you to shift from macaroni to manuscript. Put a dresser, two-drawer file or cardboard box nearby so when dinner's ready you can efficiently transfer all your work to one place. Otherwise, you may have to dig through the garbage after dinner to find a missing page that's stuck to the pasta.

Wherever you finally put your office, remember that it should be yours as much as possible, ready and available for you at a moment's notice so that, just like Superman, you can make the transformation whenever it's needed. If you have to set up shop each day or unpack your tools before working, chances are you'll find it too easy to procrastinate and put off writing for another day. Give yourself that "room of one's own," even if it's only part of a room. You'll find having that special spot makes it easier for you to get into your new role as a writer. You'll begin to think of yourself as a writer. Do it today.

Protecting Your Turf

Once you have identified the space you're going to call your own, you must protect it from invaders. Begin by calling a family meeting and letting the others in your family know where you plan to set up shop and why. If it encroaches on public space, such as the kitchen or family room, be prepared to make some concessions, such as you won't use it during special favorite television shows or if you do, you'll do quiet work with earphones so you don't disturb the rest of the family.

Remind the rest of the family that you'll need specific items to do your job properly (described more fully in chapter eight). Just because they'll know that you have scissors, computer paper, paper clips and so on doesn't give them permission to borrow your things without your say-so. Assure them that you'll have duplicates available for their use in other "public" rooms.

Don't be surprised if your hideaway becomes attractive to others because it is somewhat secluded. I think it's what lawyers call an attractive nuisance. Your kids may wander in to make private calls behind closed doors. Your spouse may prefer it because it's quiet and conducive to thinking or meditating. Whether you permit visitors or not is up to you, but warn trespassers that doodling on your manuscripts and other papers is punishable by something so awful they don't even want to know about it.

In the precomputer days I left a completed manuscript on my desk, only to come back and find that some unknown agent who had used the phone in my office had doodled on the top sheet. (Yes, Virginia, it is true that once upon a time writers wrote on typewriters and that some of us dinosaurs even used something known as a manual typewriter.)

Never let your kids play games on your computer. It's a tool of your work. A surgeon wouldn't let her kids use the scalpel to do woodworking. Get a secondhand computer for game playing and keep yours for writing.

If your spouse also needs or uses a home office, try to find a different location for yours. If that doesn't seem possible, at least erect some type of barrier to delineate each area. You can share the fax, duplicating machine and postage scale, but never share desks, computers or supplies. That way no one else will move your papers and if you run out of toner just as you're printing your final draft, it's your fault, not your spouse's.

SETTLING IN

Once you find your little bit of heaven, don't be concerned if you find it difficult to focus at first. There's a lot of emotion packed into your home, and you may feel a little schizophrenic at first. You're calling the laundry room your workplace, but you're staring at a pile of dirty laundry and wondering, who's fooling whom? Or you're in the extra bedroom and as you're looking up, thinking of something incredibly wise to write, you suddenly remember that you never fixed the ceiling fan. It's normal.

But you can help improve your concentration and begin to develop the writing habit by clearing the decks. Toss those dirty clothes in the washer. Don't turn it on yet because (1) the sound will be distracting and (2) when the washer stops, you'll then have to put the wash in the dryer, fold it, put it away, put new liner paper in the dressers drawers and so on. Clear the dishes off the kitchen table and let them soak in the sink if you'll be writing in the kitchen. If you're in that second bedroom with the broken fan, tell yourself that you don't need the overhead fan working because your papers will blow around. If you're lucky enough to have found that room of your own, don't think about how dirty the windows are or whether you should wash the dog before you start writing.

It takes tremendous willpower and determination to write at home with all of your life, memories and emotions swirling around you, but it can be done and *is* being done by thousands of other writers just like you. Don't be discouraged by beginning failures or allow yourself to be frustrated by constant interruptions.

Although you'll probably find that interruptions are distracting for you in the beginning, the longer you keep at your task, the more you'll find yourself focusing inward on your work. Your concentration will deepen and you'll be able to write despite the chaos around you. If you have toddlers, don't postpone your writing, waiting until the children grow up, because you'll be wasting valuable training time that you could be writing about—what else?—your kids.

If you're retired, what are you waiting for? Use those big blocks of time to write. If you're stumped for ideas, write about how people can make the most of their retirement years. You'll have plenty of readers for your work.

For those of you who work at other jobs during the daytime, seek out that special space where you can make the most of your evening and weekend hours as a writer. As with so many things in life, practice makes it so much easier. If you want to become a writer, you have to begin, don't you?

So hang up your shingle, shut the door on the outside world and begin this first day as a writer.

CHAPTER 8

Equipping Your Office (and Keeping the Stuff There)

My two fingers on a typewriter have never connected with my brain. My hand on a pen does. A fountain pen, of course. Ball-point pens are only good for filling out forms on a place.

— Graham Greene

If you were going to be a painter, you wouldn't keep your easel upstairs in the bedroom, your paints in the living room and your brushes in the kitchen. Yet many a writer has his tools scattered throughout the house, requiring him to run all over the place looking for the stapler, paper clips, manila envelopes, extra computer paper and postage.

It's not only more efficient to have all your supplies in one area, but it is also more professional and helps you think of yourself as a professional writer, which is what you are or hope to become.

Furniture, of course, is your big-ticket item. But there is a wide range in cost, depending, for example, on whether you purchase a leather-topped partner's desk or use your dining room table. And although I'm giving you my personal preferences, it doesn't mean they're the best choices by any means, but they work for me. Everyone's unique and works in diverse ways. Besides, I'm left-handed and everyone says that makes a difference. Come to think of it, it's mostly right-handed folks who say that.

DESK

Desks come in a wide variety and your choice will be dependent on how you work. I like a vast surface so I can spread my papers. The dining table works well for me when I'm doing research because there's room for me to shuffle my books, papers, pens and so on. There is an electrical outlet nearby so I can plug in the computer without others tripping over the cord and pulling my computer off the table. (This also keeps them from falling and hurting themselves. I don't want you to think my priorities are messed up.)

My desk in the condo is a pine table with a flat surface and one drawer. I had the legs sawed down so the top is only 26 inches from the floor. That way my hands are comfortable and at a 90° angle on the computer keys, and my shoulders aren't raised. Before a friendly neurologist (whose father was a writer) shared that secret with me, I had terrible neck and shoulder pain. In our Maine home, my desk is an extension of the kitchen counter that also has been lowered in that area to 26 inches from the floor.

Your keyboard should be lower than most standard desktops. Sit with your hands poised over the keyboard and check to be sure your shoulders aren't raised. Then have someone measure the distance from the floor. You need to prevent straining your neck and shoulder muscles. On the other hand, if you lower the keyboard too much, you'll compress your wrists, a sure way to encourage carpal tunnel syndrome.

Many people put a flat door over two two-drawer file cabinets to make a desk. While that height may be good for some tasks, for most people it's too high for comfortable typing. Often you can find inexpensive library tables or dining tables in secondhand stores, used office furniture stores and thrift shops, and you can cut a table to (your) size. Art supply stores are a good source for drafting tables, which can be raised or lowered as well as slanted for when you are editing by hand.

Consider, too, the idea of a standing desk. Both Ernest Hemingway and Thomas Jefferson did much of their writing standing up. I opted for sitting, but I do have my dictionary on a stand and that forces me to pop up and down frequently.

DESK CHAIR

Once there was a king of Ergonomicland who said, "My kingdom for a comfortable desk chair." Well, if there wasn't, there should have been. You spend a lot of time sitting in your desk chair, and if it's not comfortable and doesn't support your back properly, you not only won't want to sit in it and work but if you do sit and suffer, you may actually do physical harm to yourself. Don't opt for a dining room or kitchen chair. They're not made for sitting as long as I hope you'll be sitting, and you'll find your legs cramping, your neck cricking and your shoulders aching. I know. I've tried it.

Select an office secretarial chair that can be adjusted up or down and has a back support. I prefer a five-point base on rollers, rather than just four legs, because I tend to roll around grabbing a book or a file and the five-point is less apt to topple over. You can buy one in a used office supply store or new from companies such as Office Depot and Staples or even through a variety of catalogs but be sure the companies guarantee satisfaction or your money back. Some chairs have to be put together, but if I can do it—and did—anyone can. It really wasn't that hard, even if I first put the arms on backward.

Be sure to take your time actually sitting in various chairs before you buy one. All people are not equal in size or shape. Even Goldilocks had to try three chairs before finding the one that was "just right."

If you're short like me and your legs dangle, even with the chair adjusted really low, get a foot rest. It keeps the pressure off your thighs and prevents muscle cramps and nerve pinches.

You also might consider using a kneeler chair. You rest on a seat but most of your weight is on your knees. It puts your back in a comfortable position. I used to use one all the time, but as it didn't have rollers, I found I was putting my back in uncomfortable positions as I reached for the telephone or more stationery. Now I use it from time to time when I've been sitting a long time and want a change.

BOOKSHELVES

A number of companies make tower shelves that go almost to the ceiling. They're great for storing paper supplies, books, file folders and other paper goods that multiply like rabbits. Be careful if you have small children or grandchildren though, as the tower shelves could topple over if pulled.

You also can buy used office bookshelves, secondhand book-shelves, ready-made cabinets or custom-made cabinets with shelving above. You'll need to make provision for storing all your supplies in one spot. If you don't, you'll end up like me with enough yellow writing pads to last two lifetimes. I kept ordering more because I couldn't find where I had put the others.

FILE CABINETS

Unless you have a great reason (like also being a lawyer), use letter-size not legal-size files and folders. It's not that I have anything against lawyers; one of my daughters graduated from law school. It's just that legal-size materials cost more and take up more room.

I prefer hanging files because then when I remove the folder, the hanging file is there to remind me that the folder is still languishing somewhere on my desk. I also think it's easier to find your folders. You can buy the hanging file attachment in most office supply stores. I used to buy labels for my files because they looked professional. Then I realized that (1) they were expensive, (2) they often dried out and fell off, (3) I had to find a place to store them while I was waiting to use them and (4) it was faster to just write on the folder.

The best place to buy file cabinets is in a used office furniture store. They tend to be sturdier than the ones you buy in discount stores and don't stick as easily. If you have a place to put it, I suggest getting a horizontal four-drawer file, rather than a two-drawer or tall file cabinets. You'll be amazed how quickly you can fill these little fellows. File drawers are good for road maps from trips you've taken, brochures from attractions you think you may write about or just ideas for articles. If you still have empty file drawers, stick the knitting or needlepoint work in a drawer so nobody sees how little of it you've done.

LIGHTING

Depending on where your office is, you may not have adequate lighting for working at your computer or typewriter. Or if your room is well lighted, it may be glaring on your computer screen. Poor lighting can cause eyestrain and actually limit your productivity.

Tall desk lamps offer good lighting, especially at night. Although many people swear by the gooseneck lamp or drafting table lamp that you can twist around to shine directly on your work, I find them too glaring. Lamps with halogen bulbs tend to be too hot to have close to your computer and some have a tendency to shatter. Look around your home to find a lamp that lights your work on the screen or paper without glaring, but never use a lamp simply because it's there. Buy a new one instead. They aren't that expensive, and it's important to find the right lamp at the right height for you. But before you buy something new, ask the salesperson if you can return it if it isn't the right height. Most reputable lighting or department stores will let you take a lamp out on approval.

If you have overhead fluorescent lights that flicker, check the starter, be sure the tube's resting in its holder properly or, if all else fails, buy a new tube. Fluorescent bulbs are expensive, but they last a long time.

Natural lighting, especially if it's coming in over your back, is relaxing to work by. Don't face the sunlight directly, though, as it can cause glare and give you a headache.

COMPUTER OR TYPEWRITER?

I'm not getting involved in the computer vs. typewriter debate other than to say that if you continue to write and be published, eventually you'll find an editor who wants your manuscript on a disk or sent electronically by modem. That obviously presents problems if you're still using a typewriter. That said, there are many writers who still use typewriters. My friend, the lyricist Hal Hackady, often types his lyrics on not only a typewriter but a manual typewriter.

I began my career on an old manual Remington typewriter. It had metal-rimmed keys that you had to pound, which explains why I still hammer my computer keys. Old habits die hard. My first book was written on an IBM Selectric electric typewriter that my husband had given me for my birthday. (Promise her anything, but give her an electric typewriter.) I was thrilled with it until, fickle me, I got an Olivetti 501 word processor, a massive machine that took up most of my office space, and wrote my second book on it. It was strictly a word processor using 7.5-inch floppy disks. You couldn't do block moves or scroll backward on my magic machine, but I thought it was grand.

I soon itched to be able to do more, however, and after a fling with a Mac, began my love affairs with PCs. After a few desktop models, I switched to a laptop that attaches to a 17-inch monitor. I prefer a laptop because it offers me the flexibility to take my computer with me to Maine, on a plane or to a grandchild's house. But you pay for this adaptability because they're more expensive than a standard desktop model. I also think they have more problems because of all the traveling they do.

In the name of love (and a pushy computer genius son who wanted to bring his mother into the twentieth century before the twenty-first arrived), I first mastered the WordStar word processing program, then WordPerfect and finally Microsoft Word. The latter program marks my many typos and misspelled words and reminds me to stay in the active voice when I lapse into passive. It also counts words so I don't have to and would create an index for me if I ever had time to figure out how to do it. There is also a thesaurus program, but I find it somewhat limited and prefer my trusty *The Synonym Finder* by J.I. Rodale. (It's now published in paperback.) Now my laptop, word processing program and I are content, and I swear I'll roam never more—until I'm tempted by my son to try something new.

The point I'm making is that I really cannot recommend what computer and software or typewriter to buy because everyone is different and each person's needs are different. Also, you will probably go through more than one computer and word processing software program in your writing career. Some people also use their computers to handle their families financial planning, bookkeeping and check writing. I know there are writers who let their kids play computer games on their office computers, but the very thought makes me shudder. I'm very possessive about my computer. To let kids play on it would be like sharing my toothbrush, which I would do before sharing my computer.

Many writers get totally caught up in the vast computer world and spend many nonwriting hours investigating the Internet or just playing games. I'll admit it's tempting, but it doesn't get pages written when you have a book to write. Chat rooms are fun from time to time and you can gather good information as long as you remember that some of the people chatting may not be real experts and the information they give may not be valid.

Although I do use the Internet for research and use E-mail to talk to editors, my nieces and nephews and a few friends, I'm basically a real dummy about both computers and my software. I know just enough to write my books, insert page numbers, headers and footnotes, and print the darn things. Only recently I learned how to backup an entire book folder without going chapter by chapter. One day I want to learn how to have the computer make the indexes for my books. For now, I've acccpted that my computer and software can do far more than I'll ever understand.

Although I've hung onto my typewriter to type envelopes, since I can't figure out how to do them on the computer, I seldom use it for anything else, and it sits with its dusty cover alongside a dresser in my office. But if you want to use yours for writing, be sure you have a clean ribbon and self-correcting ribbon or tape. Even if you can change fonts (typefaces) on your typewriter, keep the fancy script and italic fonts for personal correspondence and use a standard one, such as Courier or Times New Roman, for your professional work.

Though I'm as far from being a computer guru as Dustin Hoffman is from playing linebacker in the NFL, I will offer this advice pertaining to computers:

- Go to a number of computer stores before you make a decision.
- Talk to friends (who are writers, if possible) about how they like their particular computers and word processing software. If they're unhappy with either, ask why.
- If you have access to any major company, talk to the business manager to see if the company has old computers awaiting disposal. Often businesses will upgrade their entire computer systems and then don't know what to do with the older models. They may sell one to you at a greatly reduced price and perhaps, if you're lucky, even be willing to give it to you for free. It's worth asking.
- Consider how and where you'll be working.
- Be sure you're working with a knowledgeable salesperson. Obviously, she wants to sell you as much as possible, especially if

there's commission involved. But a good salesperson also knows that if she does a good job for you, you'll be back again and again. Computers (and software) are addictive.

• Remember that the computer is the hardware. It runs the software, which is the program, so be sure the computer you buy can handle the software you have, need or plan to purchase.

• Get the name of a computer genius (not my son because he's even too busy to help me) because you'll often have frantic questions on how to install a program, what to do when the whole screen freezes and you can't shut your computer off or what to do when you hear grinding sounds coming out of your computer's innards. Call your local high school or college for the name of one of these young people. (You probably could get the same help from your local middle school or elementary school, but that would really make you feel lousy.)

• Always get more memory than you think you'll need. Otherwise, the following week you'll want a new type of software for which your computer doesn't have enough memory.

• Buy the best printer you can afford, such as a laser or ink-jet. The pages from inexpensive dot matrix printers are hard to read, and many editors won't even bother trying.

• If you have cats, try to keep them off your computer and monitor. I once had a 22-pound gray cat that used to sit on top of my old word processor shaking his head slowly as I wrote. I thought he was a little too critical of my work. What I didn't think about was all the cat hair flying into the disk drive or how his rubbing up the computer could create static electricity and mess up something inside the computer.

The Other Electric Equipment
• **Fax machines**

If your computer software doesn't give you the capacity to send faxes, you'll eventually want to get a fax machine, as it's a quick and convenient way for editors to send your copy back for corrections. Some faxes come with telephones and memory for speed dialing. If you buy a fax, my preference is for a machine that uses plain copy paper rather than thermal paper that comes in rolls. The latter feels like wax paper the butcher uses and it curls. Some fax machines can duplicate letters, although you won't be able to make copies of newspaper articles or a page of text from a book.

- **Duplicating machines**

You may be able to purchase secondhand copying machines at used office furniture stores, but you might be better off with getting a new one from an office supply store because the new ones come with warranties. Unless you buy an expensive version, you probably won't be able to enlarge or reduce copies.

Electric Outlets and Extra Phone Lines

All of the electrical equipment requires more outlets than most homes enjoy. Ask an electrician to add a few more for you so you don't have to use extension cords, which can be tripped over. Also get a surge protector for your computer and fax machine to protect them against power surges and power failures. Living in both Florida and Maine, I have experienced both and was very happy to have my computer and fax machine protected.

I also suggest getting one and preferably two extra phone lines if financially possible. One line is your business line so you can talk to editors without your call-waiting clicking or your phone being tied up by others in the household. The other line is for your modem and fax machine. Many people combine these two extra phone lines, but your business phone will ring busy when you're sending or receiving a fax.

Storing the "Little Stuff"

It's the "little stuff" that can overwhelm you when you're writing at home. It's the pencils, pens, computer or typing paper, reference books, stamps and staples. That's also the stuff that disappears; everyone in the family knows you have it, so it seems to be fair game. In most "real" businesses, there are supply closets with wonderful shelves ready to hold all these supplies. At home, unless you are most fortunate, the "supply" closet also holds your clothes, linens, dishes or kids' puzzles and games. So you need to be resourceful about finding a place to store these items. They *are* the tools of your trade, you know, so treat them with as much respect as you would your stethoscope if you were (are) a physician or your drill and screwdrivers if you were (are) a carpenter. Fortunately, many companies and other writers have been creative for you so you don't need to reinvent (or store) the wheel.

If you're like me, you go crazy when you go into office supply stores. I feel a longing for all the little pads, stickers, files and pens, absolutely convinced that each of them will help me become a better writer. While it's sometimes cheaper to buy in bulk, and you do need to stock up on many of these items so you don't have to run out every time you need a file folder or an envelope to mail in an article, beware of overbuying. Make sure you have places to store these items so the paper doesn't get wrinkled and the toner or glue sticks dry up.

Try to keep your writing supplies as close to your work area as possible so you don't have to run upstairs for envelopes and into the kitchen for the scissors. Use mugs or silverware dividers to keep your pens and pencils united. I prefer the latter and separate types of pens by their function, such as markers for highlighting, red for corrections (I told you I was a creature of habit), black for signing letters and taking notes, and pencils for marking dates in my Filofax. Empty baby food jars or mugs are useful for storing paper clips, rubber bands and business cards. If yours is a traveling office that has to give way for the table to be set for dinner, use a small muffin tin for these small items. When you're finished writing, put your papers in a box or plastic washtub, lay the cupcake tin on top and move your office to a nearby chest or buffet.

If your actual work space is limited, put your stapler, extra staples, scissors, letter opener and correction fluid in a shoe box with a lid to hide it from prying eyes and impatient hands, and keep it in a nearby cupboard. Use a permanent pen to mark your name and "Do Not Remove From Office" on the scissors, stapler and anything else that might walk. Keep your business postage separate from what you use for bills and personal correspondence by hiding the stamps in the front of a reference book or dictionary. Otherwise there won't be a stamp around when you're ready to mail your manuscript ahead of deadline. Postage stamps have a way of disappearing just like brownies or fudge, one piece at a time until you suddenly realize you're all out.

I used to recommend having a bulletin board to hang some of the stuff that cluttered the desk. Now I realize that my desk still continued to be cluttered by other papers, and, in addition, I also had a cluttered bulletin board that I seldom, if ever, looked at. Instead, I now keep phone numbers in twin Rolodexes and have a third that I use strictly for medical writing which has physician experts alphabetized by specialties rather than their last names. That way I can quickly contact two or three gastroenterologists from different parts of the country for input on an article about gastroesophageal reflux disease (GERD), for example, rather than having to try to remember their names or worse, thumb through a Rolodex trying to discover them.

For those of us who write at home, necessity truly is the mother of invention. A woman whose office is basically her kitchen table told me that she uses the inside of the cupboard by the telephone as her bulletin board. When she's working, she opens the cupboard door and checks on her writing progress on the chart there, gets a phone number from the list pasted there and tracks her articles making the rounds of magazine editors. When her working day is over, she shuts the cupboard door, puts all her supplies back into her giant roaster pan, slides it back on its shelf under the sink and fixes dinner.

"I only use that roasting pan on Thanksgiving," she explained. "It seemed like such a waste for it to be sitting there the rest of the year, so I put it to work." Although she still uses a typewriter so it's easy to transfer it to a countertop after writing, many people have computers in their kitchens so the same idea would work for them.

There are many catalog companies that cater to those of us trying to get organized. Ask your catalog-ordering friends about those companies. As they come and go, I hesitate to list any by name. Check on the Web for updated information.

Wastebasket

This is no time to be timid. Move the tiny decorative wastebasket out of your writing area, and replace it with the biggest one you can find. The larger it is, the more likely you will toss papers you don't really need and reduce some of the clutter most writers tend to accumulate.

Reference Books

I'm totally biased when it comes to books. I've had a love affair with them since I was four years old and got my first library card in Fort Dodge, Iowa, as soon as the librarian would give it to me.

Some of my reference books have been part of my life since I was in college. A few, even before that. It's difficult to make specific suggestions on what you need because that varies according to your finances, available space, the type of writing you do (fiction, nonfiction, health care, etc.) and your personal interests. Since I began writing medical articles and books, my reference library has expanded greatly. As medical definitions vary greatly in clarity, I have both *Dorland's Illustrated Medical Dictionary* (Saunders) and *Stedman's Medical Dictionary* (Williams & Wilkins). I also have *The Merck Manual* and *Gray's Anatomy*, as well as many others. I haunt library sales, garage sales and secondhand bookstores for reference material because even if the data is obsolete, the books can be helpful for background information.

There are, however, a few basic reference books I would suggest you have handy (this means in or near your office, not somewhere in the house or in the library).

* **Dictionary**

Even if you won every spelling bee in grade school and junior high and your software program has a spelling checker, you still need a dictionary to check a definition to be sure it's the exact meaning you intended. Buy a hardback dictionary, not a paperback, and get the most extensive one you can afford. You'll use it often.

* **Book of synonyms**

When you proof your manuscript, you may be amazed to discover how often you use the same word over and over again. We all have favorites that tend to pop up in our writing like the targets in a shooting gallery. You can shoot these ducks down and use a synonym if you have a good reference book. Although I prefer *The Synonym Finder* by J.I. Rodale, now available in paperback, there are many others. Take your time looking through them at your local bookstore before buying. Many word processing software programs offer this service, which is better than not having it, although at times the choices seem limited.

- **Stylebook**

Although some book publishers have their particular styles and will send you stylebooks to follow, most of them just prefer you pick a style and stick with it. Since I went to college in the Midwest (Northwestern University), I use *The Chicago Manual of Style*. There are other good ones, including *The Associated Press Stylebook and Libel Manual*.

- **Book of quotations**

Whether you're writing a speech, article or book, it's always advisable to have a couple of good quotation books on hand. I have about five, including *Bartlett's Familiar Quotations*, *Dictionary of Quotations* by the late Bergen Evans (one of my professors at Northwestern University) and *The Fairview Guide to Positive Quotations*. There is quite an array of specialized quotation books, such as only women's quotes, Jewish quotations, biblical quotations, sports quotations and so on, and many are available in paperback.

- **Marketing book**

One of the most important books you'll need is *Writer's Market* published by Writer's Digest Books. Printed annually since 1921, it describes markets for your books, articles, plays and even greeting cards. It also includes information about royalties and advances, along with names, addresses, phone numbers and E-mail addresses for over four thousand potential markets. It's now available in paperback and on CD-ROM. If you buy only one book for your writing, this is the one to get. I don't say so because Writer's Digest Books is also my publisher for this book; I say so because without it, I don't know how you'll sell your work. I've been using it for almost forty years, so I don't argue with success.

- **Encyclopedia**

I have an old set of the *World Book Encyclopedia*, which I use for background information. There are many other fine encyclopedias, and for this purpose, they don't need to be up-to-date, although you need to keep that in mind when you check facts. You can buy old encyclopedia sets at garage sales, in thrift shops and in secondhand bookstores. Just be sure you have room for them as they do take up a lot of space. You can also get encyclopedias on CD-ROM.

- **Personal interest books**

Most of my writing today centers on health care and women and family interests. My library tends to reflect that. When I wrote greeting cards, I collected joke books that could trigger an idea. I frequently haunt the markdown tables in bookstores, at library sales and in secondhand bookstores and get fifteen and twenty dollar books for a few dollars or less. If you get one salable idea from a book, it's paid for itself.

If you write about gardening, cooking, travel or sports, you should start gathering books on those subjects. The best advice I can give is that if you find yourself checking the same book out of the library all the time or having to run to the library to look something up, you probably should buy that reference item for your personal library. It is a business expense, you know.

In some fields, however, you might be able to get reference books free. A doctor's office gives me its old *Physician's Desk Reference* (*PDR*) when the new one arrives. You also can contact publicity departments of publishers who handle books on topics you write about and ask for review copies. If you mention the names of their books in your article or book, it not only may boost those sales but it also may bring your name to an editor's attention who then could ask you to write a book.

- **Ledger**

In case you've forgotten, the art of writing is also a business. You need to keep up-to-date and accurate records. Record all your expenses (with receipts) as well as checks as they come in. If you have an office in transit and need to move your work to make way for another household function, put your ledger in a safe drawer nearby. It needs to have a permanent home so you can find it quickly.

- **Personal organizer**

I wish I had a dollar for every personal organizer (used to be called calendar) I've purchased in the hopes that this one would be the one to keep me organized and on time. When my children lived at home, I had two calendars. One of them was in my purse, and the other stayed by the phone with everyone's appointments in it. I also used it to keep track of friends' and relatives' birthdays and anniversaries. Don't just write down "doctor's appointment," though. Put a name or initial by it. I once took the wrong kid in for a checkup.

Now I have only one personal organizer, and it stays by the telephone until I go out. Then it tags along with me. Mine is a Filofax brand, but there are many others, such as Day-Timer and At-a-Glance. They all come in a wide variety: day at a glance, two days, a week or a month. Some versions are loose-leaf so you can add special sections, such as addresses, phone and fax numbers, motivational quotes and "to do" lists. I have additional personal divisions in mine for lists of the shirt sizes of all my sons and sons-in-law, my children's china and crystal patterns, books I've heard about and want to read and notes for the next book I'm going to do. (There's always a next book, or at least, I hope for one.)

Take your time looking over the personal organizers until you find one that seems to suit your needs. Don't be surprised if you have to try a few until you find one that fits perfectly. Try to use just one at a time, however. Otherwise you may find that you've forgotten to transfer an appointment and are double-booked for the same time.

- **Business stationery**

You'll need business stationery sooner than you may think. Although you can make letterhead on your computer in the beginning, you quickly will want to have matching stationery and envelopes when you query editors or write for information. The more professional you appear, the more professional you will begin to feel. Any quick-print shop can help you design something that looks professional. Look over samples or collect letterheads from businesses that write to you. Stay away from neon colors. Choose white, cream or light beige. If you feel the need for a logo, make it a simple one. You really don't need a fancy logo, though. Just put the words "Freelance Writer" under your name as many of us do.

- **Business cards**

If you're going into the business of writing, you'll need to have a business card. It's as important as developing a firm handshake and eye contact. Don't spend money on anything fancy. A business card simply needs to have your name, the word "Writer" or "Freelance Writer" under your name, your address, telephone number and, if you have them, fax number and E-mail address. Don't get oddly shaped or oversize cards as they won't fit into standard card holders. The one exception to this is if your card is one that can be put into a rolling address file, such as a Rolodex. In that case, consider having them made in two sizes, as many people, including me, use the 3″ × 5″ card rather than the smaller 2″ × 3″.

- **Business checking account**

It helps when it's time to figure your taxes to be able to pinpoint your business expenses and to account for them separately from your household expenses. A separate checking account for your writing is the easiest way to do this. It also is the account to receive the money you'll make writing. Isn't that a pleasant thought? Hopefully, it won't be too long before your writing income more than offsets your writing expenses.

- **Address labels**

"To" and "From" labels with your printed return address look professional when you send manuscripts in manila envelopes. While the labels are not a necessity, they save time. You also can cut out your printed return address to use on the self-addressed envelopes you include with manuscripts, although a rubber stamp works just as well.

- **Memo paper**

Ask a print shop to make you memo pads on colored paper that's cut to half the size of a standard 8½″ × 11″ sheet. Often a print shop has rejected print jobs containing errors, and you can buy this paper cheaply and use the back side. The colored paper stands out in a sea of white manuscript paper on your desk so you won't waste time searching for a scrap of white paper on which you wrote an important phone number.

- **Correspondence file folder**

Keep a printed copy of your correspondence in a special folder marked "correspondence." If you keep these pages in chronological order, you can quickly find one when you need to refer back to it.

I start a new folder each year and file the previous ones in case I need them in the future.

Keeping Track of Pencils and Pennies

Keeping track of writing supplies has always been harder for me to master than the writing itself. When my kids were little, I would try reason: "These are Mommy's business things. You can't touch them because I need them for my work."

I tried threats: "I'll do something drastic to anyone who touches my scissors again. Now I'm going to close my eyes and when I open them, I want to see the scissors on my desk." When I opened my eyes, my stapler was missing too.

Pens and pencils disappear like the Cheshire Cat but without the smile. I keep replacing them, now buying them by the box. But I have to wonder if by some psychic phenomenon they're in the same place as the socks I lose in the dryer and my extra set of car keys.

You could lock everything in a drawer, but you might lose the key. I've found that the best bet when you're not writing is to keep your writing tools hidden in a drawer or cupboard. Out of sight means they still may be there when you return the next day.

It isn't a matter of being selfish with your things. It's a waste of time, that precious commodity, to have to hunt down your pens, paper clips or scissors. Having to replace lost items is costly to you in both time and money.

When my kids were preschoolers, I sensed they sometimes considered my work as a competitor. It took Mommy away from them. Rather than quitting out of guilt, I set them up in businesses by giving each kid a cigar box with his or her name on it. The boxes were filled with their own office supplies (crayons, safety scissors, paste, paper, etc.) so they could "write" when I was working. It kept them out of my things, and I only remember one time that I had to borrow from them.

As the youngsters grew older, I often proofed my work while they were doing their homework or watching television. I was with them yet working. That seemed to satisfy everyone, although all of them complained that I never read any of their written work without automatically picking up a red pen. Occupational hazard, I guess.

SETTING AND FOLLOWING BUSINESS HOURS

In the beginning you need to be strict about keeping definite working hours. After a few months of following whatever schedule you've devised, you will have developed the writing habit and will find yourself expecting to go to your work space to write. It's really not much different than starting an exercise program. You'll often find yourself making excuses about why you don't have time to write. But make yourself sit down and do it. Schedule it into your day like any other important appointment.

By setting and sticking to a regular writing schedule, you'll also be training your family and friends. They'll know not to bother you between 8:30 A.M. and noon or from 8 P.M. to 10 P.M.. The downside, of course, is that they'll know they can get hold of you then and may call with "just one quick question."

***

Once you've amassed all the tools of your trade, you're set. Look around your office. You've got a computer or typewriter, paper, reference materials, market guide and so on. You've even purchased stationery and business cards that identify you as a freelance writer. Start thinking of yourself as one, even if you have to resort to a game of Let's Pretend. Someone once said, "There are no amateurs in freelance writing; there are only writers who haven't been published yet." So what's next? Start writing.

CHAPTER 9

Laying the Groundwork

Our plans miscarry because they have no aim. When a man does not know
what harbor he is making for, no wind is the right wind.

— Seneca

KNOW YOUR MARKETS

You may think it's odd for me to talk about markets when you
haven't written a word. But it's important that *before* you write
you know where you plan to send your work, because you'll have
to slant it for particular markets. In order to do that, you need to
have an understanding of your potential markets. And while fiction
may be less market specific than nonfiction, you still need to know
which publishing houses handle romances or mysteries and which
wouldn't touch them with the proverbial 10-foot pole.

While knowing your markets sounds like a given, you'd be surprised how many people submit poems, articles and story ideas that
are totally foreign to the targeted magazines or book publishers.
Don't figure that just because a magazine has never published
poetry, for example, that it will make an exception for your work
or that a magazine for women between twenty-five and fifty will
love your story about male action adventures.

If You Don't Read Them, It's Hard to Write Them

People often ask me why I don't write mysteries, science fiction or
romances. The answer is simple: I don't read them. Any true mystery fan would immediately see through any plot I might create.
My feeble attempts at science fiction would be laughable, and my
romantic tales, awkward and high schoolish. There is a certain

format for writing a specific genre, and if you don't even read it, it's doubtful you'll be able to write it.

If I ever needed to write a mystery, however, you can be sure that the first thing I would do is to check out every good mystery book and buy every mystery magazine and immerse myself in them.

Check Market Guides

Market guides, such as those found in writing magazines and the most recent edition of *Writer's Market*, will give you an idea of the readership, preferred slants and number of words or pages required by each magazine or book publisher. Don't waste your time and postage sending to a market that doesn't publish the type of material you want to write.

Don't use last year's copy of *Writer's Market*, as publications frequently go out of business or change their focuses. You need the most up-to-date information you can get. You can also write directly to the editor of a book or magazine and ask for a copy of that particular publication's guidelines. You'll be surprised how specific they are, often even to the age range, educational level and income status of typical readers. Be sure to include a stamped, self-addressed envelope.

Read the Actual Magazine

To really get a handle on a particular magazine, however, you need to buy a few copies and read them carefully. Also check some back issues (available at your library). Analyze the lengths of the various articles. Are most of them 500 words or 1,500? Longer? Do they use anecdotal material, information from experts or a preponderance of statistics? What types of stories do they run? Self-help? Mind-body relationship? Humorous? Political? Fashion oriented? Recreation and out-of-doors? Which articles are hyped on the cover? Who are the advertisers? What does that tell you about readership? How often is this particular magazine published? Are there special editions for holidays, weddings or back-to-school?

If you want to write a book, go to the library or bookstore and study other books a particular publisher has printed. Write or call and ask for a current catalog or check *Publishers Weekly*. Study the books' lengths and subjects. Don't try to sell a self-help or inspirational book to a publisher that specializes in history, cookbooks and mysteries.

Make a list of two or three potential markets for your work so that if it's rejected by the first one, you'll be able to make the necessary changes and then send it to the next one. If you're not immediately prepared with a second possible home for your work, you'll be more likely to stick the manuscript in a drawer and give up.

DON'T WRITE ABOUT THE WORLD— JUST ONE SMALL SECTION OF IT

Chances are you now need to narrow your focus. The topic that excited you probably is too big for you to get your arms around, let alone handle adequately in 1,500 words or even in a book. It's not just a matter of thinking small. It's more that you need to select one aspect of the overall topic that you'd like to write about.

When I wanted to write about strokes, for example, I limited my focus to what a family of someone who had a stroke needed to know. Rather than going into great scientific detail about the neurological changes, I wrote about how these changes manifested themselves in ways a family could understand, such as how it altered their loved one's thinking and physical abilities and what the family could do to help. I explained the need for speech and physical therapy and what it was but did not write about how it was carried out. Specific selection of one aspect of a subject is like looking at a slide through a microscope. You know there's a lot more material available, but you're just focusing on one particular aspect.

CHECK THE COMPETITION

Before you spend too much time researching and writing a book or magazine article on a particular subject, you need to check what's already been done. The presence of another book on the same subject doesn't necessarily mean the death of your idea, but you need to be aware that one has been published so you can (1) tell a prospective editor that you know about the competition and (2) know how yours will differ from the existing book or books. Use the library or Internet to check *Subject Guide to Books in Print*. You also can use Amazon.com, an on-line bookstore, to see what titles exist on your topic. If the most recent book on your subject is old or out of print, it may be time for a new one (yours) to appear. On the other hand, if there are twenty other books on your topic, think of a way to make yours different or back away.

To see if an article on your subject has recently appeared in a magazine, ask if your library has access to Magazine ASAP. If not, use the *Readers' Guide to Periodical Literature*. It comes out monthly so you'll have to painstakingly search each volume. At the end of every year, the information comes out in one big volume. It's worth the time, however, so you don't send your terrific magazine article idea to a publisher that ran a story like it four months before.

DON'T OUTLAW OUTLINES

I can hear groans already. "Not outlining! I did that in high school and I hated it. All those little 1s and 2s, Roman numerals and little *a*s and *b*s. Nasty business."

Well, you can stop moaning and start tearing up your preconceived formal outline notions. You won't need them. But you will need an informal outline to use as a road map for your writing. Otherwise you will zigzag all over and eventually crash.

What I am about to suggest to you is the way that *I* outline a project. It works for me, but it may not for you. Everyone's different. There are many other ways writers outline. I'll mention some of them to you, and then you can borrow a bit here and a piece there to develop an outlining style that is efficient and helpful to you.

Expand to the Wide-Open Spaces

I have an easel that holds paper 27″ × 34″. You can use a blackboard or just a big drawing tablet, anything that's oversize. You need this free-form space so you're not inhibited. Working on a tablet with lines is constrictive, at least to me. (I always did color outside the lines.)

In the center of the pad, write your idea for an article or book. Then, like spokes in a wheel, write everything you can think of that supports the idea. Write all around the pad in no particular order; that will come later. For example, the idea for this book was "writing at home." Most of the chapters now in this book originally were jotted down on the easel when I began to plan the project. Some topics (such as child care, finding ideas, where to find illustrations, and publicity) were dropped from the list because of space limitations or were folded into other chapters.

Then, with a red pen (an old habit, but I'm not sure I could work with green or purple), I begin to number the spokes in what seems to be a logical order. Often that order is altered once I actually begin writing. When that's complete, I turn to a clean page and write the topic for chapter one (or section one of an article) in the middle of the page and begin to list, again in no particular place or order, thoughts that should come under that heading. Naturally, once I begin to research and interview, I'll find more points to list under each heading.

If I can't think of anything to write for a particular topic, I'll ask myself how important that chapter or section really is. If I still think it's important to the book or article, I'll leave it, assuming that my research and interviews will flesh out that point. Sometimes it does, but more frequently, it doesn't.

I continue to repeat the same procedure with each of the remaining chapters or sections. For me, the importance of having the oversize pad of paper is that I can brainstorm with myself without feeling that it has to be an orderly progression. I have the freedom to throw ideas on the pad as fast as they come, without subconsciously censoring any topics at that point.

Other writers use index cards and then spread them all over a table or the floor to arrange them. I used to use that system, but my writing's too big to put everything on an index card and too often a dog, cat or kid would come in and trample all over my "outline."

Print Your Outline

Your outline may look great on the giant pad, but how does it read in context? You really won't know that until you type your outline as a table of contents. In writing this book, I've not only moved chapters from one place to another, but I've also added chapters once I began to write the book and even combined two. Books tend to develop lives of their own once you begin writing, but right now you're in your planning stage. Editors expect that a finished project may look somewhat different from its outlined version. Nevertheless, spend time and thought in this preplanning stage.

An outline helps whether you're writing nonfiction or fiction. It gives you some idea where your story is going, and you won't end up with a *Perils of Pauline* ending with no way to get your heroine off the railroad track.

TITLES, OR "WHAT'S IN A NAME?"
I'll be the first to admit that I'm lousy at titles. I had no trouble in naming our five children, although I had two left over—names, not kids. But titles for writing projects remain a challenge. I appreciate good ones but seldom think of them myself. Nevertheless, you have to call your work in progress something even if the name gets changed as you work on it. And if you don't change the title yourself, chances are good that your editor will.

Working Title
The name you give to your article or book is called a working title. It means just that: It's the title as you're working on the story, understanding that the name may only be tentative and could be changed when the piece "grows up" and leaves home. The working title gives you something to call it rather than "a book about writing and being at home along with some time management principles and other organizational stuff." The fact that you've named it also makes it more real in your mind. Just don't be surprised if the title undergoes a few alterations as you begin to research and interview people. You may even find a title from something one of your interviewees says.

Alliteration
Alliteration often works well for a title, especially for an article. *Family Circle* featured a cover story titled "Chefs' Secrets for Delicious Diet Dishes." I used alliteration for a children's story, "The

Missing Matzoh," that appeared in *Highlights for Children.* Readers like alliteration because it plays nicely on the tongue. My favorite alliteration title, which really wasn't a title because it was for a radio commercial I wrote, is "Little Lambs Love Lacey Lingerie." It was for children's underwear and nightwear. I wrote it for an obnoxious disk jockey who had trouble saying his Ls. It's been forty years, but I still feel guilty about it. I'd publicly apologize to him, but I've forgotten his name.

Numbers
If you check the covers of many magazines, you'll see articles titled "13 Ways to . . ." or "5 Methods to Help You . . ." That's because numbers, especially odd numbers, seem to catch a reader's eye. *Prevention* used numbers in titles twice in one issue, with "See 20/ 20 at 40-Plus," and "3 Minutes to Total Relaxation." You have only to look at the success of Stephen R. Covey's *The 7 Habits of Highly Effective Families* for a good example of the same technique in books.

I've used that approach for many of my own articles, including "10 Ways to Help Your Child Adjust to Camp" in *Family Weekly* and "29 Ways to Create Your Own Job" for *Glamour.* In a recent issue of *Men's Health*, numbers were featured in the titles of three articles: "50 Healthy Junk Foods," "10 Signs You're Not Eating Right" "and 4 Exercise Bets You Can Win." The cover of a recent *Woman's Day* also had three articles with numbers in the titles: "79 Spring Cleaning Tips," "620 Great Ideas" and "Two Months of Menus." Obviously, for many writers, using numbers in titles add up to sales.

Comparisons
It's eye-catching to use comparisons for titles as well. Some of the ones I've used include "From Rags to Enrichment" for *Today's Catholic Teacher*, "Mess/Stress" for *Ladycom*, and "Little Whoppers to Big Lies" for *Glamour. Prevention* ran an article titled "Cheer Up and Slim Down. One of the best recent examples of comparsions in book titles is *Midnight in the Garden of Good and Evil.*

Be Brief

Despite the advice to keep your title short, there have been very successful books with long titles. The ones that quickly come to mind are *Everything You Always Wanted to Know About Sex, but Were Afraid to Ask*; *When I Say No, I Feel Guilty*; *Don't Sweat the Small Stuff . . . and It's All Small Stuff* and *Men Are From Mars, Women Are From Venus*. Nevertheless, now, with the advent of computers, you're better off keeping the titles short enough to fit into the bookstores' computer data banks. I learned this firsthand with my first book, *How to Be a Successful Housewife/Writer*. The title was so long that the *Writer* part of the title was omitted in many bookstore computers. Obviously, that omission changed the main focus of the book for many potential buyers.

Since that first effort, I've tried to keep my titles five words or less. That "keep it simple" theory is ascribed to by many top-selling authors, including John Grisham whose book titles are usually two or three words, as in *The Firm*, *The Street Lawyer*, *The Client*, *The Partner* and *The Runaway Jury*. Other brief titles on the best-sellers list at this writing are *Cold Mountain*, *The Notebook* and *Simple Abundance*.

How To

Many successful article and book titles begin with *How to* because most of us are interested in bettering ourselves and finding ways to do so. One of my recent titles, *How to Get Out of the Hospital Alive*, was one that captured the interest of buyers and the media alike. No, it wasn't my idea, but rather that of my most creative agent, Faith Hamlin. I used a reversal of a how-to title in my article "How Not to Poison Your Child." *Woman's Day* recently ran, "How to Give Your Kids Confidence," while *Time* published "Asteroids: How to Stop Them."

Superlatives

It's hard to pass up reading a book or article whose title includes "The Best Way to . . ." or "The Biggest Books of . . ." or "The World's Greatest . . ." Just be sure that if you use this type of title, your work can live up to the boast. I personally don't use a superlative unless it's for a humorous story.

What You See Is What You Get

Don't be too cute when it comes to titling your writing or the editor won't have any idea what you're selling. Describe what your book or article is about through your title. That's why some of my titles are clear-cut, such as "Mother Was a Soccer Player," "Step by Step Back Into the Working World," *Relief From IBS* and *Depression: What Families Should Know.*

Be Open to Catchphrases and Plays on Words

Sometimes during an interview or general conversation, you'll hear a phrase that is the perfect title for your book or article. Keep your mind open to it. Write it down, or you'll never remember it.

You also can use a well-known quote and change just one word to create a pun or play on words. I did this for an article about a ranch-style preschool, titling it "School on the Range." A recent issue of *Food & Wine* ran two articles with this type of title, "Seeing Stars in Italy," a story about Michelin-starred restaurants in Mantua, Italy, and "Keller Instincts," an article about one of America's top chefs, Thomas Keller. *Variety*, the show business magazine, and *Time* both use this technique frequently. Look through a few back issues to see experts at work.

Ask a Question

You'll find question titles more often in magazine articles than as book titles. Nevertheless, they are effective. I asked, "Will You Poison Your Child?" for an article on how to prevent accidental childhood poisonings that was published in *Essence*. Questions are used frequently for magazine articles' titles because they speak directly to the reader.

Have a Gimmick

Some fiction writers who write series, usually mysteries, develop gimmicks for their titles. Two authors who quickly come to mind are John D. MacDonald, who used a different color in each of his

Travis McGee book titles, and Sue Grafton, whose titles follow the alphabet, such as *A Is for Alibi, B Is for Burglar* and *C Is for Corpse*.

THE QUERY

The first thrust of your research will be to give you enough information to write the query. That's a fancy name for a proposal. The query is your display piece, a sample of your writing wares. It is the selling piece that you use to convince an editor that you not only have a great idea (and are a fantastic writer) but that you know a great deal about your subject and have already interviewed a few experts.

You can write the query before you complete all your research, but never send a query before you have a good feel for your topic. If the editor calls you and asks a few questions, you want to sound as though this topic is your passion and that you think about nothing else. I know a few writers who hurried with their queries and mailed them prematurely. They had egg on their faces when they had to sell their ideas on the phone to editors and had little information to pass along.

You'll find more about how to write a query in chapter twelve. Just keep the query letter in mind as you begin your research. If you find something that's specifically interesting to you, make note of it on a separate pad. If it caught your attention, it probably would the editor's as well.

And now, it's time to roll up your sleeves and dig in. Don't panic. Research can be fun. It's a lot like learning to swim: You can't just put on a swimsuit and go to the pool, lake or ocean; eventually, you have to get wet.

CHAPTER 10

Researching

I will try to cram these paragraphs full of facts and give them a weight and shape no greater than that of a cloud of blue butterflies.
— Brendan Gill

R*esearch!* The word has a musty ring to it, conjuring up visions of long library tables piled high with dusty volumes, stacks of index cards and term papers soon to be overdue. Even the thought of researching through the Internet fails to make it sound like fun to many writers. But unless your writing is confined to greeting cards, inspirational writing and humorous articles, chances are you'll have to roll up your sleeves and learn how to dig out the facts you'll need to support your article or book.

FINDING THE ANSWERS

Now that you know what you're going to write about, have narrowed the focus and have selected a few potential markets, it's time to start collecting information. You need background material, experts, anecdotes, statistics and other data. You'll want to find answers for all the questions you would have if you were the reader, and because you've already studied your markets, you have a good image of your potential reader in your mind's eye.

How much research is enough? More than you'll need. Just don't get so engrossed in doing your research that you never get around to writing. It's called the dissertation syndrome, and doctoral students are not the only ones susceptible to it.

WHY DO YOU NEED RESEARCH?

The most basic reason for research is that it adds substance and validity to your work regardless if it's fiction or nonfiction. If you're writing about the evolution of football uniforms, for example, your manuscript might be strengthened by including specific facts such as "the first football uniform numerals sewn on the players' uniforms to enable the spectators easily to distinguish the players were used by the University of Pittsburgh, Pittsburgh, PA, on December 5, 1908, for the game against Washington and Jefferson. The score was 14-0 in favor of Washington and Jefferson." (This and other gems can be found in Joseph Nathan Kane's book *Famous First Facts*. It's great rainy day reading.)

Although research is most important in nonfiction, it helps make your fictional work more believable too. It keeps you from making mistakes that someone's bound to catch, such as having your hero fly on the Concorde five years before its maiden voyage or using the wrong date for a well-known event. When you describe a specific town, restaurant or museum accurately, your editor and readers will nod and say, "Yes, that's exactly right."

Sometimes, especially in health care articles, you'll discover that the "facts" don't agree. Experts may have differing opinions about the cause of a disorder or, more often, its treatment. Take time to discover both sides of an issue, and present them for a balanced piece.

HOW TO BEGIN YOUR SEARCH

I begin my research by listing what I already know about a subject. Sometimes I find it's a great deal. Other times, I know very little but am curious to learn more. When both of my parents suffered strokes, for example, I knew how helpless I felt. It made me realize that even with my previous medical writing experience and a long-time interest in medicine, I was fairly ignorant about what actually was happening and what I as a family member could do to help.

I interviewed over one hundred stroke survivors and their families; physicians; speech, occupational and physical therapists; nurses; psychologists and psychiatrists; social workers; and members of the clergy. I visited leading rehabilitation centers and talked with the experts there. I read everything—both lay and professional—I could get my hands on about strokes. I learned at that time there were more than 500,000 new stroke patients each year. I knew I could write a book that would be helpful to their families. The result was *Strokes: What Families Should Know*, which was published by Ballantine Books.

Tell People About Your Project

While you don't want to talk your idea out before it's written, you should tell others what you're working on. Many times I've learned of an important new source from someone who knew someone or had letters or other documents I could use.

Years ago I was writing an article about people who collect things and mentioned at a meeting that I personally had accumulated more than two hundred hippo figurines. A woman next to me said that she had even more bulldog figurines. And she knew someone who collected miniature china shoes. That lady knew someone who collected doorknobs and she knew . . . well, you get the idea. Before long I had more than enough examples to use in my article. Although that article was published almost twenty years ago, people still come up to me asking when I'll do another and feature their collections.

Check Your Personal Library

If you are interested enough in writing about something, there's a good chance you've already collected a few books on that subject. Wander through the house and check your personal library. Don't forget your children's books. You'll often find good basic information in the kids' nonfiction titles.

Over the years I've amassed a number of reference books. Additional information may also be on-line or available on CD-ROM, but if you don't have a computer or you need to go to the library to use one, you may want to get some of these and other books mentioned in chapter eight.

- *The New York Public Library Desk Reference*
- various "experts" lists from universities' news services or media relations offices
- *World Book* or some other encyclopedia
- books on your areas of expertise and interest

- *The World Almanac and Book of Facts* or some other type of an annual almanac
- an atlas

Use the Telephone Directory

Sometimes one of your best resources is right in your home: the telephone directory. Many businesses are affiliated with state or national organizations or associations with staffs available to help disseminate information to writers. If you're not sure how to get in touch with these resources or whether a particular industry has such an organization, call a local business and ask how to get hold of its state or national association. Often you'll even get the name of someone to contact.

Check the yellow-page classifications for the names of local experts too. We tend to take the telephone book for granted because it's always there, but it's a valuable research tool.

Make Friends With Your Public Librarian

Forget that nonsense about dogs being a man's best friend. Librarians are your best friends when you're a writer. Introduce yourself to the staff and tell them what you're working on. Not only will they probably suggest sources you've probably never even heard of, but they also often will help you begin and narrow your search.

As most libraries now have computers for the use of their patrons, the librarian can also show you how to navigate the Internet to find specific information. Don't be embarrassed if you're a novice. Everyone was once.

Ask to use the library's vertical files on a particular subject too. This is usually one or more folders containing newspaper clippings, brochures and other information on a particular subject.

If there is a college or university nearby, ask for permission to use its library. Most state institutions will let you use their facilities, although you may need a special permit to check out books.

If you can't find a particular book you want, ask the librarian to use the interlibrary loan system, through which libraries borrow books from other libraries.

Networking

Often the hardest part of doing research is finding the right people to talk to. In 1990 there was a hit stage play on Broadway called *Six Degrees of Separation* by playwright John Guare. One of its main contentions was that we're often just six people away from anybody we want or need to talk to. In the play, one of Guare's characters says, "I read somewhere that everybody on this planet is separated by only six other people. Six degrees of separation . . . you have to find the right six people to make the connection. It's not just big names. It's *anyone.*" I've found that to be quite true.

Johann van Goethe said, "Go to the place where the thing you wish to know is native; your best teacher is there . . . You acquire a language most readily in the country where it is spoken; you study mineralogy best among miners; and so with everything else." It's still good advice. Most professions have their own special dialects that you'll need to acquire to write knowledgeably about those subjects. If you're writing about learning disabilities, for example, talk to teachers, principals and parents of children with learning disabilities. Contact psychologists, special education teachers and social workers who deal with youngsters with learning disabilities. Learn the lingo. Educators are famous for using acronyms such as IEP, SED, LD and LRE, which you'll need to be able to translate into individualized education plan, social or emotionally disturbed, learning disabled and least restrictive environment.

In your reading, watch for names that keep coming up as authors of articles or as experts being interviewed. Don't feel that even some of the big names are out of your reach. Often, the more prominent the individuals are, the more responsive they will be in talking to a writer, once you've convinced their secretaries or assistants that you're a professional. How do you reach these people? Look them up in *Who's Who*. Often the business address is listed and you can write to them with your request.

Once you've made your contacts, keep their names and phone numbers on your Rolodex, in a special folder or in some safe place. You may be using them again. If you got the name from someone, make a note of it so you can refresh the expert's memory when you call again. Also, note the names of the experts' secretaries or assistants, and be nice to them. These people often are the gatekeepers and can block your way to the gurus or open the doors.

The Internet has made it easier to find experts and get exactly the information you're looking for. You can quickly develop a virtual community, which is computer talk for networking.

Get on the Internet

I'm hardly a computer whiz, but I have learned to use the Internet, electronic mail (E-mail) and the World Wide Web to help with research for my writing. These seemingly scary haunts quickly feel like home once you frequent them a few times.

For a general understanding of how the Internet, World Wide Web and E-mail all work, you can read one of dozens of books on the subject. I suggest you take about half an hour to browse through them at your favorite bookstore and buy at least two so that if you don't understand an explanation in one, you can turn to the other. Since new books constantly hit the bookshelves, I won't recommend one but rather tell you how I have used the computer to help me, even with my somewhat limited knowledge of its capabilities. That's the good news, you realize: You don't have to be a computer genius to take advantage of its magic.

First you need a gadget called a modem to get you onto the Internet. The modem is your electronic bridge. It helps you to connect with an on-line information network through your telephone line. Modems operate at different speeds reflected by their bps (bits per second). The higher the number, the faster the information is transferred. Since all this happens over the telephone line, it helps to have a second line so you won't disturb your on-line session if call-waiting interrupts. There are a number of these on-line information networks, although the best known are American Online (AOL), CompuServe, which is now owned by AOL, and Microsoft Network (MSN). You pay these companies monthly fees for usage.

Once you've gone on-line, you can create an E-mail address and password and begin to "talk" to people all over the world. It's much faster than using the U.S. Postal Service, often referred to as snail mail, and keeps you from playing telephone tag with those you need to talk to. I conducted many of the interviews for this book using E-mail. There also are chat areas and special interest forums where a number of people can communicate at the same time. Just remember that information given in these areas may not be factual but rather the individuals' personal opinions.

You can quickly use the Internet to gather information from a variety of sources. The famous World Wide Web you've heard so much about is only a part of the Internet. To get around, you need a search engine (Hey, I didn't come up with these names!) I begin with one called Yahoo! You call it up by typing http://www.yahoo.com. There is also one called Lycos, http://www.lycos.com, and another known as AltaVista, http://www.altavista.digital.com.

With Yahoo!, you pick from a selection of topics. If you want information that isn't listed among those topics, type in a word or two that describes what you want, being as specific as you can. Otherwise you may get thousands of matches. Warning: You can spend hours playing on the Web, using your entire writing time allotment if you're not careful. Remember what happened to the fly that got caught in the web.

You also can learn what books have been published on a specific topic you're writing on by checking Amazon.com, one of my favorite Web sites. Type http://www.amazon.com. You can search by author, subject or topic. (My other books are listed there.) You also can order books at a discount through Amazon without ever leaving home.

While it sounds futuristic to those of us not familiar with the Internet, chances are your kids or grandkids are already surfing the Net, playing games, talking to peers in Europe and gathering information for their history reports. If they can do it, so can we.

Let Government Agencies Help You

Uncle Sam wants to help with your research. As a taxpayer, you've been supporting your government for some time. Now, as a writer, it's time to get something back.

There are virtually thousands of government agencies on local, state and federal levels. Each of these agencies has a full-time staff on your payroll as Boss Taxpayer. They're available to answer your questions and send you all sorts of printed material. It may take a while to find the right person, but once you do, it's well worth the effort. To save long-distance costs, start at your local level and get referals to the right departments of particular agencies. Keep those phone numbers; you might need them again. The Government Printing Office in Washington is a good source for basic information on a number of topics. As its phone number keeps changing, call information to get the most recent working number.

If you write fiction or your writing is travel oriented, contact a state's Department of Tourism, a community's Chamber of Commerce, travel agents, the American Automobile Association (AAA) or the Canadian Automobile Association (CAA). For foreign travel information, you can write or call the country's tourist bureau, usually located in Washington, DC, or New York City. The latter will give you brochures and printed material plus give or loan you photographs to illustrate your article.

KEEP TRACK OF YOUR SOURCES

After you find the information you need for your manuscript, you must decide where to put it within the article or book, and then you must store the information and the facts identifying the source. Publishers have research assistants whose sole job it is to call authors at the least convenient time possible and ask, "Where did you get this fact?"

A shrug won't do. You have to be able to come up with the answer if you want your work published. You'll sound far more professional and less hysterical if you can pull that quote or statistic from your notes and locate the source written neatly beside it. I also date my notes from interviews for the same reason. It makes my life less stressful, and I'm sure it helps the research assistant have a nicer day.

It used to be difficult for me to keep track of my research. I used index cards, charts, the computer, and I finally have arrived at a way that works for me. When I begin a book or article, I create separate files for every chapter, marking them with the names, but not numbers, of the chapters. I don't number the files because chapters, like kids at a family reunion photo session, have a way of constantly changing positions as you write.

As I research, I put my notes, articles from magazines or the name of a book with a particular page number or numbers in the proper chapter file. When it's time to write that chapter, I arrange the research into some semblance of order within the file. After completing a draft of that chapter, I return everything to that particular file. When the editor calls with questions, I can (usually) quickly find the source of a quote, statistic or bit of general information.

If you clip something out of the newspaper or a magazine, be sure to write the name of the publication, the date and the page the article was on. You'll often need that information for a footnote or to satisfy the publisher's need for verification.

RESEARCH REMINDERS

1. If you quote material from another source, you must put it in quotation marks and credit that source either in the body of the text or as a footnote or endnote. If it's a great deal of material (more than three or four sentences), write for permission from the publisher, in care of the permissions editor. Tell the editor what you want to use the material for, exactly what you want to quote (I duplicate the page from my manuscript and include it with my letter) and how it will be used. Usually the editor will grant you permission, although sometimes this may require a small fee.

- If you omit material, use ellipsis points to show you haven't used the entire quote.
- Always put quotations around a quote when you're taking notes to remind yourself that you're quoting someone else's work.

2. Don't copy someone else's errors. Be careful when you copy another's facts so you don't pass along incorrect information. I often have discovered errors in dates, inaccurate statistics and quotes attributed to the wrong person. Get as much verified with a second source as possible.

3. Authenticate your quotes. When you find an expert named in one of your research sources, try to get your own fresh and original quotes. Usually an article will say something like, "Dr. Ocelot from Zoology Department of Cage University says. . ." All you have to

do is to write or call Dr. Ocelot and mention the article you read concerning his theory of mating leopards with ostriches. He may tell you that he was misquoted in that publication and that it was orangutans not ostriches and then reveal to your ears alone that he's currently into shortening giraffe necks. Now you've got a totally different slant to your article. More importantly, you've received fresh material from an expert rather than passing along another writer's old (and inaccurate) "facts."

4. Give yourself a deadline. You need a specific deadline to complete your book or article, even if the deadline is self-imposed. You need a cutoff time for doing research too. Otherwise you may get so engrossed in researching that you never get around to writing the piece.

- Having a deadline makes it easier to work with others who are sending you information because it creates a sense of urgency.
- Set the deadline a little earlier than it actually needs to be, as many people wait until the last moment to fill your request for information.

5. Don't make your notes perfect. Because we writers tend to be experts in procrastination, it's tempting to perfect complex forms of note taking, transfer dates onto charts and graphs, recopy information on different-color index cards, type it into the computer and use a variety of file folders. Like carefully showing everyone how to squeeze toothpaste from the bottom of the tube not the middle, this process is a lesson in futility. It keeps us from our main business, which is writing, not becoming professional note takers.

- Find a system that works for you and stick to it.
- Stay alert for time-wasting activities.

6. Don't overresearch. I'm fascinated by research and find that one thing seems to lead to another. I get carried away, wanting to check one more expert, one more source. So when do you have enough? When do you call it quits? Obviously, when you have enough to first write a strong query and then to write your book or article. When is that? Sorry, there's no definite point. You have to sense it and be alert for it.

When you finally sit down to write and you feel as though you'd like to keep researching because it's the easier of the two tasks, you probably have enough material to begin. We all know so-called writers who have been "researching my book" for ten years. Chances are that's all they'll ever do. Fear of failure has kept many would-be writers riding into the sunset on the research trail, fearing failure if they got out of those saddles and actually tried to write.

Research can be a frustration and a chore, or it can be a fascination and a delight. The secret is in using research as merely one of the many steps in writing and not letting it become a safe harbor in which to drop anchor.

CHAPTER 11

Interviewing

[Sometimes] the interviewed has nothing to say, and the interviewer does not know how to make him say it. Sometimes in despair they write up a lot the man never said, never intended to say, and couldn't say if he thought of it.

— Mark Twain

For many of us, interviewing is a lot like public speaking; just the thought of it makes butterflies take flight in our stomachs and our throats to become parched. But, just as with public speaking, the better prepared you are, the more effective you'll be.

WHY INTERVIEW?

You may feel you haven't the time to set up and conduct interviews. After all, why not just get the information from journals and books? You can, of course, and many successful writers do, but their work often lacks immediacy and is flat. For the most part, probably the only writers who can get away without interviewing anyone are those who write from their personal experiences (and even there, additional expert opinions are helpful), those who write humor bits, such as the dear late Erma Bombeck, and those who write fillers. Even fiction writers often need to hone their interviewing skills to learn more about their characters' backgrounds, job skills and locations.

There are three major reasons you need to develop interviewing skills.

1. Interviewing Makes You More of an Expert

When James Michener was writing his novel *Recessional*, about a retirement community, he came to the Tampa Bay area to see such residences for himself. A friend of mine drove him around.

She was impressed by what he had already learned through research but even more so by the questions he asked of the residents, the staff and others.

When I wrote my book *Relief From IBS: Irritable Bowel Syndrome*, I did a great deal of reading on the subject. Then I interviewed patients who suffered from this chronic disorder, physicians who treated it and psychologists who treated the emotional issues that arise from the disorder. They told me of personal experiences and gave me poignant quotes that no reference material offered.

Regardless of how well you write, most magazine and book editors want to know that you've contacted "experts" on whatever subject you're covering. It could be a local television anchor, architect, physician or dog groomer, but a quote from someone other than yourself adds credibility to your work. It lets the editor know that you haven't written your piece off the top of your head or merely adapted reference material written by someone else.

2. Interviewing Gives You Quotes and a Style of Expressing Things Different From Your Own Voice

Often your interviewee expresses things far better than you ever could. The person's natural phrasing or choice of words gives life to your writing. When I wrote *Gifts of Time* with pediatric neurosurgeon Fred J. Epstein, he was both my coauthor and a primary interviewee. His personal comments set the tone for the book about his work with kids who had severe brain stem and spinal cord tumors and made the book come alive. When asked why he offered hope to families of children with brain and nervous system tumors when he knew there wasn't any and other surgeons had been unable or unwilling to operate, Epstein replied, "You have to believe. Miracles do happen. I've seen them happen." His quote, "Kids aren't meant to be sick. They're certainly not meant to die," said more about his stubborn optimism and his successful surgeries than anything I could have said.

3. Your Interviewee is the Subject of Your Article

Although Dr. Epstein was the subject of the book we wrote together, I also interviewed a number of other people. The list included the parents of some of his patients, parents of children whom Epstein had been unable to save, peers, nurses, social workers and even his wife and three of his five children.

Often, however, we interview only one person for an article that stands on its own. It may be an inspirational article on how an individual overcomes a problem; a how-to article about someone unusual who makes houses out of seashells and bits of driftwood; or a personality story, as with an entertainer or athlete.

One of my favorite personality interviews was with television and stage actor Peter Falk in 1971. He was appearing on Broadway at the Eugene O'Neil Theatre in *The Prisoner of Second Avenue*. I had written to him requesting an interview but hadn't gotten any response. Nevertheless, I went backstage after the show and told the wizened stage door attendant that I had an interview with Peter Falk. He shrugged as though he didn't believe me but went to check. Shortly, he returned and motioned for me to follow him.

I walked to Falk's dressing room on trembling legs and entered. He just stared at me. "I'm here for the interview," I said weakly.

"You're kidding," he said, giving me a bemused look. "I thought you were just coming backstage so you could say you had met me and then write whatever you wanted to."

"Nobody wants to read that I met you," I answered, gaining courage and a sense of professionalism. "They want to know what Peter Falk really has to say." He wrinkled up his face comically as viewers have seen on Falk's television hit *Columbo*. "You make me crazy," he said in his gravel-like voice. "But you're on. Give me ten minutes and we'll talk." And he did. I sold the story to *Screen Stars* and used his opening comments to me as my lead.

Many articles for local newspapers and city or regional magazines are no more than interviews with interesting local people. I've interviewed a number of local noncelebrities, including a silversmith, describing how he repaired sterling and silver-plate items, and a man who taught troubled teens at a juvenile home how to repair lawn mowers, cars and vans and to build bicycles out of donated odd parts. Think about the interesting people in your community. If you find them engaging, chances are readers might also.

WHOM SHOULD YOU INTERVIEW?

Your time is best spent interviewing people who are experts in their field, people who are personalities whom others want to read about or those ordinary people like you and me who have had extraordinary experiences, such as surviving a month on a desert island, adopting triplets or serving gourmet meals to fifty people at once in a one-room efficiency. Of course their experiences don't have to be quite that unusual, just those that your readers can identify with or be glad or sad that they weren't their experiences.

Depending on your article or book, you might want to check out some of the following interview subjects.

Professors at Colleges or Universities

Most institutions of higher learning have public relations or media relations departments that are responsible for working with the media to get the schools' names mentioned in positive ways. You can either call those departments directly or, if you have enough time, write explaining what you are writing and what type of expertise you are looking for. Don't call professors unless you know them. Some are most learned but are terrible interviewees. Go through the media relations departments. They know who is a "good talker" and who mumbles or is too academic.

Ask the media relations person to put you on mailing lists for releases pertaining to whatever subjects you are interested in, even if you aren't writing on those topics just then. I've pulled out fifteen-year-old releases and called to check if a particular professor quoted in the release was still on campus. Usually the answer was yes.

Business Executives

Most businesses are also happy to work with writers to get the companies' names mentioned prominently (in positive stories). Call the office of a company's president, manager or top executive. Explain to the secretary or administrative assistant that you're a writer, describe what you're working on and approximately how much time you'd need for the interview. Always figure less time than you really would like. If the interview goes well, you'll probably be invited to stay longer. You may have to wait until the person goes to check with the boss. Chances are, however, that the boss will say yes.

If you already have a commitment from an editor, say so. Never try to fake it by saying you have an assignment when you don't. The person you're talking to may be that editor's best friend or brother-in-law, and if he finds out you've lied, your credibility as a writer is ruined.

If you have no assignment and the person asks who you're writing for, say, "I plan to submit it to *X* and *Y* magazines." Don't add that it's on speculation or that it's the first article you've tried to write.

Read business journals or the business section of your local paper and keep a list of businesspeople who are guest speakers for different organizations. Note their topics and the companies they represent. If they're in demand as speakers, they're probably also considered experts. Mention to the gatekeeper, "I see that Ms. Buzz spoke to the Wednesday Luncheon Club about beekeeping. Since I'm doing an article on how to prevent bee stings, I thought she'd have something important for me to include in my story." The secretary is bound to be impressed that you keep up with his boss's public appearance, and that will help your request for the interview.

Physicians and Other Health Care Workers

In the many years I have done medical writing, I have never been refused an interview with a physician or any health care worker. Sometimes, the first person I speak to suggests others for me to meet.

That happened when I was collecting background information for my book on irritable bowel syndrome (IBS). I was visiting Baltimore with my husband and decided to call Johns Hopkins University School of Medicine to ask for the name of a physician who saw patients with that disorder. I obtained the name of Marvin M. Schuster, M.D., professor of medicine and psychiatry at the medical school and chief of the Division of Digestive Diseases at Francis Scott Key Medical Center. Dr. Schuster not only was in but agreed to see me that day. I hurried over.

After a most enlightening interview, Schuster insisted I meet with his co-worker, William E. Whitehead, Ph.D. He also was available and I came out of that interview not only with books and a stack of research data on IBS, but also the name of another physician, Douglas A. Drossman, who was an associate professor of medicine and psychiatry in the Division of Digestive Diseases and Nutrition at the University of North Carolina School of Medicine at Chapel Hill. He also agreed to see me and, as with the others, was most instructive and helpful.

Why did these three (and other) health care professionals give so much time to a writer they had never heard of? Because the diagnosis and treatment of IBS was a passion with them. They cared about their suffering patients and welcomed the formation of a layperson's book on the subject. I think they sensed that I wanted to do a careful and accurate job, and they wanted to help me achieve that goal. After I finished writing the book, I sent each of them the manuscript to check for accuracy. I am indebted to them for their help and contributions. The book's still in print and selling well.

I've had the same experience with psychologists, nurses, social workers, nutritionists and other health care workers. If the thought of calling someone of national repute scares you silly, start with those you know locally. But don't be afraid to contact some of the leading medical centers and ask to speak to the experts on a particular subject. They usually love what they're doing and probably will be delighted to share their knowledge with an interested writer.

Do remember, however, that theories, diagnoses and treatments in medicine differ widely. Don't assume that your experts' opinions are shared with all of their colleagues. Ask if there are differing viewpoints and who else you should talk to for a balanced article.

Writers

As you do your research, you may find that certain writers' names keep coming up because they have written on your subject. These authors are good potential interview subjects because they not only know the topic, but they know what information you're looking for. They also may identify additional contacts. To locate a particular writer, look for clues among the credits listed at the end of the article or on the book jacket. You also can call the editor of the magazine or book, but an editor often won't—and probably isn't allowed to—give out the requested information. You also can go on the Internet and type www.four11.com. If the writer has a registered E-mail address, you could find it there.

Personalities

Most magazines are eager for articles based on the lives of well-known personalities. If Robin Williams lives next door to you or you work out at the gym with Whitney Houston, you can probably sell an article *if* you can get one of them to agree to an interview. Sports figures, well-known authors and other popular figures are not only interesting topics in themselves, but if they also happen to be experts on a particular subject—such as Paul Newman and racing cars, Mary Tyler Moore and diabetes or Jim Eisenreich with Tourette Syndrome—you have an excellent slant for your story. Although you may have to work harder to get permission for the interview, often going through an agent, manager or publicity person, you'll find most of these personalities are just ordinary people like you and me. Treat them as fellow human beings and with respect for their time and you may get wonderful interviews.

"Ordinary" People

Never underestimate the power of an "ordinary" person's story. Readers easily identify with an unknown someone who succeeds despite overwhelming odds, performs a courageous act or is just plain interesting. Think about the success of talk shows on both radio and television. Most of the guests are just ordinary people who have stories to tell. Encourage those people to tell their stories to you.

National Organizations and Associations

There are thousands of experts paid by someone else to answer your questions. These are the men and women who work for national organizations and associations. They are available for interviews, plus they often can put you in touch with other experts and laypeople alike to help flesh out your article or book. Just a few I have worked with include the Tourette Syndrome Association, American Medical

Association, American Academy of Pediatrics, National Association of Home Builders, and Shriners Hospitals for Children. Their representatives have all been most helpful and cooperative. Check in Gale Research's *Encyclopedia of Associations* for the names of those organizations and associations that can answer your needs. Like the lonely Maytag repairman, they're waiting for your call.

RESEARCH YOUR SUBJECT

Always give your interviewee the courtesy of doing some homework beforehand so you don't ask questions that you could and should have answered for yourself. When television and movie actor Len Cariou was in Tampa rehearsing for the musical *Teddy and Alice*, he agreed to give an interview to a local reporter. "She began with, 'And what shows have you been in, Mr. Cariou,' " he said. "I was furious that she hadn't done her homework." And he was well within his rights.

The various *Who's Who* books and computer searches of articles on your potential interviewee can help fill you in on details such as education, past accomplishments and so on. I think I gained rapport with Peter Falk, who spent a summer at the University of Wisconsin, by mentioning that my husband had attended that school as well. Falk smiled at obviously happy memories. How did I know he had gone there? From a previous article about him.

WHAT MODE OF INTERVIEW SHOULD YOU USE?

Your circumstances may determine what type of interview you want to conduct. If you're collecting information for statistical purposes, you may want to send out a questionnaire. If you have an invalid parent and twelve kids at home, you may have to opt for a telephone interview. And if you prefer face-to-face encounters and can travel as needed, you probably will use the personal interview. Each type has its pros and cons.

Mail and E-mail Interviews

If your expert lives too far away for you to visit, you can write to ask for a telephone interview or to ask if you can send questions by mail. If you get a positive response, carefully develop a list of questions and prepare your correspondence.

- Address your letter by name. If you don't know who's in charge, make up a title, such as Director of Trash and Disposables, or Manager of Designing, Perfume Division.
- Include the name of the publication you're writing for, if you have a definite assignment. Don't fake it.
- Do not send more than ten questions. Respect your expert's time.
- Leave plenty of room between questions so the person can answer right on the paper rather than typing the responses separately.
- Include a deadline for the response. Make it a few weeks before the time you actually need it.
- Give your telephone number, and encourage your expert to call you collect. Also include your E-mail address and fax number if you have these capabilities.
- Always include a stamped, self-addressed envelope.
- Send a thank-you note after you receive a reply.
- Send a copy of the article after it's published.
- Keep the names of those who responded. You may want to contact them again for another story.

I've interviewed successfully by mail many times. It's expensive, sometimes more than telephoning, because of printing and postage costs. Usually you get no more than one response for every ten requests. Mailed questionnaires are useful, however, when you need many opinions or a wide geographic representation.

Using E-mail for interviews is far easier and faster than using "snail mail" because you can quickly respond to your interviewee's answers to ask for clarification or pose additional questions. I've used E-mail interviewing for my book on stepparenting and this one. I've found that individuals seem freer with their responses with E-mail, are more willing to flesh out their answers and often ask questions about my work in progress. Many times they then offer names of additional people for me to contact.

Telephone Interviews

Be ready with your questions when you call to set up a telephone interview because often the individual will say, "Well, right now's a good time." If it isn't a good time for you or you really don't feel prepared, say that you'd prefer to call back at a time that's convenient for you both.

When you conduct a telephone interview, put the dog outside, make arrangements to have the kids out of the house, either at school or with a baby-sitter, and tell your spouse that you're making a business call. It's hard to sound professional during a phone interview with a dog barking at your feet, a child screaming, "He hit me and I didn't do nothin'!" or your mate hollering, "Honey, where's the extra toilet paper?" or "When are you going to take this darn garbage out?"

If you have call-waiting on your telephone, disconnect it so the clicking that tells you of an incoming call doesn't interrupt your expert's train of thought.

Schedule enough time for the interview so you don't have to break it off when it's time to pick up the kids from soccer practice or meet your spouse's train.

I've found that standing up while I talk on the phone makes me sound more energetic. I also keep a mirror nearby so I can look at it and remember to smile. Yes, I know most of us don't have videophones yet, but when you have a smile on your face, you tend to have a lift in your voice. Ban the monotone and smile.

Personal Interviews

My preference is for the personal interview because then I can see my interviewees as they speak and study their body language. Are they distracted? Do they doodle as they talk or tap a finger? What personal mannerisms describe each subject? How are the interviewees dressed? What jewelry do they wear? By actually eyeballing your subjects, you'll know if they are speaking from notes or have the facts at their command.

Before I leave, I always ask, "Is there anything else you'd like to add?" and, "Is there anyone else I should talk to?" After interviewing a periodontist for an article about periodontal surgery, which he claimed was a painless ordeal, I asked him if he could suggest a few patients I could talk with. He checked with two and then said I had their permission to interview them. The first patient I called gave a very different reaction to her surgery—and a wonderful quote: "It was the most painful experience I've ever gone through," she said. It certainly gave balance and a firsthand report from someone who had been there, and best of all, she was someone whom the periodontist had personally selected for me to contact.

Another physician did more than recommend names for me; he picked up the phone, dialed a colleague in another city and handed me the receiver. "Here," he said. "Ask him what he thinks."

WHERE TO HOLD THE INTERVIEW

If you're doing a personal interview, arrange for it to be conducted somewhere other that your own home. Even if you have a separate entrance to your office, many people don't think of an at home writer as a professional. If you have young children at home, they may bounce in just when you're ready to ask the "big question." You're better off seeing your subjects on their own turfs or at neutral locations, such as quiet restaurants, parks or beaches.

The positive aspect of interviewing people in their own homes or offices is that you get an added sense of who they are and what they do by noticing the plaques and pictures on the wall, the books in the bookcases and other personal touches. Also, interviewees should be more relaxed in their own environments and may let down their guards for you. A negative about home- or office-based interviews is that your subjects may be interrupted by phone calls or people popping in and out.

PLAN SPECIFIC QUESTIONS

Before any interview, plan specific questions you want answered. Have more than you'll need in case your subject wants to keep talking and what is being said is of value for your story. It also helps keep you on track when your interviewee begins to wander off on side paths. If you know the slant of your piece, you can gently lead your expert back to where you want to go. If you like the new direction, however, be flexible enough to adjust your questions accordingly.

Word your questions so you ask for the expert's own opinion, feelings and experience, not just the company line. Ask, "Why did you . . .?" or, "How did you . . .?" All of us are flattered by attention, and most people are pleased to talk about themselves if encouraged. If your subject keeps telling you about, "The company thought that . . . ," ask what the inverviewee's own contribution was.

Don't be so focused on your questions, however, that you fail to hear an opening for another line of questioning. One of the many times I interviewed pediatric neurosurgeon Fred Epstein, he said, almost as an aside, "Of course, I can't save them all. I wish I could." Sensing that he was ready to talk about the kids he couldn't save, I asked him, "How do you feel when you lose a patient?" He opened up with such apparent anguish that it gave a most human view of a gifted neurosurgeon. Had I said, "I'm sure you do," and then gone on with my list of prepared questions, I would have missed some telling emotional quotes and anecdotes that gave a depth of understanding about the man and the work he performs.

Also, don't let your interviewee off easily by asking questions that can be answered with yes or no. These responses lend little to your story and negate any chance you might have for your subject to give you useful quotes.

HOW TO DRESS FOR THE INTERVIEW
Neither overdress nor underdress for a personal interview. What does that mean? It means not wearing a cocktail dress, dangling diamond earrings and spike heels if you're a woman nor showing up in your favorite pair of jeans and a sweatshirt, regardless of your gender. For most interviews in homes or offices, business attire is preferable. If your interview is being held on a farm, on the beach or at a ski resort, however, you should dress accordingly. The goal is to look professional without standing out because of what you're wearing.

While tailored pantsuits for women are fine, I advise females to avoid wearing short skirts at interviews. If you're constantly worrying if your skirt is crawling up your thighs, you can't concentrate on the interview, and it may be distracting for your subject as well. Leave the sheer blouse in the closet along with the one that pulls too tightly across your bust. Dangling bracelets and earrings are another distraction for both you and your interviewee. Leave your bulky tote bag at home and bring a small tailored handbag where you can quickly find your pen or handkerchief without digging around, muttering, "I know it's in here somewhere." Many women just use a briefcase and slip their billfolds and combs in the bottom. Put your purse or briefcase on the floor next to you, never on your expert's desk. Use a moderate amount of makeup, and never wear perfume. Your expert may be allergic to it and could quickly cancel your interview.

If you're male, leave the earring and body-piercing jewelry at home unless you're interviewing someone who also is into that type of body adornment. Don't wear flashy ties, sleeveless shirts or sandals. Sport shirts may be all right if the occasion calls for it. Match your attire to the type of clothing your expert wears. If you're interviewing a lifeguard at the beach, sportswear obviously would be preferable to a dark suit. If you're in someone's paneled office, your good suit or at least a conservative sports jacket is recommended.

While the following should be obvious, I'll add them anyway: Arrive on time (or a few minutes early so you have time to collect your thoughts before seeing the expert), and don't chew gum or smoke during a personal interview. I never accept a cup of coffee as it's too hard to juggle a cup and saucer, notepad and pen. You don't want to spill coffee on your expert's antique rug now, do you?

TO TAPE OR NOT TO TAPE

Writers are split on the question of whether or not to use a tape recorder for a personal interview. There are advantages to taping an interview.

- You don't have to take copious notes, which frees you to listen more closely and interact directly with your expert.

- You get a good sense of the rhythm of the person's speech pattern.
- You get a permanent record of exactly what was said, which is helpful if you don't remember the exact words or the person claims to have been misquoted.

But there are disadvantages to taping an interview as well.

- Some people, who may have been chatty and friendly earlier, clam up as soon as you press the "record" button.
- If you have to change tapes, you lose the mood and natural rhythm of the interview, as the expert becomes self-conscious again, realizing that she is being taped.
- The tape can break or the machine not record for some reason known only to the gods of mechanical things. If you haven't taken written notes, your interview is lost.
- You have to listen to or have someone transcribe the entire interview, which may include a lot of small talk and other useless material.

As you may surmise, my bias is not to use a tape recorder. I prefer written notes when conducting interviews and have used them successfully for most of my writing career.

HOW TO TAKE WRITTEN NOTES

Before you arrive at your interview destination, be sure you have more than one pen or pencil. Ink can dry up and a pencil lead can break. You lose an aura of professionalism when you have to ask your expert for a pen or pencil. Rather than using a standard-size yellow pad, I use a reporter's notebook, which measures 4″ × 8″, or a steno pad, either of which can be purchased at an office supply store. The reporter's notebook fits in the palm of my hand and is less conspicuous than a large tablet.

As you take notes of what's being said, add information about the speaker's clothes, gestures, mannerisms and voice patterns. Over the years, I've developed my own personal brand of shorthand and so will you as you do more interviewing. Here are a few tips to consider as you take notes.

- Abbreviate words, use symbols for commonly used words and omit what you don't need. For example, I use *p* for *people,* ^ for *of,* and *adv* for *advantage.* If you're interviewing an advertising executive, however, you might want to use *adv* for *advertising.* Make your shorthand work for you.

- Only write what's important. Look at your subject and react to what's being said.

- If your expert throws a zinger as an aside, don't note it right then because the subject may pause to rethink what just popped out. Wait until your expert is saying something else, then write the quote so you don't forget.

- Repeat facts to be sure you note them accurately. "Thirteen thousand units a day? That's amazing." With luck, your expert might add, "That's nothing. Next month we add our X-128 machine and it can produce twice that. . . ." And then you have information the expert may not have wanted to share just yet. On the other hand, if you misunderstood and the figure was thirteen hundred not thousand, your expert has the opportunity to make a correction.

- Ask if you can send the expert's quotes to be checked for accuracy, not writing style. You'll always get a positive response. When you do send them, include a stamped, self-addressed envelope as well as the deadline for returning the corrected information.

- Ask for the correct spelling of names and terms with which you are not familiar.

- Date your notes. Then if you have to check with the expert later, you can say, "On May 14 when we met . . ."

- Stay alert for good quotes. One of them might become the title for your article or book.

- If you sense that your expert is reluctant to talk, put down your pen and ask conversationally, "What made you decide to quit Sage Brush, Inc., and start your own company?" or, "What characteristics do you think are necessary for success in your field?" Television's Barbara Walters is an expert at opening up even the most hesitant speaker.

- If you feel your expert is giving you a snow job from the public relations department, prepared pap the company wants you to hear, ask the interviewee directly, "I understand that this is the party line, but what do you really think about the feasibility of that plan? Is there some tweaking you'd like to see taking place?" That puts the ball directly in the subject's lap and offers the opportunity for your expert to tell you the way he would like to see a project carried out. It also appeals to the ego, the fact that we all like to talk about ourselves and the work we love.

• As soon as your interview is over, go to your car, the rest room or some quiet place and quickly fill in any information you want to remember. Check through your notes to add data you may have omitted. You'll find that you have almost total recall at that point.

LISTEN

Listen for the unique way people express themselves. You can learn a lot about individuals by the words they select and the ways they put them together.

Some executives talk as though they're quoting from the company manual when they describe their employees and how they interact with management, even when the administrators say it's a family-type atmosphere. You get a far different impression when an executive says, "Oh, we've all grown up together, sort of like a large family. Old Orvis Ossolinkee has been here going on twenty-five years. Started in the mailroom and now he's the head of the broken bottle division. His kid, Orvis Jr., is working in the mailroom now. His wife, Junella, was my assistant for ten years."

Other experts use peppery language to show you they're tough. Some use *me*, *mine*, and *I* throughout their conversations to emphasize how single-handedly they have transformed their industries or professions.

Listen for the quotes that say something in a unique way, tell something about the speaker or give facts or statistics in an interesting way. Good quotes aren't made (unless someone's public relations department manufactures them); they just happen. If you ask your experts to give you a good quote, they'll just look at you in panic. But listen and you'll hear them. Often the best quotes come just when you've put away your pen and are walking to the door.

"I'm glad you're doing this story," the head of a blood bank told me. "We're always in need of donations. Blood is the medicine no pharmacy can make."

I used his quote as my title for an article about donating blood, published in *The Rotarian*.

DON'T TALK ABOUT YOURSELF

It's always been hard for me to shut up about myself. We all love to talk about ourselves and what we do, so there's nothing wrong with answering a few friendly questions on what you're writing and how you became a writer. Just remember that you are the interviewer, not the interviewee.

I once left an interview thinking how great my subject had been. It wasn't until I was driving home that I realized that he knew a great deal more about me than I did about him. Often an expert will purposely question the interviewer to postpone having to answer any questions. Be on guard. If necessary, say, "Enough abut me. What do you think about . . . ?" and get the conversation back on a professional level.

If asked about your kids, it's OK to say that you have sixteen between the ages of two weeks and five years, but stop there or you'll never discover how your expert made billions by adding strings to the tea bag. Don't bring out pictures, talk about the kids' athletic prowess or do anything else that delays getting the information you came for. If Mr. Expert pulls out snapshots dating to when the oldest of his brood was six days old, admire them and then get back to business.

If it's appropriate, you can begin a question by saying, "My parents both had strokes, so I realize how devastating it can be for the family. What advice would you have . . ?" That tells your expert that you know a little about her specialty and that you're interested in knowing more. Don't start telling your own story of frustrations and trauma or you'll lose control of your interview.

You may find that you and your expert have interests in common. Ask a few questions to get a little color and interest for your article, then get back on track. If your subject gives information in anecdotes, put down your pen and listen. Jot down enough to jolt your memory later, but don't let your interviewee wander too long or your time will be up and you won't have gotten answers to your "hard" questions.

Don't be afraid of the pregnant pause. Use it to your advantage. If your subject stops talking, don't feel you have to fill the void. Just sit there, smiling pleasantly. Usually, the expert will feel uncomfortable with the silence and begin talking again, often saying just what you've been waiting to hear.

"SAY GOOD NIGHT, GRACIE"

George Burns, the straight man in the George Burns–Gracie Allen comedy team, used to say, "Say good night, Gracie," when it was time to end the show. Remember those farewell lines. Don't sit until cobwebs form between you and your chair or your expert quietly rings for the secretary to come in for a rescue. Stand up, hand the person your business card and say, "In case you think of anything else you'd like to add, here's where I can be reached." Sometimes I've received printed material with a note that reads, "Thought this might be useful for your article."

Always ask, "Is there anyone else I should talk to?" It not only will help you with your research, but it also gives you an opening with the new person to say, "Dr. Very Important Mann suggested I call you about an article I'm writing on . . ."

Be sure to follow up with thank-you notes to all your interviewees and send copies of the articles or books when they come out. You may never get thank-you notes from them, even when you've spent your own money (minus author's discount) to buy them the books, but they will remember when you call the next time.

Don't be afraid of the interview. If you've done your homework, you'll be in charge. People—even famous people—are just like the rest of us: They're concerned about what you're going to ask, are willing to talk about what usually are their favorite subjects (or they wouldn't have agreed to the interviews) and are a little curious about you as a writer, unless, of course, *they* also are writers. In that case, be careful you don't fall into just talking shop.

An interview is a lot like childbirth: It may be painful at the time, but the final result makes it all worthwhile.

CHAPTER 12

Showtime! Time to Write

In a mood of faith and hope my work goes on. A ream of fresh paper lies on my desk waiting for the next book. I am a writer and I take up my pen to write.
— Pearl Buck

You've come a long way. You've made the commitment to write, found a place to do it and amassed the tools you'll need to get the job done. You've completed the bulk of your research. You're almost there. Like an actor who's been cast in a role, learned the lines, rehearsed the role, been fitted for the costumes and mastered the stage business, it's showtime. The curtain's about to go up on one of the most rewarding parts you'll ever perform: The Writer at Work. Don't be put off by a few butterflies in your stomach. It's natural. I still get them every time I begin page one of a new book.

THE QUERY

Although some writers toss off quick query letters without much thought, most of us know that carefully thought-out proposals increase our chances of making sales.

Don't get uptight over your query letter. Just think of it as your sales presentation. It's your opportunity to pitch your idea, the slant or approach, why you have special qualifications that make you the perfect one to write this story, why your book or article is different from others recently published and what's going to be in your article or book.

If it's an article, let the editor know if you can furnish photos or other illustrations. I used to use my children as photographic models for many of my magazine articles. The kids were always around, and I didn't have to pay a model's fee.

Don't Promise the Moon

There's a tendency to want to promise anything—that you'll interview a number of national and international experts for your story, that you can have it written in three days or that you can include illustrative photographs—just to get a go-ahead. But don't promise more than you can deliver. Writing a query is a lot like flirting: You need to have a good idea of how far you want to go before you begin.

Be Specific

Don't say you want to write an article about dogs, for example; say you want to write about dogs working in the health care industry as companion dogs that visit hospital patients, Seeing Eye dogs and so on. If you work as a trainer for these canines, be sure to say so in the query.

Don't be discouraged if you get rejections from editors. They might have just purchased similar articles or may not think your subject is a good one for their particular magazines. If you get a handwritten note from an editor that says something like, "Sorry we can't use this, but I like your style. Please send me something else," don't assume it's what they all say. It isn't. Take that for what it is—encouragement—and put together another query for that editor. Do it quickly, as editors change faster than the seasons and one who likes your stuff today may have moved on in two months.

How to Handle an Acceptance

Once you get a go-ahead from an editor, reread your query to be sure you remember *exactly* what you promised to write. I once strayed from the slant of an article for *Today's Health*. When I turned in my manuscript, it was rejected with a note that said, "This isn't what you said you'd deliver." The magazine was on a tight deadline and didn't have time for me to attempt a rewrite. I was devastated, of course. But it was a good lesson, albeit a painful one, and I've never repeated that mistake.

THE LEAD

The lead (rhymes with *need*) is the opening paragraph of your book or article, the hook that makes the readers bite and want to continue reading. Often the lead is the same one used in the query. To be effective, a lead really has to zing, to pull in the reader just like the carnival hawkers at the fair.

Anecdotes

The lead can be a shocker or dramatic anecdote. For my article on how to prevent accidental childhood poisonings, my lead was simply, "Will you poison your child? I did." I then told how my toddler had climbed on a chair and gotten into the baby aspirin that I had left on top of a dresser. The rest of the article was true to my lead. It included statistics and ways to keep children from ingesting common poisonous substances found around the house. I think readers could easily identify with my experience, and thus, various versions of the article sold to a newspaper, to *Essence* and to a British women's magazine.

Follow the Tone of the Article

Your lead must follow the tone of your article too. For a light newspaper piece, my lead was, "Three little words. That's all they are. But they can cast a decided pallor over the face of the most resolute Ladies' Day golfer and hurl havoc into a harried housewife-turned-working woman's day. Those seemingly innocent words—'school is out'—might have changed the history of the world." The remainder of the piece speculated on what would have happened if the Wright Brothers had had to carpool the kids to Kitty Hawk Day Camp or if Madam Curie's youngsters had wanted to make a lemonade stand. The piece was humorous and a bit of fluff, but the lead promised just that.

Humanize Statistics

You can use statistics in your lead if you can put them in human terms. One of my favorite examples is a 1977 article from *Reader's Digest* by James Lincoln Collier. It is titled "Asimov, the Human Writing Machine" and tells about the prolific author, Isaac Asimov. The lead draws readers in by saying, "Most of us find writing a four-line thank-you note troublesome. Even professional writers often have to drag themselves to the typewriter to face that blank page. What then are we to say about a man who would rather write than do anything else? A man who usually starts to write at eight o'clock in the morning and often goes on until ten o'clock at night, typing steadily at the rate of 90 words a minute." In just four well-written sentences, Collier catches and holds our attention.

CONFETTI YOUR WORK

No, I don't mean tear your writing into little pieces, although there certainly is a time and a place to do that too. I'm referring to breaking down your writing into smaller bits so all the writing you have to do doesn't overwhelm you. Every writer has own tricks to keep her from thinking, "I'll never be able to write an entire book." I'll share mine, but they may not work for you. If not, tweak them a bit until you create something that does work.

Four a Day

I divide my writing load into manageable parts by convincing myself that I only have to write four pages a day. Figuring an average of 250 words on a page, that's approximately 1,000 words a day. I've written many newspaper and magazine articles of that length. The procedure's always the same. You write a word, then a sentence, then a paragraph and so on. The trick is to keep your eye on the short term so you don't panic.

My contract for this book was 70,000–90,000 words. That's a minimum of 280 pages. Scary? Not really, because I've broken them down into four-page segments, which seem doable to me. Some days I write more than four pages. A good day is six, and a great day is ten. Some days I only write two pages, and yes, there are days that I write nothing. I'll even goof off and go baby clothes shopping with my daughter-in-law who is expecting any day, or help my daughter house hunt, or just have lunch with the ladies. The trick, of course, is not to play hooky too often.

Keep a Running Total

I keep track of my pages on an easel that sits in front of my desk. On the top of the paper, I have the title of my book, the number of words/pages it requires and my deadline. On the left side, I write the date. The next column is for how many pages I write that day. The third column shows how many total pages I have written, and the last column, the number of pages I have left to write. On days I write less than my quota of four, I'll chastise myself by drawing a little frowning face by the date. Corny, but it works for me.

On the right-hand side of my easel paper, I list each chapter by name (not number because that tends to change as I write) and the number of pages in that chapter. Although it isn't important to have the same number in every chapter, I try to keep them somewhat even.

LEAVE SOMETHING TO PRIME THE PUMP

Some writers disagree with this method to bring you back to work, but it works for me and you should at least try it. When I'm writing well but it's time to quit to fix dinner or go somewhere, I'll leave in the middle of a paragraph. If I've finished a chapter, I'll type in the heading for the next one and, in the case of this book, actually find the right quote to head the chapter. That way I don't have to gear up the next day. I jump right in and finish the paragraph in question. It's like a hiker marking the path so he can find the way back.

I'll also leave notes for the next chapter on top of the computer so I don't have to think where I put them. Sometimes I'll write memos to myself to help jump-start the process. Whatever helps you cut down on the delay time means more time spent on writing. Don't worry if it's weird or sounds strange. Writers are an unusual group, so welcome. You'll fit right in.

BEGIN IN THE MIDDLE

Having trouble getting started? Don't spend too much time agonizing over it. Books and even articles don't have to be written in order. I often write the first chapter last or pick out an "easy" chapter to write to get myself going. Start in the middle and go backward, or write the last chapter first. As long as you then rewrite carefully to erase all the seams, no one will be the wiser.

READ YOUR WORK ALOUD

Most writers develop a definite rhythm in their writing, but you may not be aware of it unless you read your work aloud. Read it to the baby, the dog or cat, your spouse or just aloud to yourself. That's really the only way to detect sentences that are too complex, difficult to understand or just sound clumsy.

Sometimes the rhythm connotes a particular mood. In a book for beginning writers, I was trying to describe how you need to keep writing in order to become a better writer. I used the example of my daughter's cat that, at first, didn't purr. My daughter had told me, "You need to keep stroking him and then he'll purr." My written anecdote was, "She knows of kittens and their ways." When I got my manuscript back from the publisher, the copyeditor had changed my phrasing to, "She knows a lot about cats." For the first (and presently only) time ever, I disagreed with the copyeditor, and I refused to make that change. The rhythm was different, and the corrected version didn't express the mood for what I was trying to say.

REWRITE

Rewriting—the secret to a writer's success. There are few writers who can sit down and write a clean manuscript without doing any rewriting. Sometimes I'll find very little that needs to be changed, but usually I'll stare at one or two paragraphs and wonder aloud (I often talk to myself), "What on earth does this mean?" If *I* don't know, you can rest assured an editor won't either.

When you're figuring how long it will take you to write an article or book, always leave ample time for rewriting. It not only corrects obvious mistakes, but it also helps you smooth out wrinkles. Usually you write a book or even an article over an extended period of time. Rewriting lets you be certain that the last few chapters have the same tone, rhythm and feeling as the earlier ones, which, in some cases, you could have written almost a year before.

REJECTION

Let's be honest about it. Nobody likes being rejected. And when an editor rejects your writing, it's like having one of your children criticized. Your first reaction may be to think, *What do you mean you don't like it? What makes you think you know better than my spouse or best friend, who said it was great?* Your second reaction may be to write an angry letter to the editor suggesting that she find another line of work—but don't do that. Follow your third and more professional reaction by taking another look at your manuscript and seeing if you could improve it before sending it to the second publisher on your list. Contrary to what you're feeling with that rejection slip in your hand, it isn't a personal rejection but rather a business decision. And yes, editors do make mistakes and reject manuscripts that go on to become best-sellers. (There's more about rejection and how to handle it in chapter sixteen.)

Paying Your Dues

Take heart in realizing that you're in excellent company when your work's rejected. John Grisham's *A Time to Kill* was rejected many times before it was finally published. So was Tom Clancy's *The Hunt for Red October*. (And now the first edition of that same book is worth a great deal of money.) *Love Story, Jonathan Livingston Seagull, Talking to Heaven* and *All Things Bright and Beautiful* were all rejected a dozen times before finding a home. *To Kill a Mockingbird, The Road Less Traveled* and *The Fountainhead* had multiple rejections too. Robert Pirsig's *Zen and the Art of Motorcycle Maintenance* was rejected 124 times before finally being published.

Taylor Caldwell spent eighteen years trying to find a publisher for her first book, while *The Doctor's Quick Weight Loss Diet* by Samm Sinclair Baker and Dr. Irwin M. Stillman was rejected sixteen times before it was finally published and became a best-seller. Patrick Dennis, author of *Auntie Mame*, admitted wryly that his manuscript circulated for five years before finding a publisher. "It finally ended up with the Vanguard Press," he said, "which, as you can see, is rather deep into the alphabet." Even Beatrix Potter's well-known *The Tale of Peter Rabbit* was rejected seven times before the author published it herself.

The moral: There's no shame in being rejected. Just don't give up.

Get Back on the Horse

Allow yourself a little grieving time as you study the rejection slip to try to ferret out its exact meaning. If the message reads, "Nicely done. Wish we could use this," I usually wonder: So why didn't you so we'd both feel better? My writer friends and I suffer from the same paranoia: Did they mean they loved it when they said they liked it, or did they mean they only liked it? We go round and round, contemplating the meaning of life and wondering about a profession in which a faceless "they" two thousand miles away can make or break our day.

Believe in your work. Be willing to rework it, cut, edit, add or totally rewrite it, if necessary, but keep it circulating. It won't sell in your desk drawer. It may not be as good as it will be next year when you have another year's writing under your belt, but it's as good as it can be at this moment. And you must write, because nobody can read your work (or judge it, reject it or buy and publish it) until it's written.

There must be a slight masochistic tendency in those of us who want to be writers. We place our fragile egos in the hands of others while we sit at home and wait (or, hopefully, work on another project). And yet, if our work's rejected, we don't curse the gods or a distant editor for long, but rather we bounce back up again like those plastic dolls with weighted bottoms that kids use as punching bags. We do that because that's what writers do.

CHAPTER 13

Making It Your Business to Be Businesslike

If you don't drive your business, you will be driven out of business.
— B.C. Forbes

riting is an art, not a business! I hear you thinking. Yes, it *is* an art, but there's an important business side to it, and even if you have an agent, you still have to learn to be businesslike if you're going to be successful. Adopting a businesslike attitude helps you to think like a professional, and the more you think like a professional, the more quickly you'll become one.

BECOME PART OF MANAGEMENT *AND* LABOR

If you're going to write at home, you'll have to become a little schizophrenic and work both sides of the street, thinking like both management and labor. As management, you're charged with the responsibility of setting up sound business systems and demanding punctuality and performance from your labor pool (which also happens to be you).

As a member of the labor force, you need to get organized so you can work to your potential, regardless of what hours you put into your job as a writer. Put down your placard. This kind of labor organization doesn't involve staging a strike or a slowdown but rather creates some type of order in the workplace so you can become more efficient and effective. Tell management that you want a plan, and then work that plan to the best of your ability. Go ahead and talk to yourself if it helps. I do, and it does.

PRACTICE PUNCTUALITY AND PEAK PERFORMANCE

How long do you think most companies would keep an employee who came late and left early? Who missed deadlines and didn't complete jobs to the best of his ability? Who couldn't find important papers amidst the mess on the desk? The answer is obvious. It probably wouldn't be too long before that employee found a pink slip in the pay envelope.

Expect better from your employee (you). Offer your boss (also you) a job well done, completed as per schedule and in an efficient manner. Set definite working hours and stick to them, regardless if it's a 9–5 schedule, two hours on Saturday morning or three hours every evening. Guard against the normal inclination to procrastinate by reading the newspaper, talking on the telephone, baking cookies or performing any of the other tasks we tend to create for ourselves when we should be writing. I've even cleaned out my closet and rearranged kitchen cabinets rather than facing the empty monitor screen.

FOLLOW A ROUTINE

Although my work habits may seem somewhat erratic or driven to an outsider, they've been working for me for a long time. But these routines didn't just happen. They evolved over the years as I discovered what worked well for me and what didn't. Routines are personalized, depending on your other responsibilities and your personality. That's why I sadly cannot offer you any suggestions of what *your* routine should be. It's really something you'll have to work out for yourself through trial and error. My only advice is that when you find something that feels right and helps you become more productive, it's probably a keeper.

Routines Maximize Your Writing Time

My self-created and honed routine helps me to focus on my writing—two books, two articles and a brochure this year. Yet I'm not a workaholic. I still have time to plan a wedding for one daughter, help another with house hunting, spend days playing with my step-grandson and a new baby grandson, visit an out-of-town granddaughter and see almost every movie in town with my husband.

While I obviously don't spend every waking minute writing, the minutes I do spend are extremely productive.

Routines created to fit your personal schedule and time commitments can quickly become work habits. These habits help you to assume the professional persona as soon as you enter your office space, regardless if it's a large wood-paneled library or a section of your living room delineated by the back of the couch. Routines help you prevent sliding into procrastination because you know what you're supposed to do next. If you dawdle, your conscience will whisper, "Aren't you supposed to be answering mail right now?"

Routines Act as a Jump Start, Banishing Procrastination

When I first started writing, I handled my correspondence in the morning. Then one day I had a lightbulb experience. I asked myself why I was using the time of day I felt most alert and creative to open mail and answer letters. It made no sense. I switched my schedule and began writing at 8:30 A.M., as soon as the kids were out the door for school. When they were home, I could easily handle the no-brainer types of chores, such as filing, making copies, stamping envelopes and so on.

Schedule blocks of activity to fit your internal clock's peak hours. Experts, called chronobiologists, who study this sort of thing, say that each person has peak periods in which he has great energy, is most creative and so on. Experiment to see when your inner clock ticks best for you so you can do your writing then if at all possible.

Bundle the mundane chores as well. Make your telephone calls once or twice during the day, save filing for two or three times a week and order supplies once a month if possible. Do your most important creative work, your writing, whenever you are freshest.

Allow Flexibility in Your Routines

While it may seem contradictory to tell you to be flexible in your routines, it really isn't. Just as you need to weed out your closet from time to time, you also need to be flexible enough to weed out writing routines that you may have outgrown. Don't stubbornly stick to a routine that worked for you in the past. Your home situation may have changed over the years—your spouse is retired now and is around the home for longer periods of time, your kids are now in school or have left home to be on their own or you have an older parent to care for. Expect your routine to change and evolve frequently as technology or your responsibilities change.

Although I used to answer my mail and calls later in the day when I had children at home, my first task now in the morning is to check my voice mail and E-mail messages. I find that by quickly answering my E-mail, I get warmed up for writing. It's easy then for me to bring up whatever file I'm working on and continue writing.

Build Breaks Into Your Writing Routine

Remember that old saying about all work and no play? Well, as part of the management team, you want your labor force to have scheduled breaks, even if the workers don't think they need to relax occasionally. You know that regularly scheduled, frequent breaks prevent mental and physical fatigue.

As part of the labor force, I often don't practice what I preach. I often get so caught up in the mood of a story or the rhythm of a chapter that I just keep on writing. It used to exhaust me and probably is what lead to my developing carpal tunnel syndrome long before it was a popular disorder.

I've learned to force myself to take breaks by having my dictionary across the room so I have to get up to use it. I also finally put a clock (a quiet one) in my office so I would realize when it was around lunchtime. Otherwise, I'd work right through lunch and then wonder why I felt queasy. I no longer grab a sandwich (or a candy bar) and eat as I work. I either schedule a lunch date with an upbeat friend or make myself sit down at the table at eat a proper lunch. I'll read a magazine or a chapter of a book but not anything that has to do with my writing.

Occasionally, even on a deadline, I'll take a day off from writing and go shopping with a friend or with one of my daughters or daughters-in-law. I'll spend the day with a grandchild. I'll just re-charge my batteries and come back to work with a vengeance. It's always been worth it. Breaks are important as long as they remain just that—breaks—and don't become major parts of your routine.

Establish a Quitting Time Routine

Since you're the one who blows the quitting time whistle, get your work in order before punching out. Before I end my day's work I write a "to do tomorrow" list, then straighten up (which for me means putting the pencils away) and turn off the computer. By having my "to do" list sitting out in front of me, there's no delay the next day when I sit down to write. I know exactly what "management" has planned for me to complete.

On Friday, before starting the weekend, I back up my working files onto a disk. I learned the hard way that it takes a lot of typing to retype a book manuscript when your hard drive takes a dive. As a book progresses, I become very neurotic. I make additional backups, which I give to friends for safekeeping in case my house catches on fire, the computer is stolen or I'm abducted by aliens.

HANDLING MAIL

Have you ever read stories in the newspaper about bodies of recluses discovered in their homes buried under piles of magazines and mail? I knew I was doomed to suffer that same fate if I didn't change my mail-handling procedures. I bought about ten how-to books, all of which said the same thing and also added to my pile of potentially deadly paper. I'll happily pass along a compilation of their tips.

Sort Your Mail Over a Wastebasket

Remember back in chapter eight when I suggested getting a large wastebasket for your office? That was to tempt you to throw things away, because the more you write, the more mailing lists you'll find yourself on. That means more mail coming in on a daily basis and more back strain for your delivery person.

Somewhere I came across an acronym—TRAF—that helps you remember what to do with mail. I'd credit this idea to the creator if I could only find the slip of paper I wrote the source on. (The issue of filing so you can quickly retrieve information comes later. Do as I say . . .)

The *T* is for *toss*. Toss flyers or junk mail that you know you have no need for. That is the mail the experts say you should only handle once. It's almost impossible to follow that advice for your remaining mail.

Toss your bills, not in the wastebasket as you would prefer but into a box or file marked "to pay." Be sure to open them first to be certain the store hasn't made any mistakes. Before I had a specific spot for my unpaid bills, they often ended up as bookmarks or hidden in manuscript files and were never more seen. Don't do that. It plays havoc with your credit rating and does not endear you to your creditors.

R is for *reference*. You may get a flyer about a writers conference you'd like to attend. Jot the date on your calendar, and put that flyer into a folder marked "appointments." I also do that with information I need for board meetings, speaking engagements and book-signing appearances. Then I don't have to panic when I can't remember the program chairperson's name or telephone number. It's all in that file.

A is for *answer* or *action*. This includes skimming your trade magazines and tearing out and filing articles of interest. It includes responding to invitations. If you accept one, do so and then put the date and time in your calendar and place the invitation in your appointment file. If you must send regrets, do so and toss the invitation.

Take action on a manuscript that has been rejected by making any necessary changes, typing a new cover letter and sending the package to the next publisher on your list. Answer your correspondence, either by E-mail, fax or, if possible, jotting your answer on the bottom of the person's letter. Make a copy for your file so you have both the letter and your answer.

If you don't take action on your mail as it comes in, it tends to pile up like snowdrifts. Resist the temptation to just heap it on one side of the desk or on the floor. It breeds.

F is for *file*. That's what I do with the myriad of medical newsletters I receive, the articles I've clipped on topics of interest to me and correspondence from readers. As I'm primarily a medical writer, I have a separate file cabinet for my medical information with more than two hundred topics separately indexed. The other topics on which I collect information include women's interests, family issues, learning disabilities, safety and children's issues. I also have a file for future ideas for books and articles.

Remember that the purpose of filing is to be able to retrieve something at a later date. Unfortunately, I've often spent a great deal of time trying to remember how I filed something. Don't get too creative or use too much of an abbreviation.

Purge Your Files Semiannually
Go through your files every six months to weed out anything you really don't need anymore. It's a lot cheaper than buying new files. Having said that, however, I've often found something I wrote ten or more years ago that still had something to say as background material or that was important enough for me to update. It's a judgment call. I fear I err on the side of keeping too much, although I have purged some of my medical files of material dating back to the sixties, so there's hope for all of us.

Use Color Coding
To help jog my memory, I use color codes for my file folders. My medical files are red, my business-related files are green and my volunteer work is in blue files; each nonmedical article or book gets a color of its own. (The material for this book is housed in pink file folders.) That way when I see a green file sitting on my desk, I immediately know what it is and where it belongs. When I've completed a book and it's gone through the copyediting and proofing stages, I put all my notes and other information in a file box, mark it well and use the old file folders for the next job.

CREATE A PRIORITY TELEPHONE LIST
I keep a list by my telephone with the names of editors who have my work along with the names of the projects they are considering. That saves a great deal of embarrassment when Wendy Waxstein-Weiss of the *Greatest Digest Digest* calls and says, "I love your article," and you can't remember if it's the one on building houses from Popsicle sticks or the piece on training butterflies to pull plows. And no, this has nothing to do with age. I couldn't keep track of my manuscripts even when I was younger. I tried faking it

from time to time until I created this foolproof method, and now I can say, "Ah, yes, the story about . . ."

MONEY IN, MONEY OUT

If you're going into the business of writing, you need to be business-like when it comes to your money too. You may think that you could record your sales from writing on the head of a pin, but before you know it, you'll need a good paper trail for yourself and for those folks at the IRS.

Have a Separate Business Account

As soon as you can afford to, set up a separate business account. It will help with taxes because you'll have all the checks written for expenses right in one place. You'll also have your deposit information there, until you start making so much money that you need to invest it somewhere to make more interest. (Think positively.)

Use this business account to pay for all your writing expenditures from the extra phone line(s) and computer software programs to paper and postage. I used to keep a ledger to record expenses, such as parking fees, tolls, reference books and supplies. Now I just put those receipts in an accordion file separated by month. At the end of each year, I categorize them for taxes and gather them together in a large manila envelope, writing the year on the back of the envelope. If there's ever an audit, I can quickly produce evidence of my expenses.

Ask Your Accountant What Can Be Deducted

There are many things that can be deducted as legitimate business expenses when you're writing at home. Your equipment, such as a computer, fax machine, second telephone line and answering machine can be depreciated *if* you can prove without a doubt that they are used for business. If they are used partly for business, be prepared to keep detailed documentation. Books, pens, business stationery and other supplies can also be deducted, as can travel expenses from home to see people for interviews or to visit your editor. For your office space to qualify, however, it has to be exclusively for writing and not for any other function. That disqualifies your dining room unless you *never* eat there. To be sure what is or is not a legitimate deductible expense, *always* contact a knowledgeable accountant. Rules change frequently.

Use More Logs Than a Beaver

You need to keep meticulous records, not only for tax purposes but to help you find things such as letters from editors, research data and contracts. I once collaborated on a book with someone who called me after the project was completed to see if I had a copy of our contract with the publisher. He had misplaced his. It made me wonder about the accuracy of the data he had given me.

• **Telephone log**

Create a telephone log to track your long-distance calls. It doesn't need to be anything fancy. Even a loose-leaf notebook will do fine. Just list the date, the person you called, the telephone number and a brief note as to what was discussed. Then when you get your long-distance phone bill, you can check the calls to be sure nothing was billed to you in error. It also gives you a quick way to find a phone number when you have to call that person again.

• **Message log**

I use a small notebook to jot down my voice mail messages, listing the person calling, the date and what the call was about. I also note the telephone number so I don't have to look it up if the line is busy the first time I call back. It gives me a complete history of my messages so that if someone says it's been four weeks since our conversation, I can check and see that it was only a week.

• **Permissions log**

If you quote more than a few sentences from a book or article, you need to get permission from the publisher of that material. I keep a separate file with the letters for permission I've written and the copy of the permission when it's received. I immediately make a copy of that permission letter because you need to include all permissions with your manuscript. Never send your original letter because it could get lost.

• **Correspondence log**

I've learned to keep a separate chronological file for copies of all my business correspondence so I can quickly find a letter when it's needed. Often, I make a second copy and put it in the file with the article or book it pertains to so I can find it that way if necessary.

When I'm conducting mail interviews, I keep copies of the original letters as well as a log of the recipients of my letters and who answered, along with the date each responded.

- **Billing log**

Once you begin making sales, you usually need to send invoices to remind your publishers or clients that they owe you money. I use a billing log with the name of the publisher or client, a description of the work done, when I was hired, when the work was completed and how much I am owed. When the check arrives, I note that as well, usually with a flourish.

When I record each check, I list the name of the company issuing the check and the name of the publication or publisher. In this age of mergers, it's often difficult to know who's who or where the "bookkeeper" actually works. I also enter the amount of the check, the date the check was issued and the check number. All that data may be important if you have correspondence with the publisher about your check. I also list the name of the article. If the title was changed by the editor, which is often the case, I list both.

WATCH YOUR PENNIES

When you're in business for yourself, which we in the writing business are, every penny counts. Invest in a postage scale so you don't overpay postage on letters and manuscripts. If you send copies of books through the mail, remember to use the reduced book rate. Since postage rates change frequently, contact your local post office to check the present cost.

Check rates for rapid delivery services, such as Federal Express (FedEx), Airborne Express, United Parcel Service (UPS) and Express Mail, but only use them when you really need the quick service. Don't automatically send things by the next-day rate unless the material really must be received the next morning. If your manuscript sits on the editor's desk for two days, you've wasted your money.

Buying in bulk is a savings only if you have a place to store reams of paper and boxes of envelopes and stationery. Remember that area codes, phone numbers and ZIP codes are subject to change, and if you have five hundred more boxes of preprinted stationery, envelopes and address labels when your address changes, you'll spend more time in the coming months correcting your address than writing.

CUSHION YOUR DEADLINES

When you're agreeing to a deadline for a writing project, always include some emergency padding, in case you or someone in your family becomes ill or your grandchild comes early and you've promised to help with the new baby for a few days.

On this book, I needed that extra time when a pipe burst and ruined my new wood floor. I had to spend valuable time coordinating the furniture being moved so the ruined floor could be torn up and a new one laid. Who says high-rise buildings can't be in a flood zone?

In addition, while writing this, my daughter-in-law had a baby, which we anticipated and I had built in a time allowance for, and my daughter got engaged and we're planning a wedding for the week after my deadline, which I hadn't anticipated and had not planned for.

Be realistic about time, and don't plan to write during your two-week vacation at the beach or during the winter holidays when all the family's coming and you have to entertain them. Allowing yourself some flexibility also keeps you from panicking if your computer gets cranky and won't do what it's supposed to do.

Building in some wiggle room for your deadline allows you to be conscientious about meeting your deadlines. It's a good business practice.

CHAPTER 14

Making It Pay

Write out of love, write out of instinct, write out of reason. But always for money.

— Louis Untermeyer

All writers develop their own tricks for turning plain paper into greenbacks. A few lucky ones, I guess (for I've never met them), sit down at the computer or typewriter and effortlessly pound out the required number of words, stick the pages in a manila envelope and send them off to be published.

I wish it were that easy for me. The only way I know to write (and to rewrite) is through hard work. I write, crumple up wads of rejected thoughts and sentence fragments fresh from the printer and write some more. My wastebasket fills like a popcorn popper at the movie theater. Finally, when I think I've done it, I read it aloud. If it "sounds" right, I let it stand. I confess it's a lot like the way my grandmother made omelets, sticking her hand in the oven until the temperature "felt" right.

Certainly in this field, as with many others, time is money. The faster (and better) you write, the more opportunity you have to sell your writing. Your manuscript will never sell if it's stuck in your bottom desk drawer or if you're still revising it after ten years. Yes, I know there are stories about authors who have done just that— sold what became a major best-seller after laboring on it for more than a decade. It's said that Margaret Mitchell spent ten years writing *Gone With the Wind*. But the reason we know that and other similar stories is that it just doesn't happen that often.

To help you earn more at your craft, you need to write more, publicize yourself, expand your abilities and learn to diversify. All this takes time, and you probably already feel that you don't have

enough time for your writing. But the more time you save, the more
time you'll have to devote to your writing. The more writing you
do, the more you'll sell and the more money you'll make.

TIME IS MONEY

Always be alert for ways you can save time through time management, better organization and a businesslike attitude.

- Use E-mail, send postcards or jot a reply on a letter to save time.
- File so you can retrieve things quickly. Don't adopt someone
  else's filing system; adapt it to your own needs.
- Have one spot for supplies so you don't waste time looking
  for them or waste money buying extras when you don't need
  to. (See my 8-inch stack of yellow legal pads for evidence).
- When you figure the cost of a proposed writing project, include
  what your time is worth.
- Keep travel expenses and other costs low when you know a
  potential market won't pay enough to cover them.
- Consider secondary markets to spread the expenses attributed
  to an article.
- Remember what Dr. Samuel Johnson, English author and lexi-
  cographer, said: "Nobody but a blockhead ever wrote except
  for money." While many of us must be blockheads because
  we write for many reasons, money just being one of them, it's
  also true that we often give too much away for less than its
  true value.

HOW TO DETERMINE THE COST OF A PROJECT

Figuring your expenses for a piece of writing is no different than a
retailer knowing what it will cost to sell a piece of goods. Unfortunately, a writer usually isn't in a position to dictate a price tag and
so has to work the other way and keep costs in line.

If an article involves questionnaires, for example, you need to
consider the cost of duplicating them, either on your printer or
using a quick-print shop; your postage; and your time tabulating
them.

Interviewing can also run up costs, for your travel, in actual
money as well as time expended; food; parking; baby-sitting fees if

you have small children; and time you spend in the interview. Try to spread that cost by writing more than one article using the information gained. If you interview a business executive, for example, one article could focus on his new product that has taken the world by storm and another could be slanted to a hobby magazine, describing this same executive's amazing beetle and water bug collection.

MULTIPLE SALES: GETTING MORE MILEAGE FROM ONE MANUSCRIPT

Don't file an article once you've sold it. After all that research, you can usually squeeze a lot more salability out of an article.

Reprints

There are many markets, listed in *Writer's Market*, that buy reprint rights. Get permission from your original publisher, and submit proof of publication to the reprint publisher.

Second Rights

Many newspapers and Sunday supplements will buy second rights for an article published elsewhere, providing it was in a noncompeting market.

Rewrites With Different Slants

You can always rewrite your research material for different markets. This is different from selling reprint rights because in this scenario, you are actually rewriting. You're changing the slant or focus of the article, changing the contents, adding new quotes and changing the organization of the material to fit a new market.

For example, the subject of time management is of interest to many people—and would be of interest to markets in widely different, nonoverlapping readerships. Take the original research you did for your article on time management for businesspeople and write a second article, this one geared to stay-at-home moms and dads. Tell them how they can apply those same proven theories in their homes to get more out of their working days.

Youngsters also can benefit from learning efficient use of their time. All teenagers would be interested in ways to expand their after-school hours to make time for homework, sports, part-time jobs, dinner, television and social lives. By using the same principles as in the other articles, you could write another piece, this one showing teens how to take control of their lives.

In each case, you'd slant your writing for your particular readership. It could be farmers, theater students or doctors who need to see more patients with managed care but still want to keep up with their medical journals, spend time with their families, finish their paperwork and play golf. With each story you'll need different examples, peer interviews and statistics to interest each publication. But the basic information doesn't change. Just answer your reader's main question, Why should I care about this? and you can recycle the same information into income for you.

USE YOUR EXPERTISE

Once you've researched and written on a subject a few times, you may be surprised to find that people consider you an expert. Since the publication of my book *Depression: What Families Should Know*, newspaper reporters on both coasts looking for a few quotes to add to their stories have interviewed me. Articles in local newspapers about my writing led to my being hired to teach a noncredit course, Writing for Publication and Profit, at our local community college. I've also given numerous speeches on a myriad of topics I've used as subjects of my writing.

Speak Up

When you've had an article published, think about local groups who might be interested in having you as a speaker. While you probably won't be paid for your talks, other than possibly a small honorarium or gift, you will be getting your name out, which will come in handy when you begin to write books, want to write brochures and press releases or otherwise need a market for your work. People enjoy meeting a writer, and when they see something with your byline, they'll read it. That's why book publishers try to showcase their authors on national television talk shows. They know people are more likely to buy a book when they've seen and heard the author.

Write a letter to the program chairpeople of luncheon clubs, service organizations and other groups telling them of your topic and qualifications as a speaker. The best time to send these letters is in the spring so the new program chairperson can consider you as one of the organization's speakers. But you can always write and offer your services as a fill-in in case a scheduled speaker becomes ill or otherwise is unable to fulfill an obligation. You may be surprised to realize that you're really an expert on many subjects. I've talked to a newcomers' group about volunteerism, to a business organization about better ways to communicate, and to hospital staffs about time management.

Have copies of your article, including your name and phone number, to distribute to your audience so they can call you with story ideas or to ask if you'd tackle writing assignments for them. If you've published a book, be sure there are copies available for the members of the audience to buy after your talk.

One caveat: Don't get so caught up with speaking engagements that you don't have time to write. Your speeches should support, not dominate, your writing. They are the cherry on top of the sundae.

Don't Be Shy, Publicize

Promoting yourself as a writer isn't bragging. It's a way of letting folks know you're around so they begin to think of you as a writer. I had written seven books for nationally known publishers before people stopped asking, "Are you still writing?" I'll confess, I once snapped back at a local surgeon, "Yes. Are you still doing surgery?"

When people begin to think of you as a "real" writer (as opposed to a fake one?), they begin to open doors for you. I once received free publicity assistance from the subject of one of my articles. I had written about the owner of a quick-print shop who also was a talented artist. In addition to interviewing him, I took some pictures and submitted the entire package to one of the printing industry's small publications, which bought the article. The shop owner was so pleased with the published article that he reprinted it and included it with all of his completed orders. I couldn't have paid for that kind of publicity.

So, if the features editor calls you from your local paper and wants to do an article about you and how you manage to write, entertain one hundred for a sit-down authentic Ukrainian dinner and teach concert violin and brain surgery to all of your eight pre-school children, say yes.

Remember what Hillel said in the Talmud: "If I am not for my-self, who will be for me? If I am only for myself, what am I? If not now, when?"

EXPAND YOUR TALENTS

There are two sides to the question of whether or not you should expand your talents when you become a writer. Some say you should concentrate solely on writing. Let the experts handle the ancillary chores, such as photography and desktop publishing. They take up too much time, time that you could and should spend on your writing.

Wrong, say the opponents. It's important to expand your talents. Everything you learn makes you a more desirable writer and opens up the opportunities for new and more diverse assignments.

Me? I'm undecided. I know a little about both photography and desktop publishing. My expertise is just enough to let me expand my talents a little, without taking too much time from my writing.

Photography

With today's new cameras, you can get good photos by just pointing and clicking (once you've removed the lens cover, of course). I've taken many of my own pictures to illustrate travel stories and fam-ily-oriented articles, usually using my family members as models. When I did a great deal of travel writing, I probably used 80 percent of my own photos and 20 percent canned shots supplied by travel bureaus, embassies and photo companies. I even had two of my colored slides of Switzerland purchased by a film company that made calendars and sold the slides to others needing that type of illustration.

My photography experience was and still is very slim. I took a course in photojournalism at our local state university and learned how to crop a photo both with the lens, and later, with the enlarger. I also learned the vocabulary I need to tell printers exactly what I want done when they develop photos for me. In addition, I purchased and read a few books on picture taking for profit. I haven't illustrated any work lately because most of my recent work has been medical in nature and I didn't think I should take the 35mm into the OR.

Yet it's fair to say that throughout my writing career I made sales that I may not otherwise have made had I not been able to furnish my own photos. What's more, I often was paid more for the photos than I was for the articles.

Desktop Publishing

I have a couple of desktop publishing software programs. They probably can do a great deal more than I've discovered thus far. I am only somewhat proficient in making brochures and less so for newsletters. Some day I'll take time to explore all the other goodies that came with the program. But what I do know about the software is enough to turn out professional-looking brochures and newsletters. I do more of the former than the latter because I don't like waiting for others to send me the material needed for a newsletter. Nevertheless, these programs are not complicated and you can quickly learn to use them to help add to your writing income.

Hobbies

Why did I include hobbies with ways to make extra money writing? Because if you have a hobby, such as woodworking, toy trains, doll collecting, knitting, lapidary or quilting, there are thousands of others spending their time enjoying the same hobby. There are even magazines dedicated to your hobby, and they depend on articles to fill their pages. Study the markets as described in *Writer's Market* and write or call for a sample magazine. You're an expert in your particular hobby, so you have all the prerequisites to turn out an interesting article:

- You know something about your subject.
- You are interested in your subject.
- You can write.

DIVERSIFY

Most of the writing described so far has been for articles or books. But there are also many other types of writing, most of which can be very rewarding—both personally and financially. Sometimes you may discover that you not only enjoy a different type of writing than you've been attempting but that you are better at doing so, at least during a particular time in your life.

Advertising

I actually was trained as a copywriter, majoring in radio and television at Northwestern University. My first job after college was writing commercials for a small daytime radio station. We signed off the air at sunset, which meant a short workday during the winter months. But because there weren't many people on the staff, I ended up writing the public service announcements, the promotional material and anything else that needed writing. It was good training.

If you think you might be interested in learning to write copy, contact a nonprofit organization and volunteer to help write its public service announcements. Study the format and ask for samples. While you won't be paid as a volunteer, you will be gaining valuable experience as well as making contacts for future paying assignments from those who have heard of your writing ability.

For print advertising, analyze copies of previous ads run by a particular business and its competition. Practice rewriting copy for ads you see in the newspaper and magazines. You'll probably begin by writing ad copy as a volunteer, but once you develop an effective style, you can contact advertising agencies and offer your services. By then you'll have some professional-looking samples to show.

Annual Reports

Writing annual reports for companies and nonprofits is another good opportunity for writers. Although only public companies are required to have annual reports, now many privately owned businesses also have them. Start with a small business or nonprofit.

Ask for copies of what was done in the past and study how each section is handled. Don't try to get too creative. Chances are the executives want their new annual report written in a form similar to that of the others. Most of the financial information will be reproduced exactly as it is received, but you may be asked to rewrite the president's or CEO's letter and do some features on the individuals within the organization. Ask for at least fifteen copies of the finished product so you can use them as samples for future jobs.

Brochures

Brochures are a good way to add to your freelance writing income because so many businesses and organizations use them. Think of local groups you know that could benefit from brochures telling about their services. Just a few include art galleries, beauty shops, car dealerships, dog grooming shops, exercise clubs, furniture stores, hospitals and other health care facilities, ice-cream shops and on down through the alphabet. You can either write the copy for them to take to a printer or learn one of the desktop publishing software programs and turn out a camera-ready brochure.

If you'd like to learn this type of writing, start to collect brochures wherever you go. It won't take long for you to amass quite a pile. Study them to see what works and what doesn't. Many brochures have too much copy, too many typestyles (called fonts) and muddy illustrations.

Think about your particular contacts and the types of brochures they could use to promote their products or services. I've written brochures for physicians' offices, service organizations, nonprofits, restaurants and as publicity for my own books. With the new "dummy-proof" desktop printing programs, it's not too difficult to create professional-looking brochures.

As a beginner, you might create a few samples promoting yourself as a writer and then take them to your neighborhood quick-print shops. People often come to places such as Kinko's looking for someone to write copy for brochures. If your name and phone number are handy, you might get the jobs.

Collaborations

You could fill a book (and some authors have) about the pros and cons of writing collaborations. They are as delicate as a marriage relationship, and many of them are far stormier. It's reported that the famous musical duo of Gilbert and Sullivan collaborated on fourteen comic operas between 1871 and 1896, but because they disliked each other so much, they seldom met in person and, instead, used the mails for their collaborative efforts. I have written a number of articles and five books with collaborators. Fortunately, my experiences have, for the most part, been pleasant ones.

All of my book collaborations have been with physicians or psychologists. Usually, they provided some, but not all, of the information, and I did all or most of the actual writing and the shaping of the book. My collaborations on articles have been with one particular writer, who is also a friend. She and I split each article into sections and then write our selected sections. Then we critique each other's work and merge the parts into a united whole.

Sandy Frye, a freelance television and film scriptwriter and video producer, says that in her line of work "a great deal of tight collaboration is needed." Her advice is to "go into a collaboration with a good heart." She urges you to "defend your position if there's a disagreement, but be willing to strike a compromise." Good advice.

If you know of someone whose business, hobby or experience would make an interesting article or book topic, contact him to see if, first, you could write about it yourself or, second, if he would be interested in entering into a collaboration with you. If the subject is technical, medical or otherwise complex, you may have better luck selling your work if it's a collaborative effort.

When you enter into a collaboration, have a written agreement spelling out who does what, how expenses will be handled, how any income will be divided and whose name goes first. With the article collaborations, we alternated who got top billing. Usually with expert collaborations, the expert's name goes first and the writer's second. Also include a deadline for the work to be completed and a termination agreement in case the collaboration doesn't work out.

Columns

Although it's unlikely you may be hired to write a column for *The New York Times* right away, your local newspaper, weekly publication or city magazine may be willing to hire you to write a column. The money, although usually not excessive, is regular and something you can count on. You build up a reader base and develop a following. The negative is that you constantly have a deadline hanging over your head.

My only experience with a column (other than in high school when I wrote one under the heading "The Scribbly Scribe") was a humor column for a local weekly religious newspaper. It was fun, gave me good experience meeting a short deadline and taught me to write humor succinctly. I wrote it for two years, ending when other writing responsibilities and a lack of a pay increase convinced me to end my brief career as a columnist.

If you think you'd like to try your hand at writing a column, develop an idea that has a unique slant and that fits a specific need. Chuck Shepherd writes a column for Universal Press Syndicate called "News of the Weird," a compilation of actual news stories that are, indeed, a little weird. His advice is to get an idea that is "not something people want to read but something that people think they *need* to read."

Veteran columnist Robert Fulford of Canada's prestigious *The Globe and Mail* offered this advice:

> First, you don't have to start at the beginning. From age eighteen to age thirty-one, I believed that the way to write a column (or an article) was to begin at the beginning and stop when you got to the end. This meant I could spend hours or days worrying about the beginning and then, when finally I started, I would still have the whole thing to write.
>
> At age thirty-one, while writing a cover story for *Maclean's*, I wrote something that I thought would be the lead and realized it wasn't. I set it aside. I wrote another few paragraphs, which I also thought would be the lead, but they weren't. I set them aside. I did that a third time

and realized that these three passages were all worth putting into the final article. I still needed a lead, and I soon found it. I began structuring the piece and discovered that one of those passages made an ending. That day, writing became easier for me—not easy, mind you, but easier than it had been.

The second thing that took me years to learn: if you are writing a column, think as far in advance as you can. When I first wrote a column (six a week for the *Toronto Star* in the 1960s) I lived from hand to mouth. I did some research and wrote a column, did some research and wrote a column, and so on. On Tuesday I had no idea what column I would be writing on Friday.

Later, writing a magazine column I realized that it would be greatly enriched if I planned it far in advance. So I sat down, sometimes by myself, sometimes with colleagues, and made lists of ideas for the future. Then I began doing research in bits and pieces, thinking about these ideas in odd moments, and clipping material for them (by now I had a file for each of 15 or 20 columns on my list). Some of these ideas never worked out, but most of them did.

I've worked that way ever since. It makes me feel more secure and makes it likelier that the column will contain something worth reading.

Steve Otto, who writes a general column five days a week for *The Tampa Tribune*, gets many of his ideas from the more than five hundred E-mail messages he gets a day from readers. "You have to either be very general or very specific when you write a column," Otto said. "And you have to be careful so you're not predictable. I write about things that interest me, but I'm broad based so there's something for everyone. You have to know your audience. I find it's easier to write five columns a week because I can be more topical. If you only do one a week, it tends to stand alone. You can be more relaxed with five. They're not so formal but more episodic."

These and other columnists agree you need to determine your target. Do you want to write a column for your weekly church bulletin? For the monthly women's club, country club or medical journal? Do you have city magazines in your community? What type of column is missing from any of these potential markets that you are qualified to write?

Don't just pop into the editor's office and say you'd like to write a column. Steve Otto suggests that you need to create enough sample columns to run four to six weeks. One or two columns aren't enough. An editor has to know that you have the staying power to turn out the required number of columns on time without losing quality. Most columns run 500–900 words, approximately two to three double-spaced typed sheets. Once you are satisfied with your portfolio, then call and make an appointment to see the editor. Have you wasted your time if the answer is no? Certainly not. You've gained valuable experience, you've shown that you can write more than one or two columns and you should feel more confident when you alter your columns to fit the needs of the next editor you plan to call.

Otto suggests that you also check the *Gale Directory of Publications and Broadcast Media* to find the names and addresses of other daily and weekly newspapers and trade journals. This directory also will tell you the publication's circulation and will list the names of editors. Don't ignore the small weekly newspapers. Many of them are parts of chains, and if they buy your work, they may send it to their other papers. Some newspapers buy a great many columns. You don't need a syndicate to handle your column; you can syndicate yourself.

Corporate Histories

Many businesses and organizations celebrate special anniversary years by having company histories published that they then give away to customers and members of their staffs. Families often want family histories for their members. Someone has to write those histories, and that someone could be you.

A few years ago I wrote, gratis, a history of my synagogue to celebrate its centennial year. I collected and compiled hundreds of old and new photographs. Then I wrote copy to carry the story line along. It was a massive undertaking, especially since at the same time I was putting together a wedding for one of our daughters, selling our family home and moving into a condominium. My life, like yours, is complicated.

Although I didn't charge my congregation for my time and effort, doing good has its rewards. The printer I had worked with on this project had gotten the contract to print the Shriners Hospitals' seventy-fifth anniversary book. They needed a writer, and because of my previous efforts, my name was submitted. After being interviewed by people with the Shriners Hospitals, I got the assignment. *A Heritage of Helping*, a book with both old and new photographs celebrating the accomplishments of the "World's Greatest Philanthropy," was the result. And yes, this time I was paid for my labor.

Projects like this usually pay well, but they are extremely time-consuming. Never take on such an assignment unless you are committed to completing it by or before the deadline. If you don't, you will not only ruin the celebration for the business, organization or family, but you will also probably never be hired for another similar project. Word does get around; negative word spreads like wildfire.

Carol McEwen Dyches, a freelance advertising copywriter, finds writing corporate histories "a nice departure from advertising." She stresses that "organization is essential. So is total cooperation from your client and his or her staff. Make sure the client shares information with you, even the bad stuff. You won't use it, but you need to know the truth. Check sources and do your own research so you don't reprint errors that have been passed along throughout the years by the company scribes. Be aware that there's a lot of pressure on you when you're writing corporate histories. They sort of take over your life—not to mention the entire house."

Correspondence

Many people are frightened by a blank page and will hire writers to do the deed for them. I have written letters for businesses explaining new policies and for medical practices describing new procedures. Usually these are "hurry up and turn around" type jobs.

Again, don't try them if you don't have the time to meet your deadline.

Although there's nothing wrong with giving your opinion concerning a prospective assignment, it can backfire on you. A bank wanting me to rewrite nine hundred form letters once contacted me to ask what I would charge. Instead, I said I thought the bank had too many letters and would be happy to review the letters for consolidation purposes. No one ever called back.

Ghostwriting

Ghostwriting does not mean writing spooky tales for Halloween; it means writing something that another person puts her name on. It differs from plagiarism in that you, the author, have granted permission for the other person to get credit for something you wrote.

As your reputation as a writer grows, you may be asked to ghost letters and articles. I've been a ghost twice. Once was for an article, and the second time was for a book. I was pleased with both efforts, and it never bothered me that I got no credit for doing the writing. Remember, however, that if you ghostwrite something, you cannot tell others about it. The whole purpose of being a ghost is that you stay in the shadows while the other person takes the bows. If you can't take it, stay out of the ghosting business.

Greeting Cards

When my last child was born, I went through a two-year period when I found it impossible to concentrate with five little people bouncing around like basketballs during warm-up time. I put aside my articles for newspapers and magazines and focused on writing greeting cards. I wasn't too good with the sentimental verses. My form of humor seemed to find a niche creating what was then called studio cards. I wrote for Hallmark, Norcross, Charm Craft and a number of other card companies.

Writing greeting cards was fun and didn't require the type of concentration needed for longer work. If you think you might enjoy trying your luck, study the types of cards now on sale in pharmacies, gift shops and bookstores. Write to the various card companies and ask for their guidelines.

Be aware, however, that greeting cards pay freelancers very little and there are seldom royalties unless you're someone well known.

Manuals

Some companies hire freelance writers to write their training or instruction manuals in lay language. Those who write them say that you must be careful to include all necessary steps. If you omit even one minor step, assuming that "everyone" knows what it should be, the reader may be unsuccessful, frustrated or even injured. Stay away from this type of writing unless you have a very organized mind, one that visualizes things in sequential terms.

Newsletters

Every organization, business and social club today seems to have its own newsletter. That means job possibilities for freelance writers. It used to be that you could write copy for a newsletter, do a mock-up for the printer and then leave it for the printer to create. Now, with the advent of desktop publishing, most groups expect the writer to write the copy in newsletter form and then take it to the printer camera-ready or, at least, needing only to have photos scanned in.

As with brochures, you can easily collect more newsletters to study than you really want to read. Make note of which general layout makes for the most pleasing appearance, particular features of interest, typefaces and font sizes. Don't use unusual fonts or use too many different ones on a page. If your newsletter is for an older readership, use at least a 12-point font.

As a newsletter writer, you'll be dependent on others to turn in their stories by a set deadline, which then gives you time to edit and rewrite if necessary. Set others' deadlines far enough ahead so you don't have problems meeting yours.

To get new newsletter clients, use newsletters you have already written as samples. Contact service organizations, churches and synagogues, businesses, associations, social groups and schools, and offer your services.

Press Releases

Volunteering to write press releases for nonprofit organizations is a good way to gain expertise in this field. If you're not sure of the proper way to write a press release, contact your local newspaper and radio or television station and ask them for copies of press releases they've received that you can use as a guide.

Always date a press release with the month and year, and list a contact the media can call for more information. I keep some press releases I've received from universities and medical centers for years and use that information to call for an update.

The most useful press releases contain only one major point per page and are one, no more than two, pages long. I skim the releases I get and tend to lose interest if I have to read more than one or two pages of copy.

Speeches

If you enjoy writing speeches for yourself, you may want to try your hand at speech writing for others. Public relations departments of large companies are often most willing to farm this chore out to a competent writer who can write effectively using the speaker's voice. Usually you'll get a packet of information and this directive: "Just take what you need from this." It will be up to you to make it sound good when it's spoken aloud. That's often quite different than writing for someone to read silently.

When I write speeches for others, I try to keep the sentences shorter than I might if my words were going to be read silently. I use alliteration, anecdotes, metaphors, similes and quotations to create pictures in the minds of the listeners.

Have at least one meeting with the person who will be delivering the speech you're writing so you can get an idea of how he speaks. The tone of the speech must reflect the person giving it, not the individual who wrote it. Be sure you understand the makeup of the proposed audience so you neither write over their heads nor down to them.

These are just a few of the many ways to widen the circle of your writing. Try whichever sound interesting to you. Even if you decide later that you really don't enjoy a particular type of writing, you'll have expanded your talents and grown a little.

SUBSIDY PRESS

Many writers whose work is rejected by national publishers become frustrated and ask about having their work published by subsidy presses, also known as a vanity presses. The subsidy press is a company that charges writers high fees to have their work published. If the book is actually printed (many of these companies go out of business before fulfilling their agreements), the subsidy publisher may run one or two ads in little-read magazines or small newspapers. Most critics won't review books by subsidy presses, and most libraries don't buy them. The author is usually left with stacks of the poorly produced book languishing in the basement or attic.

SELF-PUBLISHING

If you're going to pay to have your work published, self-publishing may be a better way to go. You'll end up with better quality at a cheaper price. Find the names of quality printers in your hometown and explain what you want done. Get bids from as many printers as you can. Be ready to tell them how many pages your book will have and how many copies of the book you want. They'll discuss other pertinent information with you, such as type of stock you want for your book and whether it will be in hardback or paperback. With a printer, you pay only the cost of the layout and printing.

Many authors have used self-publishing for their work and handled their own promotion, distribution and sales. In a number of cases, a national publisher hears about the success of a particular self-published book and gives the writer a contract to have the work republished and marketed by a national company.

Each project you take on teaches you something about yourself and your ability, even if it takes so long that you lose money on that job or feel you didn't write it as well as you would have liked. But one thing's certain: You'll never know if there's a perfect fit unless you try.

SECTION THREE

Emotional Issues

CHAPTER 15

Staying in Touch With Friends

The best way to keep your friends is not to give them away.

— Wilson Mizner

One thing most writers agree upon is that writing is a lonely business. Some of us like the solitude while others quickly go stir-crazy. But basically, even if you do a great deal of interviewing, eventually you're going to end up alone in a room (or part of one) facing a blank computer screen or sheet of paper. Even if you have a room full of toddlers underfoot as you write, it isn't quite the same as having adult co-workers nearby. That's why it's so tempting to call someone on the phone or invite a neighbor in for coffee.

How can you fight the lonelies and still keep your writing on schedule? By applying the same principles to your getaway time as you do your writing time.

ORGANIZE YOUR BREAK TIME

Use your calendar to create definite break periods when you can meet with friends and relax. Don't leave the time open-ended, though. Make a date, saying when you'll meet your friends for lunch or shopping and when you need to go back to work. It's no different than if you were working in an office environment. If you don't schedule time limits, lunchtime may eat up all afternoon.

Meet With Upbeat Friends

Be sure that when you do schedule a break from writing, you meet with friends who are fun to be with, who are enthusiastic about their own work and who are interested and supportive of yours. Remember, though, that although most of your friends are probably amazed at your determination and discipline, they won't understand your need to write and likely won't even read your book or article when it comes out. Despite that, enjoy their friendship—and really listen to what they have to say about what's going on in their lives. Just don't be too hurt if they don't ask you much about what's going on in yours.

Try to limit your hours with acquaintances who criticize the time you spend on your writing, or worse, the writing itself. If you're around people who are depressed or bored with life, you'll drag back to work feeling tired and depressed yourself. Depression is contagious.

Sometimes you can mix business and pleasure. When I was working on a travel article about a destination a few hours from home, I invited a friend to go with me. She became my map reader and navigator, pointed out features of the area for me to note and even served as a model for my photos. It was a win-win situation: She had the opportunity to see me at work, and I had the opportunity to spend time with a good friend.

Schedule Time for Yourself

Spend some time just enjoying your own company, even if you've been cooped up with yourself writing all day. Do something that feels good, such as going for a brisk walk, taking a bubble bath, working in your woodworking shop or reading one chapter of a book. Be disciplined here too, though, or you'll finish the entire book and realize that you haven't written one page of yours.

Try to take the weekends (or another two days) off from writing. But don't spend all that time shopping, cleaning, and running errands or you'll be exhausted when Monday rolls around. You need time to refill the creative reservoir.

I grew up in Iowa, where farmers rotated crops so they wouldn't wear out the soil. Some years they planted nothing in a particular field and just let it lie fallow, giving it time to renourish itself. I think our creative resources need that time to rejuvenate as well. Often I've been frustrated and given up on a particular page on Friday and then come back on Monday and found that the words came pouring out. I've never questioned why that happens, but I believe that the subconscious needs time to work things out. Sometimes the weekend isn't enough and you need to give yourself an even greater break from work.

Give yourself the opportunity to enjoy the companionship of your spouse and family during your break. You may not realize how focused you can become when you're working on a project, and your loved ones may feel a little left out.

JOIN AN ORGANIZATION

It is with some trepidation that I list this advice about joining organizations, as they often become devouring monsters of your time. Organizations are a lot like the clothes in your closet: If you don't go through and weed them out occasionally, you won't be able to fit anything else in. But it's difficult. We join organizations for a variety of reasons and with varying degrees of enthusiasm. Then, since we belong, we feel we should go to the meetings (which eat large quantities of time) or we don't go and feel guilty (which also eats large quantities of time). If we wind up going to the meetings because they're the lesser of the two evils, we become involved, which means more obligations on our time. But before you throw in the towel and quit all organizations, put each one to the test. Answer these questions.

- What is the purpose of this organization?
- Am I still interested in its activities?
- Does this group really accomplish anything?
- How often does the group meet? Do I have time to remain active?
- Do I enjoy being with the members?
- What are the minimum requirements?
- Why did I originally join?
- Is my reason for joining still valid?
- Have I outgrown this particular organization?
- What are the financial obligations of membership?

Consider keeping your membership in those clubs whose aims are yours and whose members you count among your friends. It's a good way to stay in touch with friends, even though you may only see each other on the day meetings are held. Just be careful about becoming too involved. Committees can demand a tremendous amount of time.

Professional Organizations

Professional organizations are somewhat different from social clubs. In professional organizations you not only have the opportunity to meet and make friends but you also have the opportunity to be with peers who can give you advice about your writing career. Even with these groups, however, you have to protect your time and strive to balance outside activities with your writing. I recently served for two years as president of the Florida Chapter of the American Medical Writers Association. It was a wonderful experience and gave me the opportunity to be with other writers in the health care field from all over my state. It also was extremely time-consuming and took much of my focus away from the writing projects to which I was also committed.

Many writers belong to writers organizations. Some of these groups are national organizations, such as the National Writers Union, Outdoor Writers Association of America, Inc., Society of American Travel Writers, American Medical Writers Association and American Society of Journalists and Authors, the latter two to which I belong. These organizations often have regional and national meetings and seminars that nonmembers are welcome to attend. Long before I was ever asked to conduct a seminar at these meetings, I attended as a beginning writer and met many published writers (some of whose bylines I recognized) who were encouraging, supportive and willing to answer my questions.

Other writers organizations are local groups in which writers in all stages of their careers meet with other writers, exchange market information, enjoy shop talk and often read their works in progress aloud for critiquing by the other members. These groups offer the beginning writer emotional support when it's badly needed.

The only caveat is to be sure your local writers group is one in which the members are actually writing and not just talking about writing. If you find yourself in the latter organization, look around for one in which the membership consists mainly of published writers.

You also can "meet" published writers on-line at various Web sites. There also are chat rooms for writers, beginner and experienced. You'll be surprised how quickly you can develop a network of writer friends around the country. It pays to stay in touch with them for emotional support, advice and just friendship with peers who know what it's like to be a writer.

CHAPTER 16

Believing in Yourself

All that we are is the result of what we have thought. The mind is everything. What we think, we become.

— Buddha

T here is no trick to becoming a published writer. It's a matter of believing in yourself, having the confidence that you will achieve your goal and maintaining the patience to get there while you meanwhile continue writing, writing and writing. There's nothing new about this magic of persistence. Our thirtieth president of the United States, Calvin Coolidge, summed it up beautifully by saying, "Nothing in the world can take the place of persistence. Talent will not; nothing is more common than unsuccessful individuals with talent. Genius will not; unrewarded genius is almost a proverb. Education will not; the world is full of educated derelicts. Persistence and determination alone are omnipotent."

THERE IS POWER IN POSITIVE THINKING

There's a good reason the late Norman Vincent Peale's book *The Power of Positive Thinking* has been a best-seller since it was first published in 1952: It works. Your mind can't hold two thoughts at the same time. When it's filled with positive affirmations, there's no room for the negative ones. When doubts try to slip through, you can use a process called thought stopping to ban the negative thoughts from entering and reaffirm the positive ones. It's not difficult. You simply think, *Stop*, when you hear yourself thinking, I can't write this article, and reaffirm, I *can* do this. I'll just keep writing until I finish it.

Don't disregard this powerful power that you have within your being or think it's some kind of New Age nonsense. This power of positive thinking is very real and can actually trigger beneficial changes in mind and body.

Many sales and service organizations, such as Mary Kay Cosmetics and Weight Watchers, as well as self-help groups, such as Alcoholics Anonymous and Gamblers Anonymous, understand the value of the "believe in yourself and your abilities" concept. They use it as a strong motivational force with their members. Football coaches, such as Knute Rockne and Vince Lombardi, became famous for their inspirational locker-room talks, which motivated the players to believe in themselves and their ability to win games. This "you can do it" philosophy is found on playing fields throughout the world, on military bases and, happily, in many classrooms. It also launched the career of a mouse. Walt Disney most successfully put into action his belief that, "If you can dream it, you can do it."

Yet many writers fail to take advantage of this powerful but simple force: the magic of belief in yourself.

VISUALIZATION
Visualization is far more than just wanting something to happen or even imagining it occurring. It's more than an idle daydream. When you visualize something, you concentrate on each small but distinct and vital aspect of the whole until you can see yourself actually performing what you have practiced in your mind. Follow the advice of the poet Carl Sandburg who said, "Nothing happens unless first a dream."

Golfers, divers, ice-skaters and other athletes credit visualization or mind messages with sharpening their skills. One basketball coach reportedly had his team mentally watch themselves practicing different plays and found it strengthened their game more than with actual physical practice. Actors and public speakers also use visualization to aid their performances.

If your goal is to become a published writer, begin to visualize yourself as such from the moment you sit down at the computer or typewriter. As author Kurt Vonnegut Jr. put it, "We are what we imagine ourselves to be." Allow your mind to see the words flowing. Tell yourself that you will write well today, that you will easily do four (or more) quality pages this day. Remain positive about what you are writing (even if you later will rewrite it or toss it completely), and picture your long-term goal, which is to complete the article or book you are writing and to get it published. Complete the picture. Visualize yourself editing the copy to make sure it says just what you want it to. See yourself printing a clean copy and sending it to a publisher. Visualize the editor's positive reaction, a letter saying the piece has been accepted for publication. See your finished work in print, and let your mind help you to imagine how your book or magazine article feels to the touch.

Your thoughts trigger positive action. Without your even being aware of it, these positive actions will, in turn, point you toward making decisions based upon your overall goal, which will allow it to be reached.

Visualizing the process helps you to stay motivated and disciplined to stay on task until you reach your goal. I am firmly convinced that the main difference between a published writer and a nonpublished writer is that the published writer didn't give up. Call it persistence, stubbornness or self-discipline. The name doesn't really matter as long as you continue to write, to perfect this business of writing. You will succeed. But unlike the guy in the Broadway musical, you can't succeed in the writing business without really trying.

HAVE CONFIDENCE

Remember the childhood story of the Little Engine that kept saying, "I think I can, I think I can"? You need to adopt that affirmation as your own mantra. There's no time for *t*. Drop the letter *t* from the phrase, "I can't," making it the more positive, "I can." Ban the expression "I can't" from your vocabulary. Have confidence in your ability. Maintain that type of confidence for yourself because sometimes, like the little engine, you too will have to climb steep mountains toward success. If you have the confidence that you can make it, you'll have increased the odds of proving yourself to be right.

What's more, when you're confident, you give off vibrations of confidence and people begin to believe that image. They assume you will succeed because that's the aura you project. It becomes a self-fulfilling prophecy.

Years ago, when I applied for my first job in radio as a continuity writer (the person who writes commercials), the station manager asked me, "Are you any good?"

I was struck dumb. No one had ever asked me that before, and I had been brought up to be modest about my abilities. "Here are my writing samples," I stammered, pointing to the folder of radio commercials on his desk.

"I'll read them later," he said. "Are you a good writer?" he repeated.

I agonized as I quickly mulled over my possible responses. Would it seem like bragging if I said yes? Would he hire me if I said no? I took a deep breath. "Yes, I am," I answered.

"Good," he said, turning to examine my writing samples. "I'd never hire anyone who didn't think she was good. If you don't think so, why should I?"

I've never forgotten that important lesson. You can't sell yourself to others if you aren't buying you yourself. Although I didn't get that job, the next station manager who must have been convinced of my self-confidence hired me.

Yes, I know it's hard to convince yourself you're a good writer when no one is buying your work. Your spouse may think it's good and your mother may think you're next in line for a Pulitzer prize. But if you're not getting your work published, your confidence may wobble a little as you wonder, Am I good enough?

It should help you to know that many of us who *are* getting published still wonder from time to time. One writer friend of mine admitted, "Every time I get a check for something I wrote, I cash it quickly, just in case they made a mistake. I still feel that any day now I'll be 'found out.' "

Another friend who has published numerous books for young adults told me, "Every time I get a book contract, I'm sure I'll never be able to live up to the image the publisher has of me. I'm afraid that this book won't be as good as the others and that they'll find out I've been 'faking it' all this time. My voice shakes, my stomach hurts, my mouth gets dry and I know I'll never be able to write another word."

I was fascinated. "Then what happens?" I asked.

She looked at me blankly. "What happens? Why, then I sit down and I start writing."

It's a lot like the song "I Whistle a Happy Tune" from the musical *The King and I*. As long as you keep on whistling (and writing), you'll not only fool others, you'll also fool yourself into thinking you can write that article or book, because, as you know, you can.

In his book *100 Ways to Motivate Yourself*, author Steve Chandler warns against letting others define us. He suggests that we should "Travel deeper and deeper inside to find out your own potential. Your potential is your true identity—it only waits for self-motivation to come alive." Then Chandler quotes James A. Michener, who said, "For this is the journey that men and women make to find themselves. If they fail in this, it doesn't matter much else what they find."

Many natural leaders exude so much confidence that people willingly follow them up a hill even when facing gunfire on the other side, or take leaves of absence from their jobs to work on a charismatic leader's political campaign. Writers with strong confidence in their abilities have been able to convince reticent editors to take a chance with those writers on particular projects and have spread enthusiasm throughout the editorial and sales staff (which also boosts promotional financial backing from the publishing house).

It's difficult to say what makes a writer successful. Writing, like most forms of art, is in the eye of the beholder. It's subjective. There's almost no way to judge it, other than through an individual editor's personal taste and then, if it passes muster with that gatekeeper, through the purchasing power of the reading public. If many people buy your work, you're considered a good writer. If they line up to buy it even *before* it's been published, as readers do for Stephen King, John Grisham, Anne Rice, Robin Cook and others, then you're considered a great writer or, at least, a most commercial one.

That's quite different from being an electrician. In that profession, you're successful if you can (1) make electrical things work and (2) do it without electrocuting yourself. There's nothing subjective about that. In sports, you're successful if you win more games than anyone else. In politics, you're successful if you win (but of course that has little to do with if you're good or not).

But things aren't as black and white in the writing field. What makes you a "good" writer may be dependent on many factors, some of which are completely out of your hands. You may have submitted your manuscript to the wrong market or one that's just changing its focus. Your style of writing may be out of vogue just now. (There are fads in writing too.) The editor may reject your work because his prostate is acting up and he didn't sleep well the night before. Or because his teenager just got thrown out of another prep school and he's angry and upset. Or because his wife (whose first name is the same as yours) just ran off with someone in the art department. You have to keep believing in yourself and keep writing until you get by this first hurdle on your way to publication. It's difficult and sometimes discouraging, but if you give up, you'll never know if the public thinks you're a good writer too.

FIND A STRONG ROLE MODEL

Writing is not a team sport. And if there are cheerleaders for this sole event, I've never seen any at my games. Maybe that's why so many writers talk to themselves. We're cheering ourselves on to victory, and the pom-poms are in our heads.

Try to find a role model you can emulate. It may be a local writer you know personally or one whose work you enjoy reading. Having another writer to admire as you try to follow in her footsteps can have a positive influence on your writing. The late Harry S. Truman said, "I studied the lives of great men and famous women, and I found that the men and women who got to the top were those who did the jobs they had in hand, with everything they had of energy and enthusiasm and hard work."

Read all you can about your role model. Your writing styles and motivations are probably different, but the discipline and persistence that made your role model successful are probably ones you can emulate. If, however, you read that she depends upon alcohol or drugs to help bring on the muse, find yourself another role model.

Despite what you read about hard-drinking writers, the bottle usually comes between them and their goals at some point in their careers.

HANDLING REJECTIONS

Once when I was giving a talk about writing, someone in the audience asked me how I handled rejections. I answered very truthfully. "With difficulty." I was the last chosen for teams in PE class in junior high, and there remains a small place in my being that's still smarting from it. It doesn't get easier in the writing business either, although now only the mailcarrier knows your manuscript came back—again. Most of us with children are hurt when someone criticizes our children. It's no less painful with our brainchildren.

When an editor writes, "Sorry, this doesn't fit our needs," I feel like writing back, "But it fits mine. Why don't we compromise?" But I don't. When my manuscript that had been approved in query stage by my friendly editor comes back with a note that says, "Your previous editor and mentor just left our magazine to study the eating habits of hippos in African rivers and nobody else here really likes your writing," I vow aloud I will never buy that magazine again, let alone try to write for it. The cat just stares at me, contemplating his future with a mistress who talks to herself. If the editor writes a note that says, "Sorry, we just bought something like this," I kick myself for taking that play day and not getting my article completed sooner.

The bottom line is obvious: Rejections are no fun. But they're part of a writer's life. And they don't mean your work isn't publishable. You need to curse, kick and rail, and then pick up and go on writing. In his book *The Writing Business*, Donald MacCampbell writes, "Not all rejected manuscripts are bad. Just as 'many a flower is born to blush unseen and waste its sweetness on the desert air,' so many a readable manuscript is destined for the author's attic because, for any of the variety of reasons . . . it does not happen to be right for today's market."

But rather than toss your rejected manuscript in the attic, brush it off, read it with an impartial eye (if possible), make the necessary changes and help to find it a home.

Don't Get Mad; Get Even
I doubt that pouting and crying has ever made a rejection slip miraculously turn into an acceptance. (If I thought it would, I'd be the first to try.) Neither does burning your manuscript in your great-grandmother's cut glass bowl, writing a hate letter to the editor or dousing the manuscript with Whisper Yes cologne and sending it back again.

What does help is to know that even the best editors make mistakes sometimes. The first editor I sent the proposal to for my first book turned it down flat. A year later, when there was a new editor, I sent the exact same proposal back again. This time I got a contract, not a rejection. I subscribe to Sir Winston Churchill's philosophy: "Never give in! Never give in! Never, never, never, never . . ."

Believe in your work and in yourself. Take action as soon as a manuscript returns. Read it carefully as though you were the editor not the author. You may spot a weakness you didn't see before. Rework it and send the manuscript to the next market on your list. Don't let those pages sit on your desk gathering dust or getting buried under your Snickers candy bar wrappers.

Save Warm Fuzzies and Other Comforts
Fight off the glumps that come with a rejection by grabbing hold and displaying anything even close to encouragement. It could be a letter from a reader who enjoyed your letter in the "Letters to the Editor" section of your local newspaper, a copy of the fifteen dollar check you received for coming in second in the "Why I like washing with licorice-flavored soap" contest or even a rejection letter in which the editor said you were the greatest writer since Thomas Mann but that her company wasn't doing any more books on consumption and had just published one on mountains. One wall opposite my desk is covered with plaques holding my various book covers. These aren't to boost my ego; they're to remind me to be positive and to keep telling myself, "I've done it before, and I can do it again." That's how you make lemonade out of lemons.

CHAPTER 17

Preparing Your Mind and Body

I think, therefore I am.

— René Descartes

One of my sons attended a well-known theater school in which he and the other students were taught how to prepare and use their "instruments." The term referred to their bodies and included their voices. I've never forgotten that definition of the word or the context in which it was used.

Writers also use their bodies in their work, not just in the physical act of typing their words but in facial expressions and body language as well. Some writers pace as they write, talking into a tape recorder, while others stand and sway over the computer to the rhythm of their words. I've found myself frowning as I wrote some passages, smiling at others and even weeping as I completed thoughts in certain books, such as one I wrote on strokes. As there is a strong and most definite connection between the mind and body, we as writers must learn to prepare both so that we too can use our instruments most efficiently and effectively.

CONTROLLING STRESS THROUGH RELAXATION TECHNIQUES

Stress more than any other factor is probably the major detriment to the fluency and effectiveness of writing. Stress can cause our shoulders and necks to cramp and can trigger carpal tunnel syndrome, headaches, backaches and a myriad of other complaints, and play havoc with our digestive systems. Stress can also cramp us mentally, making us afraid to proceed, encouraging procrastination (known as writer's block) and creating confusion in our thought processes to the point that our thinking apparatuses just shut down in protest. But by learning to control stress in our lives, we can become better and more prolific writers as well as become healthier and less prey to numerous disorders and diseases. The late Norman Cousins, author of *Anatomy of an Illness* and *The Healing Heart*, emphasized that "positive attitudes and emotions can affect the biochemistry of the body to facilitate rejuvenation and health."

Be forewarned that there is no best way to relax, which is too bad because a "one size fits all" technique would be far easier than having to experiment to see what works best for you. But do test some of the relaxation techniques listed below. You're sure to find one or two that are effective for you and, perhaps, effective for your family members as well.

The Relaxation Response

In 1975, Harvard cardiologist Herbert Benson, M.D., wrote a groundbreaking book called *The Relaxation Response*. The book was based on studies he had conducted that revealed that by sitting quietly and focusing the mind, individuals could lower their heart rates, slow their breathing, lower blood pressure and overall reduce the speeds of their metabolisms. In his book *Beyond the Relaxation Response*, Benson noted, "In addition, the changes produced by this Response counteract the harmful effects and uncomfortable feelings of stress." He outlined the following procedures by which an individual could elicit this response:

- finding a quiet environment
- consciously relaxing the body's muscles
- focusing for ten to twenty minutes on a mental device, such as the word *one* or *peace*, or a brief prayer
- assuming a passive attitude toward intrusive thoughts

Since reading Dr. Benson's books, I have used his relaxation response technique to help me clear my mind for my writing. Many of my fellow writers use this or other relaxation techniques, such as yoga, biofeedback, massage, progressive relaxation, self-hypnosis and visualization (see chapter sixteen) to relax, to unwind and to prepare their minds and bodies to do battle with the war of words. A recent Gallup survey reports that 26 percent of Americans practice some form of meditation or relaxation techniques.

According to Dr. Benson, now Chief, Division of Behavioral Medicine at Beth Israel Deaconess Medical Center in Boston and President of its Mind/Body Medical Institute, "For more than 25 years laboratories at the Harvard Medical School have systematically studied the benefits of mind/body interactions. The research established that when a person engages in a repetitive prayer, word, sound, or phrase and when intrusive thoughts are passively disregarded, a specific set of physiologic changes ensure. . . . These changes are the opposite of those induced by stress and have been labeled the relaxation response."

Progressive Relaxation
But the relaxation response is not the only way to calm your mind and body. The end result is what's important, not the way to get to it. As you will soon discover, there are many paths to relaxation and physical and mental well-being. Which road you take to find tranquility is up to you. Ask your physician or psychologist or a mental health professional trained in relaxation techniques to help you find a method that works for you. There are also many audiotapes and books available to guide you.

Progressive relaxation is another method you can try to help you achieve this calmness of spirit and body. It isn't difficult, but as with other relaxation techniques, you have to practice it in order to master it. There are basically two forms of progressive relaxation—active and passive. Both work, so it's just a matter of which feels right and is effective for you.

  • **Active progressive relaxation**
Sit comfortably on your chair, or lie on the bed or couch. Close your eyes and let the thoughts fly out of your mind. As with the relaxation response, unwanted thoughts will pop in from time to time. Just let them dissolve into nothingness. Begin by tightening then relaxing your toes, then your ankles, and slowly work your way up your body. Feel the difference between the sensation of tenseness and that of relaxation. Let your facial and scalp muscles first tighten, then loosen. Enjoy the warm sensation you feel when you release the tension.

- **Passive progressive relaxation**

Although this type of relaxation is similar to its more active brother, it varies in that you don't first tense each muscle. Instead you talk them into relaxation by saying something like, "My toes are warm. Relaxed. So relaxed. I feel calm. Calm. So calm." Then you work up the rest of your body. Your mind messages crowd out extraneous thoughts as you relax your muscles. Focus on your breathing.

Picture a scene that means relaxation to you, such as the beach, a mountain cabin or a kite floating gently in the sky, or just concentrate on a word that connotes relaxation for you, such as *love*, *calm*, *peace*, *Jesus*, or simply a sound, such as "ahhhh" or "ummmm." What you're thinking doesn't matter, only that you are focusing on that one picture or sound. If you're concentrating on that, your mind won't have room to be distracted. If other concerns pop into your mind, let those unwanted thoughts drift by like seaweed in the surf, and return to your phrase or picture.

If you practice this or the other techniques once or twice a day for ten to twenty minutes (no more than that, experts say), you soon will be able to relax completely whenever you need to in your daily life. Be patient. You wouldn't expect to become proficient in tennis overnight. You'd struggle with your serve and forget how to do the backhand shot you learned just the day before. Learning to relax on demand is no different. Just keep practicing.

Remind yourself to practice relaxation. Put a reminder sticker by your telephone or computer screen. Before you realize it, you'll have mastered the skill. When you sense that your muscles are getting tense or feel stressful as you're writing, you'll be able to push back from your desk, allow your muscles to fall into their relaxed positions and focus for a few minutes on your favorite peaceful scene or special word or phrase. You'll be amazed to discover how good you'll feel afterward and how much your energy level has risen.

Yoga

Yoga is one of the more ancient forms of mental and physical exercise. (The actual word *yoga* means "discipline" in Sanskrit.) It includes various gentle exercises, proper deep breathing, meditation to quiet the mind, and specific body positions. In addition to assisting with relaxation, yoga helps to keep muscles limber and prevent stiffness, an ailment familiar to many writers.

Massage

Massage is another form of relaxation and therapy that was used by the ancient Greeks and Romans and for centuries by cultures in the Far East. There are various types of massage, although all include pressure, kneading or stroking. The amount of pressure used is an individual preference, so you must give the massage therapist feedback so he knows what you desire.

In many states, massage therapists must be licensed by the state. If your state is one of those, be sure to check with your state's department of professional regulation. Always check references, especially if the therapist is coming into your home.

I have weekly massages to help dissolve the tension I carry in my neck and forearms. Afterward, I feel innervated and ready to move mountains. Others prefer to curl up and take a nap. It's a very personal reaction.

If you don't feel like having a full massage in your home when you're working, ask the therapist to bring a chair you can straddle with a cushioned face hole. The therapist can work out tension knots in your back, neck and arms, and you can be back at work in thirty minutes.

T'ai Chi

T'ai Chi is an ancient health art that has been gaining popularity in the United States. It is a gentle exercise involving not only discipline and concentration but also balance, as it works every part of your body. T'ai Chi boosts your body's flexibility and mobility, aids posture and relaxation and has a calming effect on your mind, all of which make it a perfect exercise for a writer. I've been practicing it for just a short time but really find it both stimulating and relaxing at the same time. Many YMCAs, community centers and health clubs now offer classes in T'ai Chi, and you also can purchase T'ai Chi instructional videotapes.

Daydreaming

I bet you never expected to be encouraged to daydream, did you? But experts tell us that "daydreaming, for many people, is analogous to relaxation and meditation as it tends to relieve certain kinds of tension. . . . Most daydreamers admit that they feel more refreshed, stimulated and renewed when they 'come back to earth.'" Just don't let daydreaming take over your writing day, or you'll never get anything written.

Aromatherapy

When it comes to relaxation techniques for the mind and body, one of the least considered senses is that of smell. And yet the sense of smell is one of our most highly developed senses. Aromatics have long been used by most cultures to calm and relax and even to stimulate. Use citrus-scented candles or warmed oil to help fight stress and mental fatigue and lavender scents to help you to relax and sleep well. Some writers even burn scented candles as they work and find that it helps them to reduce stress.

Eighteenth century author Oliver Goldsmith knew about the powers of the sense of smell when he wrote:

> As aromatic plants bestow
> No spicy fragrance while they grow;
> But crushed or trodden to the ground,
> Diffuse their balmy sweets around.

Writing is a lot like the release of these aromatic scents. Sometimes our words flow easily, while other times they are more guarded and come freely only when coaxed and labored over. Unless you have an allergy to flowers, try the various scents to see if they help to reduce your stress level, opening your mind to further creativity.

Appreciating Nature

George Washington Carver once said, "Never a day passes but that I do myself the honor to commune with some of nature's varied forms." I've found that his advice works wonders when I'm feeling sluggish and am having trouble expressing myself in a particular paragraph or chapter.

I'll take a brief visit to the zoo or aquarium, repot a plant, take a short walk to the park and watch children at play or enjoy a time out on the "reading rock" outside our summer home and watch the seagulls float and soar. I can then return to my writing feeling refreshed and ready to write. It's as though something magical in nature has stirred and awakened my internal being. Perhaps it's a subtle reminder of the unique talents God has given all His creatures that stirs me into using mine. Perhaps it's just the fact that nature brings us back full circle to our roots, a realization that fills me with a sense of calmness and serenity. Whatever it is, reaching out to behold nature has always been a powerful stimulant for me in my work. I urge you to give it a try.

EXERCISE

It's that *E* word that frightens people: *exercise.* You may feel as though you don't have time to exercise and write too. I felt that way for a long time. But once I began walking—first, for fifteen minutes, then thirty and now forty-five minutes four times a week— I'm amazed at how much more energy I have for my writing. I use earphones and a radio/cassette player so I can listen to my favorite radio station (country) or motivation tapes. Recently I added weight training too and discovered that my arms don't ache as much as they used to after a long day at the computer. The truth is, you don't have time *not* to exercise because it not only will improve your mental and physical health, but it will make your writing time much more effective.

There really is no one best type of exercise to help you reduce stress and get back in shape. There is a wide range, including aerobics, biking, climbing, dancing, fencing, gymnastics, hiking, rowing, swimming, tennis, volleyball and walking. Some people prefer group exercise, and others, solo pursuits. Just find one or more that you enjoy.

I personally find my grandfather's "daily constitutional" (i.e., brisk walking) to be ideal because it's safe, beneficial to my mind and body and something I can do lifelong. Walking helps to protect me from osteoporosis and can be done inside on a treadmill if the weather turns bad. It doesn't take too long, and I don't have to change out of my writing clothes when it's time for a walk. I enjoy the scenery, the people and the fresh air. I also often get solutions to writing problems when I'm walking.

Note: Always get a physical checkup and an OK from your physician before beginning any exercise program.

POSITIVE SELF-TALK

Throughout this book I've described the importance of giving yourself positive mind messages. Let your antenna be on guard for negative thoughts so you can quickly banish them. They are self-defeating. Your body and mind are one. When you think a negative thought, it creates changes in your body chemistry, and these alterations can adversely affect your body.

Stop thinking, *I'll never stick to an exercise program*, and replace it with the positive affirmation, *I've walked three times this week. I can easily do that or even more next week*. It's a way of becoming your own personal health trainer. Shad Helmstetter, author of *The Self-Talk Solution* and *What to Say When You Talk to Your Self*, offers this suggestion: ". . . every day add a healthy dose of the mental nourishment that Self-Talk gives you." He calls positive self-talk "health food for the mind." I call it being your own best friend.

EAT PROPERLY

You wouldn't expect your car to run on water, but many people feed their bodies the wrong fuel and still expect them to run efficiently. They can't. And if you are malnourished, your mind can't function effectively either. According to a recent *Tufts University Health and Nutrition Letter*, experts are finding that "the consumption of a more satisfactory . . . diet is associated with better cognitive function." What makes a diet satisfactory includes such important elements as fruits, vegetables and grains.

You may become so focused on what you're writing that you forget to stop and have lunch. Or you may grab a candy bar and a cup of coffee. This is bad for your health, plus it will eventually affect your writing ability.

Plan for well-balanced lunch breaks, even if you have to set an alarm clock to remind you. Stock the refrigerator with nourishing but nonfattening snacks, such as apples and carrot sticks. Cut down on your caffeine intake, and instead, have a water bottle near your desk (but away from your computer). Stay hydrated as you work. You need at least eight 8-ounce glasses of water a day. Yes, it means more bathroom breaks, but you shouldn't sit in front of the computer all day anyway.

If you aren't sure what proper nutrition is, ask your physician, contact a local hospital and speak to a registered dietitian or call the Government Printing Office (GPO), (202) 512-1800 (government numbers change frequently). Ask for its subject bulletin, a catalog listing all the GPO's available information on nutrition or any other particular subject. Although the subject bulletin is free, there is a small charge for the materials you order.

You also can check The American Dietetic Association on the Web at http://www.eatright.org or the Tufts University Web site, http://www.navigator.tufts.edu. This latter Web site lists and discusses numerous other sites featuring information on nutrition.

By taking care of your physical and mental health, you'll not only be healthier but you'll feel better too. That can't help but be beneficial in your writing career. As you also learn to control and reduce the stress level within your home, your outside work and your at-home writing, you'll feel more at peace with yourself. You'll also have a stronger belief in your ability to be successful in your writing endeavor and be better able to focus on your writing.

CHAPTER 18

Doing Good Through Volunteerism

Without volunteers, we'd be a nation without a soul.

— Rosalynn Carter

Volunteerism is an American tradition. It is said to have formally originated in 1727 when Benjamin Franklin and a few friends started a mutual improvement society. (He also founded the nation's first subscription library, a volunteer fire company and, in 1751, the first hospital in Pennsylvania. And you thought he was only interested in flying kites.)

When I was little, my mother had a saying. All mothers do. Actually, my mother had many sayings, and as I get older, I realize that many of them were true. This particular saying had to do with refilling the ice cube trays. You see, I grew up in the olden days, before private homes had refrigerators with ice cube makers that multiplied ice cubes at a rate faster than even the most resolute Eskimo could ever use them up.

As we reached for the ice cube tray, my mother would automatically say, "Be sure to fill it up again. You have to put back what you take."

Volunteering is a lot like making ice cubes; it's a way of putting back into the community some of the good you make use of, of giving back to those less fortunate some of your good fortune, of sharing.

I personally feel strongly that we, as writers, should share our writing talents by contributing some of our efforts toward doing good deeds in our community. There are no merit badges for this type of work, but it can provide a valuable service, especially to nonprofit organizations that lack the funding to hire their own writers.

PROTECT YOUR TIME

That said, it's important to know how to protect your time so you don't end up volunteering all your writing time away and have none left for your own projects. If you don't learn how to use a four-letter word—"no-no"—you'll be swamped with requests for newsletters, brochures, press releases and other types of writing.

Just say no. Don't embellish. If someone asks you to write publicity for the silent auction, for example, just say "No." If you add, "I can't because I have a deadline Friday," you're likely to hear, "Oh, that's fine. The auction is three weeks away." If you have trouble being assertive, take a course in assertiveness training or read a book on the subject. I took a course in assertiveness training at our local state university, and it truly changed my life—for the better.

Pick one or two organizations that appeal to you and get to know their needs. Don't agree to write all of their publicity and printed material though. Start with a single project that sounds interesting to you. Speak up and say what you're willing to do and what you are not.

Although I'll do windows, I won't write newsletters. My anti-newsletter stand is twofold. First of all, newsletters have a regular deadline that keeps popping up like unwanted birthdays. With a newsletter, you are either writing one or gathering material to write one.

Secondly, with newsletters, you are dependent upon others to furnish most of the material for the upcoming issue. That means you have to spend time on the phone cajoling committee chairpeople to turn in their information so you can write it up. Then, later, you'll waste even more time listening to these same people complain that their material wasn't in the newsletter (because they turned it in the day you had the newsletter printed).

Fortunately, most writers don't share my feelings about newsletters, so give it a try. But if you're burned, don't say I didn't warn you. In fact, since I'm confessing my dislikes, I also try to avoid any type of volunteer writing assignments where personalities are involved. I've learned from experience that invariably someone's name is omitted from a list or one person feels that another one was cast in a bigger or better part in a skit. When it happens in a project I'm being paid for, I feel that these public relation issues are part of that package. But when it's a volunteer assignment, I'd rather pass.

KNOW WHEN TO SAY YES
What I do enjoy doing as a volunteer is writing brochures or booklets that I can write independently and on my own schedule. I like to interview the people in charge, understand the focus of what's needed, then go home and write. But remember that you're dealing with other volunteers. I once spent two full weeks writing a slide presentation for an organization that needed it "right away." I wrote the copy and even suggested what slides to use at each point. After two years, the committee never could agree on when and how to use the slide show, and to my knowledge, it never was presented. Nevertheless, I enjoyed the project and learned a great deal by working on it.

USE VOLUNTEER WRITING IN YOUR PORTFOLIO
One of the nicest things about writing as a volunteer (other than the good it does for the organization) is that you can use the material you've created as samples of your writing. I did a number of booklets for a local hospital, including *How to Avoid Injury in Youth Sports* and *Florida Health Hazards*. Although I received no pay for these projects, I asked for and was given multiple copies of the finished work, which I have used as examples of my work when pursuing other writing assignments on similar subjects.

As a volunteer, you'll meet interesting people in your community. Many of them may work for small businesses that cannot afford an in-house copywriter. Large companies, which often have a continuing series of freelance writing needs, may employ some of your volunteer co-workers as well. After seeing what you have written for the nonprofit group, these same people may refer you to their own companies when there are needs for freelance writers.

PUT SOMETHING BACK
In helping others through our volunteer efforts, we give our children and grandchildren an important heritage, showing by our actions

that volunteering is important. If you want to put more meaning in your life, if you want to teach your children and grandchildren the meaning of love, lead by example and become a volunteer. Perhaps Sir Wilfred Thomason Grenfell, an English physician and missionary, said it more succinctly: "The service we render to others is really the rent we pay for our room on this earth."

Yes, volunteering is a lot like making ice cubes. It's a way of putting back into your community some of the good you enjoy, therefore making your community even better. Don't wait for it to get hot where you live. Keep those ice cube trays full.

CHAPTER 19

Following the Leaders

People seldom improve when they have no model but themselves to copy after.

— Oliver Goldsmith

I've always enjoyed meeting other writers. I don't think it's that "misery loves company." Actually, most of us love what we're doing, or we certainly would have found an easier, less stressful and more lucrative way to spend our time. But trading shoptalk is a way of reaching out, to compare notes, to see if we can learn even one more secret of success or a better way to handle those darn rejections that come into almost every writer's life.

It really doesn't matter if the other writer is more or less published than you are. We writers just tend to gravitate to each other like grease spots on a new silk blouse. We feel safe with another scribe.

Writers clubs and now E-mail are two ways we can trade horror stories with each other. It's an opportunity to learn more about markets, editors' eccentricities and even ourselves and this bizarre business we're in with its extreme highs and lows.

In the almost forty years I have been a freelance writer, I have been encouraged, counseled, mentored and educated by many men and women who cared enough about the writing business to reach out to help a peer. I've tried to do the same when I've taught writing classes, lectured or just spoken one-on-one with other writers, both beginning and published. After all, we all were beginners once.

I feel extremely fortunate to be able to present comments from a number of published writers who write at home. They all took time off from their own writing projects to help me with mine. They wanted to share their expertise, experiences, frustrations and solutions with my readers. I appreciate their caring and support and thank them for their courtesy and camaraderie.

Note how all authors have unique ways of writing and vast variety in their choices of offices or writing retreats. The end product, however, is the same. They've all been published.

It doesn't matter if you write in a toolshed in the garden, a closet, a section of the living room, a barn, an oak-paneled study or on the kitchen table. The important point to remember is to keep writing so you can follow these leaders.

BETTE GREENE *Summer of My German Soldier; Morning Is a Long Time Coming; Philip Hall Likes Me, I Reckon, Maybe.*

"I live in a grand old house about fifteen minutes from Boston's freedom trail, and even before my children were off and running, there was no shortage of room. Then, as now, my offices occupy two sky-lite rooms on the third floor, and on a clear day, I can watch the flight of the Canadian geese. My offices are always mildly messy which is precisely the way I like things.

"I use a combination of clipboards, easels, and finally, a computer. My first draft is usually written with a fountain pen because a fountain pen feels more like an extension of me than a computer. I go through three bottles of Quink ink a year and the reason I keep track of my ink usage is because I know how much effort is involved in just one ink fill-up. So when I polish off a bottle of Quink in four months, it's a kind of proof that I haven't been a slacker.

"My husband, generous guy that he is, has offered to give me his Montblanc pen because it leaks, and he estimates that I'd probably use six bottles of ink annually and thereby feel twice as productive. I'm considering his offer, but not very seriously.

"And speaking of seriously . . . nobody will treat your work schedule seriously unless you first treat it seriously. So it's vital that friends, family, and associates be told that you don't take calls during your working hours. Will somebody at sometime be offended? Undoubtedly. So what to do? Practice saying, 'I'd love to talk with you, but this is my time to write. May I call you back later?' People who love you will understand, and those who don't understand don't love you. So what's the loss?

"As I read what I have written, it sounds as though it's never been a problem with me. Well, it has been a problem. For example, I once lost my closest friend because I almost never went out to lunch with her and would only speak to her before 10 A.M. or after 4 P.M. My dedication to writing my first novel, *Summer of My German Soldier* [author's note: which was rejected by eighteen publishers before it was published, so don't get discouraged], was clearly an impediment to our friendship, and while the choice was painful, it was never a hard choice.

"If I don't feel passionate about my work-in-progress, then why should anybody else? Since I will ruthlessly exploit myself by plunging my emotional reserves to write my books, am I also prepared to tell a friend that I'll call back later? Yeah, but it's not easy. Funny thing is, it's never been easy."

ERMA BOMBECK *If Life Is a Bowl of Cherries, What Am I Doing in the Pits*; *I Lost Everything in the Post-Natal Depression*; *The Grass Is Always Greener Over the Septic Tank*; *Motherhood: The Second Oldest Profession*; *At Wit's End*

Aaron M. Priest, agent for the late Erma Bombeck, granted me permission to reprint her comments from my book *How to Be a Successful Housewife/Writer*. Bombeck had written them on her way back from a publicity tour in Hawaii and made great effort to send them to me in time for my deadline. I think her thoughts are as valuable today as they were then, and I appreciate her agent's courtesy in allowing me to pass them on to you.

"The most difficult part of being a housewife/writer/mother is the /.

"The /, which is just below the question mark on my typewriter, represents the tightropes we all walk on; the three masters we try to serve. Which one gets priority, and how much do we steal from one to compensate the other?

In my case, I took all three very seriously.

"At first, I used to think I could allot time slots in the day. From 7–8/mother . . . 8–10/housewife . . . 10–3/writer . . . 3–11/housewife/mother.

"It would have worked out fine if my son hadn't bled during my deadline with *Good Housekeeping*, grocery day clashed with a parent-teacher conference, and the oven caught fire on the same day an editor told me he wasn't laughing.

"I could fill up a book for you on the frustrations of H/W/M syndrome. But I'll limit myself to just a few.

"Problem: No one takes your little part-time job seriously. Just because you write from your home, everyone assumes you have the flexibility to chuck it anytime you want. No one realizes the discipline that goes into writing. Even bad checks and grocery lists take concentration.

"Solution: I have an X-rated response for people who call me up and chirp, 'You busy?'

"Problem: It's lonely at the bottom. When you have no name, no contacts, no track records, how do you sustain enthusiasm for what you're doing?

"Solution: Save your fan letter. I lived for years on the comment of a desk editor on the *Detroit Free Press*. . . . an elderly man who said, 'I never read your stuff—but by God you have it here on time.'

"Problem: How do you know how good or how bad you are? Who do you go to for critique?

"Solution: I found that if I begged my husband, wrapping myself around his leg and dragging behind him pleading for criticism, he had the good sense to keep his mouth shut and thus save our marriage. Most people who ask for criticism don't really want it. Learn to be honest with yourself. When it's garbage, say so.

"Problem: Writing in a traffic area and being constantly interrupted by children who want you to stop and belt their sibling for humming/making faces/breathing.

"Solution: After about five or six years, I got up the courage to say, 'Your MOTHER is busy. I will talk to you when I am finished. If this is going to bruise your ID, then I will try for some part of your body the moment I complete this idea.

"My family has been very supportive of me and what I do. It helps more than you know, but don't expect too much out of them. For the most part, you are your own cheerleader, coach, psychiatrist, critic, confessor, and house mother. When something has to give, you have to make your own decision as to where you can take the time.

"I let my body go.

"In 1971, I took my daughter with me to Pittsburgh where I was to receive a Headliner Award from the Women in Communications.

"As she sat in the audience I looked at her and said, 'For all the irritability when the writing didn't go well that day; for the three-pound roast that was still breathing at dinner; for the time I ironed a blouse for the school play and asked, "Which sleeve faces the audience?"; for the uncombed hair until noon; the instant icing on the warm birthday cakes; I thank you. You've seen the agony of a mother who writes from home. I'm glad you're here to see the ecstasy.' "

Thank you, Erma. We miss you.

WENDY WASSERSTEIN *An American Daughter; Isn't It Romantic; Uncommon Women and Others; The Sisters Rosensweig;* Pulitzer prize-winning play, *The Heidi Chronicles*

"The most difficult part of writing at home is the telephone, the refrigerator, and the lack of happy isolation. One of the best ways to resolve this situation for me is going to the library. I tend to concentrate when I am surrounded by concentration.

"I write because when I do I suddenly feel in touch with myself, as if suddenly the center is not only holding, but producing. I write, I hope, to make character come alive."

SUE GRAFTON *A Is for Alibi, B Is for Burglar* and the other titles in the Kinsey Millhone mystery series

"I suppose the most difficult aspect of writing at home is the constant stream of interruptions. I can't say that I've ever found an effective way of resolving the issue.

"My office is on our property, located in a bungalow perhaps twenty-five feet from the back door. Even so slim a geographic separation gives me the illusion of 'going off to work.' I don't dress up for the occasion, but I'm always fresh from a round of exercise, a shower, and a light breakfast.

"Like any professional, I sit down at my desk promptly at nine o'clock every morning of the week (barring a head cold, a book signing, or a trip out of town). My desk is twenty-five feet long with numerous file drawers below and I prefer to work in an environment as serene as I can make it.

"My deal with myself is that at the end of each day, I clean off my desk so it's ready for the next day's work. The creative process is chaotic and I function best in the midst of order and tidiness. If my desk becomes too cluttered, I find myself distracted by the chores and responsibilities inherent in the mess.

"If I'm suffering from writer's block (which only occurs once or twice daily), I answer fan mail, or file clippings, or take out the trash. The homely activity soothes my fevered imagination and, at the same time, maintains the organization so necessary to my peace of mind.

"I consider myself fortunate that my early writing experience was done in the presence of small children at the end of a day of full-time employment outside the home. The experience was good training for the continuing struggle with interruptions. Somehow I managed then, as I do this day, to turn out a steady stream of work despite the absence of ideal conditions. Actually, by now, I've probably grown dependent on the interruptions so it's probably pointless to complain. The object of the exercise is keep writing without whining or excuses."

TERESA BLOOMINGDALE *I Should Have Seen It Coming When the Rabbit Died*

"My only advice would be the old advice: If one must write at home, build a home in the middle of the Mohave Desert and never, ever, tell anybody where you are."

MARK FUERST *Tone-a-Metrics; Sports Injury Handbook; The Couple's Guide to Fertility; Computer Phobia*

"I keep to a regular schedule. I get up, make the bed, eat, then go to my 'office' and get to work. I ease into my writing mode by first reading my e-mail. It helps me make the transition.

"Before we had a kid, my office was our second bedroom. Now I have our little dressing room that isn't too bad because it has a window facing our backyard here in Brooklyn. I have a custom-made desk with tower bookshelf and a three-drawer file cabinet all made of wood. I like background music when I write, although I know many writers don't. Unfortunately, my office doesn't have a door so I can't lock myself in. It makes it difficult when I'm on the phone talking to an editor and my five-year-old son prances in.

"When we had a small one-bedroom apartment, I used the kitchen table as a desk. The advantage was that I used a portable typewriter then. The disadvantage was that the table was too high for comfortable typing and my shoulders usually ached after even a short writing session.

"I think it takes a certain temperament to write at home. You need the self-motivation. Writing at home is a lonely occupation. I break my writing sessions up by taking our dog for a walk or going to the health club at lunch. Although I may talk to plenty of people on the phone, I need contact with real people too."

DODI SCHULTZ *Living With Lupus*; editor for *Tools of the Writer's Trade*; *The First Five Years*

"I've never had much problem writing at home. Everyone I've known has always worked. I've always had a separate room for an office. When I was considering going full-time freelance, my then editor besieged me with dire warnings suggesting that I'd be whiling away the time looking out the window, since there would be no one directing and demanding. I quickly found that getting the money was a powerful source of discipline.

"Actually, the only 'problem' I've run into—and it's really only a minor annoyance—is that when the UPS guy doesn't get an answer, he starts ringing other bells to see if someone else might be in to sign for the package. And I'm usually in.

"I honestly can't think of any other disadvantages [to writing at home]. In fact, there are many other advantages—not being interrupted by being called into editorial meetings (or whatever, depending on one's job); being able to schedule one's own day; not popping into the supermarket when it's crowded with homebound office workers; being able to take a total break for half an hour or however long to do something entirely different like garden work (or go to a movie, if that's what your psyche cries for); et al."

PATRICIA O'BRIEN *The Candidate's Wife*; *The Ladies' Lunch*; *Good Intentions*; presently working on a book about friendship with coauthor Ellen Goodman

"The most important thing about writing at home is having a routine you stick to. That's also the hardest, because diversions are many and tantalizing. So the second most important thing is focus. That means giving yourself permission to ignore unmade beds and dirty dishes; harder said than done. But the hundreds of little jobs in a home can chip away at everything creative inside you if you let them. Eventually they undermine one of the key reasons to work at home—which for me is the freedom to do what I want on my own terms.

"I've finally trained myself to ignore call waiting (it goes into a mailbox), because nine times out of ten trying to juggle two calls (maybe one is my daughter with a problem and the other is an editor) just sends my stress level soaring. It isn't always possible, but I don't see how anyone can keep focused without exerting some control over the telephone. It's the single biggest drawback to writing at home (once you've gotten past the dishes and beds . . .).

"It can be hard for people beginning this way of life to be taken seriously. If you're home, you're somehow 'not working.' This is particularly hard for women with children, so having a specific room to go to where you and your family understand you are NOT AVAILABLE is important.

"I also try always to get dressed before I work. (Sometimes, though, I'm still in my robe, writing away, at noon.) But I find I take myself more seriously if I'm sitting here in front of my computer looking like a grown-up."

JUDY BLUME *Are You There God? It's Me, Margaret*; *Forever . . .*; *Wifey*; *Summer Sisters*; many others

"I'm a morning person—not the kind who rises at 4:00 A.M. and writes for hours before breakfast—but an ordinary morning person. When my children were young and had to catch the school bus before 8:00 A.M., I would be at my desk by 8:30. Now I try to sit down to work somewhere around 9:00, following my breakfast and shower. I like to be dressed for the day, as if I am going *out* to work, even though my office is just a few rooms away from my bedroom.

". . . During the first draft of a book, which is the hardest time for me, I check my watch a lot and hope the phone will ring— anything to make the time go faster because I am determined to sit at my desk for three hours. . . . When I'm rewriting a book I work much more intensely and for longer hours. Towards the end of the second or third draft the urge to finish is so strong that it becomes harder and harder to leave the story and return to real life.

". . . For me, writing has its ups and downs. After I had written more than ten books I thought seriously about quitting. I felt I couldn't take the loneliness anymore. I thought I would rather be anything than a writer. But I've come to appreciate the freedom of writing. I accept the fact that it's hard and lonely work.

". . . During the summer months (my favorite time of the year) we go to Martha's Vineyard, an island off the coast of Massachusetts. I have a tiny writing cabin there, far enough away from the house to feel very private. I get up early in the morning and work until noon. I wrote most of my latest book, *Summer Sisters*, there. Sometimes I wish summer would last all year."

LISA IANNUCCI articles in *Parenting*, *Baby Talk*, *American Health*, *Writer's Digest* and *FDA Consumer*

"The hardest part about writing at home is trying to balance everything. For example, as I'm writing this, I'm taking a Sunday night to answer messages, post new messages on-line, research for a birth defect book, and write my real estate articles for a twice weekly column I have. In the meantime, I feel guilty because my husband is putting the children to bed tonight and I can't. I've taken way too much time not working this weekend and I'm behind, but the second I sit down to work, I miss what's going on in the other room.

"If I were in an office somewhere, working for someone else, I'd know I was committed to that person and would stay there, but here I'm so tempted to get out of my seat and be involved in what's going on in other parts of my home. I only have a sitter certain times of the week, so whatever I don't get done during those times, I have to get done during evening and weekend hours. I'm exhausted because I'm often working late since I do succumb to being with the family and have to make up for it when everyone is asleep.

"My office used to be in my baby's bedroom before I had her. I gave up my office to her and moved back to my bedroom, since it was so large it could accommodate me, including television."

SUSAN J. GORDON *Wedding Days: When and How Great Marriages Began*; articles in *Good Housekeeping, Family Circle, Ladies' Home Journal, McCall's, Reader's Digest, Victoria, Working Mother* and *The New York Times*

"The most difficult part about writing at home is keeping my writing life separated from my life as a homemaker, wife, and mother. Conscious efforts are made all the time to differentiate between my two 'lives.'

"These days, many houses with 'maids' rooms' have seen them converted into home offices. That's where I write—in the small room near my kitchen. It's located in the back of the house, and is conveniently cut off from entertainment areas; it even has its own bathroom. My office's undersized window was installed for 'hired help'—not the 'lady of the house'—so it doesn't overlook the attractive backyard, but a fairly dull side area instead. That's fine with me; otherwise, I'd probably spend too much time staring outside.

"Everything pertaining to running a household—such as paying bills, dealing with repairmen, writing grocery lists, working for the PTA—is managed in the kitchen where I have a tiny desk and a telephone. Everything which relates to my work as a writer is handled just a few steps away, in my home office. When I go upstairs or outdoors, I carry a portable phone; when it rings I walk into the appropriate room and handle matters from there."

CHRISTINE ADAMEC *The Complete Idiot's Guide to Adoption; The Unofficial Guide to Caring for Your Aging Parents; Start and Run a Profitable Freelance Writing Business; Is Adoption for You?*

"For me, the hardest part of writing at home is becoming immersed in a project and not taking time off to do things like eat, exercise, and so forth. You can get too chained to your computer, especially if you are on a tight deadline.

"How do I get my mind off work? That's a tough one. I'm rather an obsessive person and could be thinking about work, a problem one of the kids has and some current event in rapid succession. You have to develop a mindset that says, 'I'm not working now.' One good way is to leave—go to the store, the library, have lunch with a friend. Another thing I do is read escapist fiction, like anything by Anne Rice. That's a whole other ball game from the nonfiction self-help that I write.

"My home office is physically separated from the rest of the family room where it is located by the fact that I've made a narrow passageway to get to it, bounding it by a sofa facing the other way and boxes of supplies. I also use the word 'office' frequently, as in, 'What are you doing in my office?' to one of the kids. I try to keep them off the phone in here and using the phone in the kitchen instead."

SANDY FRYE executive producer and film writer

"Back (waay back) when I worked for *Cosmopolitan* magazine in New York, I had the occasion to view the home office of a freelance writer whose byline was frequently seen in several national magazines. He lived upstate about an hour and a half from Manhattan, and his office was a freestanding one-room frame building behind his home that had the contours of a five-sided gazebo with a peaked roof and windows on two facing walls. Inside, a two-foot-wide shelf ran around all five walls; It was a non-stop desktop 28″ off the floor. In the middle of each of the five sections was a typewriter with shelves above it (except for the two window walls), chair in front of it, and telephone books and papers piled next to it. Each workstation represented a project in progress.

"Not everyone can manage that kind of largess in a home work environment, but the concept of creating work stations impressed me enough to try to modify it for my own home office—which measures a mere 10×15 feet. It has only three usable walls, the fourth being taken up by French doors. I had a local handyman make an L-shaped Formica table and two mobile file carts which fit underneath, in which essential office supplies are kept. On the facing wall are two six-foot bookcases and a four-drawer file cabinet. I write articles, disseminate press releases and periodic reports for an art foundation, produce video scripts and have published a monthly newsletter for a regional film and television association. I have a Mac computer, a printer with two ports (one for Macs, the other for IBMs), a fax and a copy machine. I intend to buy a power book shortly and should have a 13″ TV monitor with built-in VCR for viewing my own and other tapes, but I don't think I have enough space to accommodate it. In this brave new Internet world, it's possible not only to create computer files, thus rendering obsolete the individual typewriters such as my author friend had, but also to do a lot of research electronically. The only books I have on hand (besides the computer and software manuals) are basics like *Who's Who in American Art*, the *Official Museum Directory*, an atlas, an unabridged *Random House* dictionary, and several 'quotables.' Any others come from the library.

"The rest of the shelves are labeled with each ongoing project, and the files correspond. Research requires notation and some people use notebooks for that, carefully dated with each entry. I prefer legal pads. One of the big differences between writing scripts and articles or press releases is it is often necessary to have many more versions of a video script. There is a time limitation to the video, and the available visuals for the project may make it necessary to compress some information or figure out ways to attach it to a visual which may not precisely match the content. Keeping track of those scripts is easier if you use colored paper. Each color represents a different draft. Just make sure you write down the color code. Between copy paper, printer paper, color papers, and legal paper, buying in bulk makes sense.

"The plan works reasonably well if you keep the work clearly labeled and you *always* put your material away after you use it. The only other challenge to the home office is to maintain the integrity of your working space (don't let anyone intrude on it for personal matters) and devise strategies to get into the work without resorting to evasion tactics like cleaning the front steps. Of course, some of my best ideas came to me while I was scrubbing those steps."

CADY BISSELL FERGUSON producer and writer for video, audio and text

"In 1984, years before the media touted home offices as the hottest trend, my husband and I began working out of our spare bedroom. As independent video producer/writers we figured working at home would not only save us money and a long commute, but best of all, we could wear our fuzzy slippers all day.

"Because we were watching our pennies, we set up our first home office as inexpensively as possible. My husband bought a circa 1930s desk at a yard sale and restored it (the matching chair was a freebie from a friend). My desk was purely functional—a door stretched between two filing cabinets. Our office equipment consisted of a computer with a tiny screen that displayed flickering green text on a black background, and a finicky daisy wheel printer. A few utilitarian metal shelves held our reference books. This was our 'corporate headquarters' for years.

"When our daughter was born in 1990, our office became her nursery and we moved to the dining room in the middle of the house. For a year we ate our meals while trying to ignore our messy desks and the stacks of video tapes on the floor. During that year we learned that the single most important element in a home office is having a door you can shut at the end of the day. Our little 1913 Atlanta craftsman-style bungalow was getting cramped, so we moved to Florida.

"Now we're back in a spare bedroom again. We still have the 1930s desk. We also have a variety of folding tables in different shapes and sizes that we use according to each particular job. We are always changing the location of the tables depending on the work. We like the flexibility. We have a relatively new desktop computer (the screen is bigger than our 1984 model and it displays text and graphics in living color) and a brand new laptop (again, for the flexibility of working anywhere). We've added a professional grade VCR and a monitor so we can view videos in our office while our daughter watches *Rugrats* in the living room.

"We have a fax machine, but we still lack a copier. It's next on our list of purchases. (To tell the truth, I think we both enjoy the excuse of having to go out to make copies every once in a while.)

We have an ever-expanding library, now housed in wooden book-shelves. Our videotape library is threatening to overrun our storage system (a closet with custom shelving that runs the length of one wall). The up side of limited storage space is that it forces us to go through our files and notebooks on a regular basis.

"After over 14 years of working at home we are now debating whether it might make sense to actually make the big move into downtown office space. For many years we have called ourselves 'word farmers.' We like the notion of living and working in the same environment, just like our rural counterparts. We enjoy the advantage of being at home while raising a child, but we struggle with a home that is increasingly work-oriented rather than family-oriented. We think we might need more separation. But then we wonder about the time lost to daily commutes, the overhead . . . and most of all, the fuzzy slippers."

DAVID SCHAEFER *Surefire Strategies for Growing Your Home-Based Business*

"I can't imagine writing anywhere but home. I closed down an office when writing became a major part of my work because some-one always wanted to chat. My personal dragon is the fact that when I'm stuck on a writing passage I stretch out on a couch to think. The bad news is that often leads to a nap. The good news is, it almost always leads to an answer to the problem, which usually comes in that misty area between being asleep and awake."

JEFF BERNER *The Joy of Working From Home: Making a Life While Making a Living; A Business of Your Own: The Small Business and Home Office Start-up Guide; The Nikon Touch Photography Guide; The Photographic Experience; others*

"The hardest part about writing at home is creating a space and time sanctuary, free from interruptions. So, the most important piece of equipment a serious (or playful!) writer needs is: a door that closes.

"I had the pleasure of designing a home to accommodate my lifelong career as an author, blending business, the arts and technology—always as a home-office based independent professional. My office is small but can be closed off from the rest of the house by a door with a window in it. It's double-glazed for soundproofing and covered with a Venetian blind. Shades of film noir.

"Although I have written a dozen of what I claim are non-fiction books—including *The Joy of Working From Home: Making a Life While Making a Living*—if I'm interrupted in the midst of inspiration, it can be hours before I can get it back. (Sure, I can keep writing, but it feels like only a cut above mere typing if the spell has been broken—no pun intended.) So, my wife cheerfully agrees that she won't interrupt me unless she wants a romantic break—I don't want to be insulated from my happiness. But no chores, errands or 'do you have a moment' intrusions.

"My 12′ × 12′ space is 'decorated' like a Pacific Islands tropical bar in the 1940s, full of junktiques and 'objects of my affection,' collected from every corner of the planet, so the many hours I spend there are filled with memories, laughs, and inspiration wherever my gaze falls. The bar has a corrugated metal roof over it, held up by bamboo poles. It accommodates fourteen elbows.

"My windows look into two bays and an ocean. As I write, I can also take long squints across the Pacific. My writing tools are a PowerMacintosh, plus a big assortment of fountain pens that I use to write short bursts and 'insights' in bustling cafes, or even at concerts. I use a PowerBook laptop on volcano rims and sailboats, but usually travel with just a pen and camera.

"But I treasure most the monkish solitude required to clearly hear the inspired passages that turn me into my own happy stenographer, hypnotically taking dictation from 'innerspace.' "

SHIRLEY LINDE *The Whole Health Catalogue*; *Sickle Cell: A Complete Guide to Prevention and Treatment*; *No More Sleepless Nights*; *No More Back Pain*; others

"Three things have worked for me in the thirty-five years I have been a professional writer:

"1. Having very, very, very extensive files. I have monthly file folders for meetings, etc., that are coming up in the future; boxes for books in progress with file folders for each chapter to toss things into; folders for medical subjects that I may anytime have the remotest possibility of writing on; active articles and queries on them go onto index cards. Projects in progress unfortunately go into piles on the floor. If I ever filed them away, I would not do them. If they sit on the floor staring at me, I am forced to get to them because I can't stand the sight of them.

"2. Being at my desk at 8:30 or 9 every morning. If you don't have self-discipline, forget about writing as a profession. You haven't a chance.

"3. A sense of humor for perspective. I have clippings and quotations stuck around my desk, stuff like

> *"My main reason for adopting literature as a profession was that, as the author is never seen by his clients, he need not dress respectably."*— George Bernard Shaw

> *"The best part about writing is stopping."*— Colin Walters

> *"Literature is an occupation in which you have to keep proving your talent to people who have none."*
> — Jules Renard

"And my favorite when I'm feeling insecure—a correspondence between Ernest Hemingway and Maxwell Perkins, part of which is Hemingway worrying, '*Or do you suppose that people think only of tolls as long distance charges and of Bell as the Bell telephone system . . . The Tolling of the Bell. . . . no, that's not right. . . .*'

Perkins' response: '*You damned fool. Go and write the novel.*' "

⋘⋙⋘⋙⋘⋙⋘⋙

These men and women didn't start their careers as successful writers. They all began their writing careers as novices, but they didn't give up, following E.L. Doctorow's observation that, "Writing is an exploration. You start from nothing and learn as you go."

CHAPTER 20

The Beginning (Not the End)

To laugh is to risk appearing the fool, To weep is to risk appearing sentimental. To reach out to another is to risk involvement. To express feelings is to risk exposing your true self. To place ideas and dreams before a crowd is to risk their loss. To love is to risk being loved in return. To live is to risk dying. To hope is to risk despair. To try is to risk failure. But risks must be taken because the greatest Hazard in life is to risk nothing. The people who ask nothing, do nothing, Have nothing and are nothing. They may avoid suffering and sorrow, but they Cannot learn, feel, change, grow, love, live. Chained by their attitudes, they are but slaves. They have forfeited their freedom. Only a person who risks is free.

— Anonymous

Of course you take a risk when you decide to write at home. But what's the worst that can happen? You won't like it, you'll lose interest or you'll be so wildly successful that you'll never go anywhere without throngs of fans hassling you for your autograph and repeating everything about your private life that they've read on one of your eight dedicated Web sites.

But think about what you stand to lose if you never give yourself the opportunity to try to write. You'll always wonder, Could I have done it? Would I have ever gotten published?

This *is* that first day of the rest of your life you keep hearing about. And like all of us, you're not getting any younger, so don't wait until "someday."

WRITE NOW

I once read a story about a man who said he really wanted to go to college to get his bachelor's degree, but in four years, when he graduated, he'd be fifty. A caring friend asked, "How old will you be in four years if you *don't* go back?"

So take that first step today. It doesn't mean you're committing yourself to a lifetime of writing at home or even a month of doing so. It doesn't mean you plan to quit your day job and write for a living, although one day, you might want to. A Chinese proverb says, "A journey of a thousand miles must begin with a single step." And it's true. Best of all, you won't be taking that step alone. There are many published writers who will cheer you along, in spirit if not in person.

YOU'RE NOT ALONE

I've often thought about why so many well-known writers were willing to take time off from their work to write a few paragraphs for my chapter nineteen on "Following the Leaders." Judy Blume summed it up best. She was between publicity tours for her new book, an adult novel called *Summer Sisters*. When I spoke to her about giving me a few words of encouragement for the readers of this book, she said, "Oh, I just love books about and for writers."

I guess that's true for most of us. Unfortunately, some writers build a wall to distance themselves from beginning writers. But most of us remember the thrill of our first magazine sale, of holding our first newly published book, of signing our name in that same book for people who were actually willing to stand in line to meet us. Each published writer began as you begin—wanting or needing to write. For most of us, the road was rocky and filled with detours. But determination, dedication and discipline became our compass. We found our way. And so will you.

THE SECRET TO BECOMING A PUBLISHED WRITER

The only way to learn to write is to write. Sorry. There's no magical incantation, no inside secrets, no shortcuts. The only way to write and to improve your writing is by doing it, the way a child learns to walk—step-by-step, stumbling and starting over, getting a few bumps and bruises along the way. The only real trick of the trade I know is to keep at it and learn to control your life so that somewhere in the twenty-four hours of your day (that's all I have in mine too), you include some time for writing.

PRAISE AND GARLANDS AT YOUR FEET

I began writing at the age of eight or ten, with a handwritten book (which I still have—I save everything), titled *Good Short Stories*. It was a gift for my mother on Mother's Day.

My older sister looked at my homemade offering and sniffed, "How do you know they're any good?"

Unshaken, I replied, "At least they're short."

The passing of the years changed nothing. No man (or woman) is a hero to his valet, nor a parent/writer to the kids.

"Gee, I'm glad you're a writer, Mom." one of my then teenage daughters told me.

"Really?" I answered feeling very pleased. Obviously, she felt I was a good role model, she was proud of my success and so on. I should have remembered that pride indeed goeth before a fall. I should have stopped while I was ahead. Instead, I asked, "Why?"

"Because," she answered in that matter-of-fact way only kids can carry off, "if you didn't write, you'd drive us all crazy." She and her four siblings are grown now, and I think they feel that way even more at this point in their lives.

Someone once asked my sister-in-law if we were related. She said that we were. "Oh," gushed my fan, "I just love her humorous articles. They're adorable. Is she fun to be around? Is she always making you laugh?"

My sister-in-law thought for a moment and then answered seriously, "I don't think she's ever made me laugh."

This wild display of adoration has not ceased over the years. Recently I asked a friend to meet me for lunch. "I finally have time," I sighed. "I finished my book."

"Oh?" she answered matter-of-factly. "What were you reading?"

So much for praise and garlands at your feet. The only things strewn in my path are my husband's walking shoes that I constantly trip over.

So why? Why do it?

WHY WRITE?

I'm often asked why I write, and I'm always at a loss for words. It sounds silly to say, "I have to. It's like breathing. It keeps me alive." But I think that's true. I've never used drugs, but I get a high from words—how they sound when I read them aloud or see them printed on my computer screen or on the printed manuscript page. I hear music in the rhythm of my computer keys and in the steady hum of my thoughts as they tumble like long rows of dominoes, one after the other. I hear my writing as I work and that's the melody of my soul, like a baby's giggle, a special voice on the telephone or a kitten's purr.

Remember my mentioning Smudge, the kitten who didn't purr? He did eventually. I was just being impatient. For fifteen years, Smudge slept nestled against the small of my back or on top of my monitor as I typed. And he purred perfectly.

Although Smudge is no longer with me, I keep his picture near my desk in my Maine summer home, reminding me that writing's a lot like it was with that little kitten. You have to believe (in yourself), and you have to have patience. Of course, you also have to keep stroking—that is, writing—while you're busy believing and being patient.

I've told that story many times over the years. Cat people nod knowingly. I've often wondered if more writers have cats than dogs. Let me hurry to add that we've always had both, but fortunately, neither Fraulein (black dachshund) nor Dollar (German shepard/malamute) ever tried to sleep on top of my monitor as the cats did.

DEFINE YOURSELF

What am I? Writer? Wife? Mother? Aunt? Grandmother? I am all that and more. We all have many different facets, like a stained-glass window, with each section reflecting differently depending on the day and the angle of the sun. I, like you, am a symbiotic blend, each part dependent on the other for nourishment. My identities are so intertwined that it would take a geneticist to break the code. My writer side continually appears outside my study. It finds its way into my kitchen popping up like toast in the toaster as my grocery list nestles compatibly beside a magazine market list like the odd couple. It even creeps into my bedroom, where a new copy of *Writer's Market* hides the latest fiction best-seller on my dresser. It curls up in my handbag, where reminders for my daughter's upcoming wedding are mixed with notes for this book.

My family has always made themselves at home in my writing, like a grown child raiding his mother's refrigerator. "Write about what you know best," the experts always advise. And so I did. What does any writer know better than her family. The love shared; the arguments fought, won and lost; the heartaches and triumphs— all are part of your life and, therefore, your writing.

Although I have always considered myself a private person, I realize (too late) that I have always revealed too much of me in my writing. I think it comes from writing from the heart, trying to share my thoughts and feelings with others, writing as I do to an unseen friend over a cup of coffee.

WRITING GIVES PLEASURE
Writing gives me pleasure. It's as simple as that. What could be nicer than being in love with your work and at the same time knowing that what you do helps others by making them laugh, helping them cry, teaching them something they may not know or just letting them know they're not alone.

If you think writing makes *you* happy, if you want to write, really want to write, then decide that today is the day you'll begin. You can make time in your busy life for writing if you feel you have to. There are no obstacles too great, no schedules too frantic, no excuse too overpowering for those who will become writers.

Motivation. Confidence. Persistence. You *can* write at home and fill the world with what you have to say. Why not get started?

SUGGESTED READING

Aslett, Don. *The Cleaning Encyclopedia.* New York: Dell Publishing, 1993.
———. *Don Aslett's Clutter-Free!: Finally and Forever.* Cincinnati: Betterway Books, 1995.
Barrett, Patti. *Too Busy to Clean?* Pownal, Vt.: Storey Communication, 1990.
Bly, Robert W. *Secrets of a Freelance Writer.* New York: Henry Holt and Co., 1997.
Campbell, Jeff, and The Clean Team. *Talking Dirt.* New York: Dell Trade Paperback, 1997.
Chandler, Steve. *100 Ways to Motivate Yourself.* Franklin Lakes, N.J.: Career Press, 1996.
Covey, Stephen R. *The Seven Habits of Highly Effective Families.* New York: Golden Books, 1997.
Doherty, William J. *The Intentional Family.* Reading, Mass.: Addison-Wesley Publishing, 1997.
Fulton, Alice, and Pauline Hatch. *It's Here . . . Somewhere.* Cincinnati: Writer's Digest Books, 1991.
Heloise. *Heloise: Household Hints for Singles.* New York: Perigee Books, 1993.
Kanarek, Lisa. *Everything's Organized.* Franklin Lakes, N.J.: Career Press, 1996.
Lehmkuhl, Dorothy, and Dolores Cotter Lamping. *Organizing for the Creative Person.* New York: Crown Publishers, 1993.
Levin, Michael. *Writer's Internet Sourcebook.* San Francisco: No Starch Press, 1997.
MacLeod, Jean B. *If I'd Only Listened to My Mom, I'd Know How to Do This.* New York: St. Martin's Press, 1997.
McClellan, Pam. *Don't Be a Slave to Housework.* Cincinnati: Betterway Books, 1995.
———. *The Organization Map.* Cincinnati: Betterway Books, 1993.
McCullough, Bonnie. *Totally Organized the Bonnie McCullough Way.* New York: St. Martin's Press, 1986.
Nuwer, Hank. *How to Write Like an Expert About Anything.* Cincinnati: Writer's Digest Books, 1995.
Winston, Stephanie. *Getting Organized.* New York: Warner Books, 1991.

INDEX

Adamec, Christine, 218-219
Advertising, as market, 170
Albert, Linda, 10
Alcoholics Anonymous, 189
American Academy of Pediatrics, 133
American Dietetic Association, 204
American Medical Association, 132-133
American Medical Writers Association (AMWA), 26, 186
American Society of Journalists and Authors (ASJA), 26, 186
Anecdotes, 146
Annual reports, 170-171
Anonymous, 70, 225
Articles. *See* Magazine article
Asimov, Isaac, 39
Aslett, Don, 70
Austen, James Edward, 24

Baker, Samm Sinclair, 150
Beck, Aaron T., 75
Benson, Herbert, 197-198
Berner, Jeff, 222-223
Beyond the Relaxation Response, 197
Billing log, 161
Blau, Sheldon, 22
Bloomingdale, Teresa, 214
Blume, Judy, 216-217, 226
Bombeck, Erma, 126, 211-213
Books
    ideas for, 19-23
    reference, 98-100, 116, 117-118
    weeding out, 55-56
Breaks, 41-42, 155, 183-185
Brochures
    as market, 171
    volunteer writing for, 207
Buck, Pearl, 144
Buddha, 189
Business expenses, 159-162
Business needs, 100-103, 159-161
Businesslike attitude, 152-162

Caldwell, Taylor, 150
Campbell, Jeff (and the Clean Team), 70
Carter, Rosalynn, 206
Carver, George Washington, 201
Chandler, Steve, 192

Cheever, John, 5
Children
    caregiving for, 16-17
    clutter from, 48
    cost of baby-sitting for, 164-165
    demands of, 45
    household help from, 49-51
    reaction to writing, 29
Chores. *See* Household chores
Churchill, Winston, 195
Clancy, Tom, 150
Cleaning, 54-70
Collier, James Lincoln, 146
Columns, 173-175
Communication with families, 31-33
Computer, 83, 91-94
Confetti your work, 43, 147-148
Confidence, 4, 190-193, 229
Cook, Robin, 192
Correspondence
    answering, 157
    log for, 160-161
    as market, 176-177
Cousins, Norman, 197
Covey, Stephen R., 22, 29, 111
Criticism, 11

Deadline
    padding, 162
    research, 124
Delivery services, 161
Dennis, Patrick, 150
Depression: What Families Should Know, 21, 113, 166
Descartes, René, 196
Desktop publishing, 169
Dictionary, 98
Diet, proper, 203-204
Direct Marketing Association, 56
Discipline, 7-12, 24-25, 199
Doctorow, E.L., 224
Doherty, William J., 22
Drossman, Douglas A., 131
Dump-it drawer, 54, 62
Dyches, Carol McEwen, 176

E-mail, 120
    answering correspondence via, 157
    ideas from, 174
    interviews, 133-134

trading horror stories via, 209
Epstein, Fred J., 127
Erasmus, 44
Evans, Bergen, 99
Exercise, 202-203

Falk, Peter, 128
Family
    histories, 175
    home office discussion with, 83-84
    as part of writing team, 29-37
    support of, 74-75
Ferguson, Cady Bissell, 221-222
First, You Cry, 22
Flexibility, 15
Forbes, B.C., 152
Friends, 183-188
Frye, Sandy, 172, 219-220
Fuerst, Mark, 214-215
Fulford, Robert, 173

Gamblers Anonymous, 189
Ghostwriting, 177
Gift box, 53
Gifts of Time, 127
Gill, Brendan, 115
Goldsmith, Oliver, 201, 209
Goodman, Ellen, 216
Gordon, Susan J., 218
Government agency research, 121-122
Government Printing Office, 204
Grafton, Sue, 114, 213-214
Greene, Bette, 210-211
Greene, Graham, 87
Greeting cards, 177-178
Grenfell, Sir Wilfred Thomason, 208
Griessman, B. Eugene, 9
Grisham, John, 150, 192
Guare, John, 119

Hackady, Hal, 91
Heritage of Helping, A, 176
Hemingway, Ernest, 224
Hobbies, 169-170
Holmes, Marjorie, 24
Home office, 78-86
    characteristics of good, 79-81
    creative location for, 81-83
    equipping, 87-104. *See also* Office
        equipment
    settling into, 84-86
Household chores, 45-70
    cleaning the house, 54-70

clutter question, 47-48
    inner clock vs., 52
    list of necessary, 46
    two-box approach, 53-54
*How to Be a Mother—and a Person,
    Too,* 46
*How to Be a Successful Housewife/
    Writer,* 112
*How to Get Control of Your Time and
    Your Life,* 41
How to Get Out of the Hospital Alive,
    22, 35, 112

Iannucci, Lisa, 217-218
Ideas, 19-23
    confessions as, 23
    from E-mail messages, 174
    journal for, 21
    listening for, 20
    reminiscence and, 22-23
    tuning into yourself for, 21-22
Intentional Family, The, 22
Internet
    market research on, 107-108
    research on, 120-121
    writers' chat rooms, 187
    See also World Wide Web
Interruptions, 38-44
Interviewing, 126-143

Johnson, Dr. Samuel, 164

Kane, Joseph Nathan, 116
Keller, Helen Adams, 28
King, Stephen, 192

Lakein, Alan, 41
Lindbergh, Anne Morrow, 5
Linde, Shirley, 223-224
Loneliness, 25-26

MacCampbell, Donald, 194
MacDonald, John D., 113
Magazine article
    ideas for, 19-23
    lead, 145-147
    multiple sales from one, 165-166
    query letters for, 114, 144-145
Mail, sorting, 156-158
Manuals, 178
Markets
    advertising, 170
    annual reports, 170-171

brochures, 171
collaborations, 172
columns, 173-175
competition and, 107-108
corporate histories, 175-176
correspondence, 176-177
ghostwriting, 177
greeting cards, 177-178
knowing your, 105-107
manuals, 178
narrowing focus for, 107
newsletters, 178
press releases, 179
rewriting for different, 165-166
speeches, 179-180
Mary Kay Cosmetics, 189
McCullers, Carson, 5
McGee, Travis, 114
Mentoring, 209
Message log, 160
Michener, James A., 126-127, 192
Mitchell, Margaret, 163
Mizner, Wilson, 183
Motivation, 4-7, 229
Motivational mission statement, 6-7

National Association of Home Builders,
    133
National Writers Union, 186
Networking, 119-120
Newsletters, 178, 206
Noise-induced hearing loss (NIHL), 81

O'Brien, Patricia, 216
Office equipment
    book shelves, 89-90
    computer, 83, 91-94
    copying machine, 95
    desk, 87-88
    desk chair, 88-89
    fax machine, 94-95
    file cabinets, 90
    lighting, 90-91
    reference books, 98-99
    telephone. *See* Telephone
    wastebasket, 97
Office supplies, 100-104
    buying in bulk, 161-162
    storing, 81, 95-97
100 Ways to Motivate Yourself, 192
Organizations, 185-187. *See also names
    of specific organizations*
Otto, Steve, 174-175

Outdoor Writers Association of
    America, Inc., 186
Outlining, 108-110
Oven surprise, 61

Parkinson's Law, 45
Patience, 12
Peak performance, 153
Peale, Norman Vincent, 189
Perkins, Maxwell, 224
Permissions, 123, 160
Persistence, 4, 12, 229
Photography, 168-170
Pirsig, Robert, 150
Positive self-talk, 203
Positive thinking, 188-189
Potter, Beatrix, 150
Power of Positive Thinking, The, 188
Press releases, 179
Priest, Aaron M., 211
Procrastination, 42-44
    planned, 46
    research and, 124
    routines vs. 154
    stress and, 196
Project, determining cost of, 164-165
Proposal. *See* Query letter
Public library, 118
Public service announcements, 170-171
Punctuality, 153

Query letter, 114, 144-145
Questionnaires, 134, 164
Quoted material, 123-124

Radl, Shirley L., 46
Records. *See* Business needs
*Relief from IBS: Irritable Bowel
    Syndrome*, 113, 127
Rejection, 149-151, 193-195
Relaxation Response, The, 197
Relaxation techniques, 196-202
Reminiscence, 22-23
Renard, Jules, 224
Reprints, 165
Research, 115-125
Rewriting, 149, 165-166
Rice, Anne, 192, 219
"Right stuff" test, 12-13
Rodale, J.I., 92, 98
Role model, 193-194
Rollin, Betty, 22
Roosevelt, Eleanor, 49

Routine. *See* Writing routine

Saboteurs, 37
Schaefer, David, 222
Schultz, Dodi, 215
Schuster, Marvin M., 130-131
Second rights, 165
Self-promotion, 167-168
Self-publishing, 180
Self-talk, positive, 203
7 Habits of Highly Effective Families, The, 22
Shaw, George Bernard, 224
Shepherd, Chuck, 173
Six Degrees of Separation, 119
Skeletonizing, 44
Society of American Travel Writers, 186
Speaking engagements, 166-167
Speeches, 179-180
Spouse
   household help from, 51
   involvement of, 35
   lack of cooperation from, 74
   reaction to writing, 30
   as saboteur, 37
Stillman, Irwin M., 150
Stress, controlling, 196-202
Strokes: What Families Should Know, 21
Subsidy presses, 180

Telephone
   directory, 118
   distractions, 38-40
   emergency code, 38
   equipment, 95
   extra lines, 95
   interviews, 135
   log, 160
   priority list, 158-159
Thoreau, Henry David, 14
Tidy box, 53-54
Time
   as limited resource, 8-10
   making (for writing), 72
   as money, 164
   protecting your, 206-207
   setting cleaning task limit, 68
Time sheet, 19
Time Tactics of Very Successful People, 9-10

Timesaving devices, 48-49, 55
Titles, 110-114
Tourette Syndrome Association, 132
Truman, Harry S., 193
Twain, Mark, 126

Untermeyer, Louis, 163
Uris, Leon, 4

Van Goethe, Johann, 119
Vanity presses, 180
Visualization, 70-71, 189-190
Volunteerism, 206-208
Vonnegut, Kurt, Jr., 189

Walters, Colin, 224
Wasserstein, Wendy, 213
Weekend work, 17-18
Weight Watchers, 189
Whitehead, William E., 131
Wiesel, Elie, 5
Williams, Tennessee, 5
Woolf, Virginia, 78
World Wide Web, 120
   meeting other writers via, 187
   nutrition Web sites, 204
   search engines, 121
   See also Internet
Writer's block, 196
Writer's Market, 99, 106, 229
Writing at home
   claiming space for, 79-84
   lifestyle changes for, 75-76
   negative aspects of, 23-25
   positive aspects of, 15-23
   removing barriers to, 72-76
   "right stuff" for, 4-13
Writing Business, The, 194
Writing routine, 153-156
   breaks in, 155
   flexibility in, 154-155
   for maximum writing time, 153
   procrastination vs., 154
   quitting time in, 156
Writing schedule
   "business hours" and, 104
   control over, 18-19
   "peak hours" and, 154
   regular, 104
   time for yourself, 184-185

"You factor," 19